ENCYCLOPEDIA OF
BRITISH HISTORY

Author
Philip Steele

Miles Kelly

First published in 2010 by Miles Kelly Publishing Ltd
Harding's Barn, Bardfield End Green, Thaxted, Essex, CM6 3PX, UK

Copyright © Miles Kelly Publishing Ltd 2010

This edition updated and printed in 2019

2 4 6 8 10 9 7 5 3 1

Publishing Director Belinda Gallagher
Creative Director Jo Cowan
Cover Designer Rob Hale
Senior Editor Becky Miles
Image Manager Liberty Newton
Indexers Jane Parker, Philip Steele
Reprographics Stephan Davis, Callum Ratcliffe-Bingham
Production Elizabeth Collins, Jenny Brunwin-Jones
Assets Lorraine King

ISBN 978-1-78617-856-5

Printed in China

British Library Cataloguing-in-Publication Data
A catalogue record for this book is available from the British Library

Made with paper from a sustainable forest

www.mileskelly.net

Contents

Castles and Knights 1066–1509

Palaces and Players 1509–1714

The Ancient Islands

500,000–700 BC

ELSEWHERE IN EUROPE

c.40,000 BC
Europe's oldest cave painting, El Castillo, Spain.

c.8000 BC
Dugout canoes are being made in the Netherlands.

c.6500 BC
Farming reaches the Balkan peninsula from Asia.

c.3400 BC
Evidence of vehicles with wheels.

c.3200 BC
Bronze Age begins in the Aegean region.

c.2700 BC
Rise of Minoan civilisation on the island of Crete, palaces and script.

c.1400 BC
Rise of Mycenaean civilisation in southern Greece, walled citadels.

c.900 BC
Rise of Etruscan civilisation in northern Italy, fine statues.

ASIA

10,500 BC
Pottery being made in southern Japan.

c.8350 BC
Foundation of Jericho, the world's oldest known walled city.

c.7500 BC
Town of Çatal Hüyük grows up in southern Turkey.

c.3500 BC
The wheel is in use in Mesopotamia, in the Middle East.

c.3250 BC
Writing is invented in Mesopotamia.

c.2500 BC
Civilisation thrives in Indus valley, at Mohenjo-Daro and Harappa.

c.2300 BC
Sargon of Akkad founds first Asian empire.

c.1600 BC
Shang emperors rule China, slaves, bronze weapons, silk.

AFRICA

c.73,000 BC
Earliest known drawing, Blombos Cave, South Africa.

c.12,00 BC
Grindstones used for making flour from wild seeds.

c.8000 BC
Start of farming in the Nile valley, Egypt.

c.7500 BC
Decorated pottery being made in the Sahara region.

c.4000 BC
Sailing boats being used in Egypt.

2530 BC
The Great Pyramid is raised at Giza in Egypt.

1325 BC
Egypt's young ruler, Tutankhamun, is buried in the Valley of the Kings.

c.1000 BC
Growth of the kingdom of Kush, in southern Nubia.

"The earliest history of Britain and Ireland is written in stone, bone, wood and clay…"

NORTH AMERICA	**SOUTH AMERICA**	**OCEANIA**
c.18,000 BC One of several possible dates for the first peopling of the Americas.	**c.12,500 BC** Possible date for human occupation of Monte Verde, Chile.	**c.50,000 BC** Aborigines settle in Australia, migrating from Southeast Asia.
c.16,800 BC Possible date of tools found at Cactus Hill site in Virginia.	**c.8600 BC** Beans, gourds and peppers are grown in Peru.	**c.28,500 BC** Humans settle the land now known as New Guinea.
c.5000 BC Maize is being grown in Mexico.	**c.3500 BC** Llamas are being used as pack animals, to transport goods.	**c.10,000 BC** New wave of Aboriginal settlement in Australia, tame dogs.
c.2300 BC Earliest pottery in Central America.	**c.3200 BC** Maize is first grown in South America.	**c.7000 BC** Taro root is grown as a food crop in New Guinea.
c.2000 BC A wave of Inuit migrations through the Arctic region.	**c.3200 BC** Dead bodies made into mummies, Chile.	**c.5000 BC** Rising sea levels, New Guinea and Tasmania become islands.
c.1200 BC Olmec civilisation in Central America, carved stone and temples.	**c.2800 BC** Villages built in the Amazon river basin.	**c.1500 BC** Ancestors of the Polynesians start to migrate eastwards across the Pacific Ocean by canoe.
c.1000 BC Rise of Adena culture in eastern woodlands of USA, burial mounds.	**c.2500 BC** Cloth is woven using looms, irrigation of fields.	**c.1000 BC** Stone settlements built in southeastern Australia.
c.800 BC Zapotec civilisation in Mexico, first writing in the Americas.	**c.1500 BC** The first metal-working in Peru.	**c.1000 BC** Polynesian ancestors reach Tonga and Samoa.
	c.900 BC Rise of Chavín civilisation in the Andes, stone temples.	

The Lonely Hunters

The British Isles are a group of small islands lying in shallow waters off the northwestern coast of Europe. The two largest islands are called Great Britain and Ireland. Today these lands are green, with a moist and mild climate. Fifteen thousand years ago, they were in the grip of Arctic weather conditions. Great Britain was roamed by reindeer and bears and by prehistoric hunters. It was still part of the European mainland and the River Thames flowed into the Rhine. There were no villages or towns and humans were very few and far between. The population of the whole world in 15,000 BC was probably about the same as that of Scotland today.

IN THE BEGINNING

We find out about human-like creatures and early ancestors of humans by studying the remains of fossilized bones and stone tools.

c.500,000 years ago
Site: Boxgrove, Sussex, England
Type: Heidelberg Man

c.400,000 years ago
Site: Swanscombe, Kent, England
Type: Neanderthal

c.40,000 years ago
Site: Kent's Cavern, Devon, England
Type: *Homo sapien* (true human)

➡ *Neanderthal skulls show they had sloping foreheads, with heavy brow ridges. Scientific tests show that some Neanderthals bred with early true humans.*

➡ *True humans did not appear in Europe until about c.43,000 years ago. They were very similar to modern humans but with marginally bigger jaws and noses, and more rounded braincases.*

⬇ *Herds of woolly mammoths were hunted during the Ice Age in northern Europe and Asia. They were a kind of elephant that had adapted to cold weather conditions.*

THE FIRST INHABITANTS

The first relatives of humans probably appeared in Britain about 814,000 years ago. Remains of later species, often referred to as Heidelberg Man, date back about 500,000 years. At times, settlers were driven away by severe Ice Ages, but the people we call Neanderthal hunted here in the warmer periods in between ('interglacials'). The first true humans (*Homo sapiens*) were living in Britain by about 40,000 years ago.

THE LONELY HUNTERS

c.40,000 BC
True human beings living in Britain. Great advances in making tools and weapons.

c.24,500 BC
Start of most extreme period within the last Ice Age.

Flint and Stone

Between about 35,000 and 8500 BC, the peoples of western Europe learned to produce fine tools and weapons. They were nomadic hunters and used all the parts of the animals they killed – meat for food, skins to make clothes, gut to make thread, bone to make needles and other tools, and fat to make grease and lamp fuel. These people took shelter in caves or made tents of hide and timber. They also made paintings of wild animals on the walls of caves and studied the stars.

⬇ *Careful chipping could turn a flint into a razor-sharp tool or weapon.*

TOOLS OF THE OLD STONE AGE

The earliest period of settlement in Britain is called the Palaeolithic (Old Stone) Age. Tools and weapons were made of chipped and flaked stone, bone and wood.

▲ *Flints were used to make knives, axes and spearheads.*

▼ *Flint scrapers could be used to scrape the flesh off the hides of wild animals.*

▶ *People became more and more skilled at making weapons of stone, bone and wood.*

c.8500 BC
Evidence of a hunter-gatherer encampment
at Crammond, near Edinburgh.

c.7150 BC
Estimated date of human remains found in Gough's
cave, Cheddar Gorge.

IN THE CHEDDAR GORGE

Hunters still needed to live nomadic lives. They set up
camps as they travelled but still used natural shelters
such as caves. Remains of an adult male found at
Gough's Cave in the Cheddar Gorge in 1903 have
now been dated to about 7150 BC. We now know
that the old ideas about primitive 'cave men' are
untrue. They had to be intelligent, skillful and
resourceful to survive.

*Gough's Cave in England's
Cheddar Gorge has offered up
hundreds of tools made of
stone, bone and antler, and
even some amber from the
Baltic region of Europe.*

c.8500 BC
Start of the Middle Stone Age in the British Isles.

c.8300 BC
Melting of the last glaciers in Britain.

The Rising Sea

Along the western coasts of Wales, Cornwall, the Scilly Isles and Brittany, there are ancient folk tales of lands lost beneath the sea. It could be that these are distant memories of real floods, for between 8000 and 3000 BC sea levels rose rapidly. As the climate warmed, the water expanded, spilling over coastal plains and filling channels. By about 6500 BC, the strip of land joining England to mainland Europe had been swallowed up by the sea for the last time.

After the mammoths had gone, people learnt how to hunt smaller animals such as deer. Hunters camped on high ground to spy out the dense forests, or by lakes and shores that offered a good supply of fresh fish.

c.8000 bc
New waves of hunters cross into Britain from
the European mainland.

c.5000 bc
Oak forests now cover much of
northwestern Europe.

THE RIDDLE OF THE SNAKES

Why are there no snakes in Ireland? An
old tale claims that snakes were banished
by a miracle carried out by St Patrick,
the Christian saint. In fact, snakes
entered Britain when it was still
linked to France by a strip of
land. However Ireland was
already an island at that time,
and snakes could not swim
across the Irish Sea.

MESOLITHIC LIFE

The Mesolithic (Middle Stone)
Age is the name given to the
prehistoric period just before
the coming of agriculture. As
the climate warmed, forests of
oak, ash and elm extended
across Britain. The human
population grew and spread
north. Hunters travelled by boat
from Scotland to Ireland.
Arrowheads are made with tiny
crafted flints called 'microliths'.

⬇ Hunters now crossed
by boat from Scotland into
Ireland. Tools and weapons
were still of stone, bone or
wood, but were made with
much greater precision.

THE RISING SEA **13**

The First Farmers

Few discoveries changed the way people lived more than farming. In southwest Asia, grain crops were being grown and sheep were being raised as early as 9000 BC. Farming soon spread into North Africa and westwards across Europe. It was first brought to southern Britain by invaders and traders from the European mainland, about 6000 years ago. They brought with them seed for planting and livestock.

⬇ The first wheat crops needed improving, to produce better yields of grain. Farmers did this by only choosing seed from the very best plants.

A SETTLED LIFE

People no longer had to live as nomads, hunting for their food. They were able to stay in one place, building permanent settlements and storing up grain to use for future food. They could exchange any extra produce they made for other goods. In the Old Stone Age, every man, woman and child had been a food producer. Now, a surplus of food allowed some people to specialise as traders, craft workers, labourers – or rulers.

THE NEW STONE AGE

Farming spread throughout the British Isles from about 4500 BC. Field patterns from about 3000 BC can be seen today at Céide Fields, above high cliffs near Ballycastle, on the west coast of Ireland. They have been excavated from layers of peat bog. The arrival of farming marks the beginning of the period known as the Neolithic (New Stone) Age. In order to grow crops, clearings had to be cut from the forests of oak that now covered large areas of the country.

New Stone Age *living rooms can be seen at Skara Brae. There are wall alcoves, dressers, stone beds and a central, smoky hearth.*

SKARA BRAE

In 1850 a severe storm battered the coast of Orkney, an island off the north coast of Scotland. When it was over, the ruins of a New Stone Age settlement were revealed in the shifting sands. Skara Brae had been inhabited from about 3200 to 2300 BC. Its people were fishermen or herders of sheep and cattle, for crops would not have grown well on this bleak and windy shore. The houses were built with stone blocks, and the roofs were made of turf and whalebone. The houses were linked by covered passages.

The first sheep in Britain were tough and wiry creatures, rather like today's Soay breed.

THE FIRST FARMERS 15

c.3500 BC
Simple wooden ploughs being used in the south of England.

c.3000 BC
Grimes Graves flint mines, Norfolk, England.

MEDICINAL PLANTS

Stone Age people relied on nature to help cure sickness or ailments. Centaury was used to help heal wounds and treat snakebites. Henbane made the patient drowsy and relieved aches and pains. Rose hips, from the dog rose, were used to boost the immune system and ward off colds.

Centaury

Rose hips

Henbane

↓ Stone hand mills, or querns, were used for grinding wheat. The central hole was filled with grain and then the top stone was turned, or ground, against the bottom one. Flour spilled out between the stones.

MAKING THINGS

New Stone Age peoples were skilled craftworkers. They produced baskets, jewellery and, from about 4500 BC, pottery. Wood was used to make farm tools. Stone was used to make hand mills called querns, for grinding grain into flour. Stone was also polished and ground to make axes for clearing the forest. In stony areas, axe-heads were produced at factory sites and exported right across the British Isles – from Northern Ireland to the southeast of England, from Cornwall to the northeast of England.

THE FIRST MINES

By about 4000 BC, flints were being mined underground. Over 360 mine shafts have been found at the Grimes Graves flint mine in Norfolk, England. It dates back to 2600 BC.

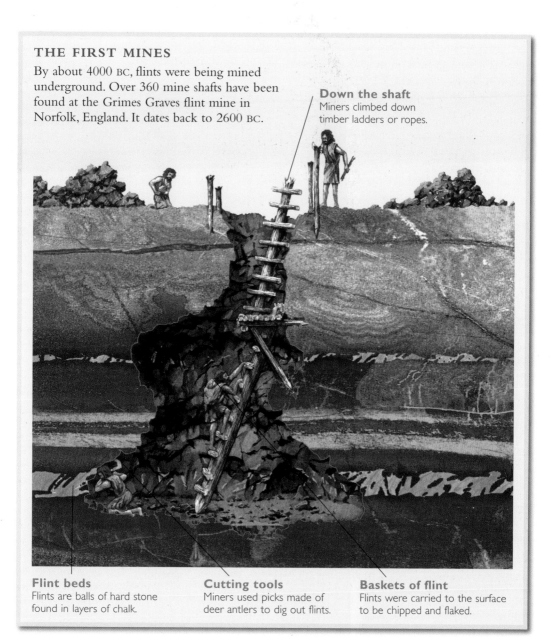

Down the shaft
Miners climbed down timber ladders or ropes.

Flint beds
Flints are balls of hard stone found in layers of chalk.

Cutting tools
Miners used picks made of deer antlers to dig out flints.

Baskets of flint
Flints were carried to the surface to be chipped and flaked.

c.3300 BC
The first stone circles are erected in
the British Isles.

c.2700 BC
A henge is in use at Llandygai, North Wales.

Stones of Mystery

In the years between about 3200 and 1500 BC, massive pillars of stone or timber were raised in the British Isles and other parts of northwestern Europe. Some were placed on their own, others were arranged in long avenues. They are called standing stones and may have been used to mark tribal borders or ceremonial routes. Some pillars were arranged within oval, ditched enclosures called henges. These seem to have been observatories, used to mark the appearance of the Sun at midsummer or midwinter, or to track the movement of the stars. They must have been sacred places where religious rituals were carried out.

c.2700 BC
Silbury Hill, an artificial mound, is built near Avebury, Wiltshire, southern England.

c.2250 BC
85 stones are transported to Stonehenge from southwest Wales.

ARTIFICIAL MOUND

Silbury Hill in southern England (not far from Stonehenge) is the biggest mound made by prehistoric people in Europe. Over 3000 years old, the mound is 40 metres high and covers an area the size of three football pitches. In 1970, a burial mound, or barrow, was discovered inside.

⬆ *Castlerigg in Cumbria is one of the most beautiful stone circles in Britain. It is also thought to be one of the earliest, and dates from around 3000 BC. The circle is made up of 38 stones, all of differing shape and size.*

⬅ *Stonehenge towers over the grasslands of Salisbury Plain in Southern England. It was built in several stages and was in use from about 3200 to 1100 BC.*

c.3700 BC
First phase of Wayland's Smithy long barrow,
Oxfordshire, England.

c.3200 BC
Passage grave at Newgrange, Boyne Valley, Ireland.

places of the Dead

The builders of henges and stone circles also used the great stones we call **megaliths to build burial chambers.** All over the British Isles, these stone slabs have survived long after the simple huts of their builders have disappeared.

➡ *Le Dehus burial chamber on Guernesy was built between c.3500–2000 BC. It was excavated between 1837 and 1847 and contained well-preserved human remains.*

⬆ *Megalithic tombs such as Newgrange are older than the pyramids of Egypt.*

BURIAL AND CREMATION

During the New Stone Age, bodies were often placed in burial chambers once they were already skeletons, or else cremated. Some burial sites could hold the remains of up to 50 bodies.

➡ *The Creevykeel tomb in Sligo, Ireland, dates from between c.4000–2500 BC.*

NEWGRANGE

The Brú Na Bóinne area of eastern Ireland includes three megalithic tombs – Dowth, Newgrange and Knowth. The Newgrange tomb was built in about 3200 BC and is made up of a huge mound over a passage grave. A slit in the roof allows the rising sun to creep into the gloomy burial chamber at midwinter. Many of the stones are decorated with swirling spiral patterns. Later peoples believed that the Newgrange site must have been made by the gods.

c.2900 BC
Copper working reaches British Isles from southeast and southwest Europe.

c.2500 BC
Early 'beaker' burials in British Isles.

Metal and Pottery

The building of stone monuments outlasted the New Stone Age, for builders of the later megalithic monuments and burial chambers used metals. Copper was worked in southeast Europe and western Asia by about 6000 BC. Within about 3000 years, smiths in these areas began to make alloys (mixtures of metals). The most useful alloy was bronze, a combination of tin and copper. Bronze-working reached the British Isles by about 2000 BC. Bronze tools and weapons were sharper than those made of stone and harder than those made of copper.

Bronze needed to reach a temperature of about 900°C before it could be poured into moulds and left to cool and harden. It was then hammered and polished.

MAKING BRONZE

About 5500 years ago, metal workers invented bronze by smelting copper ores and tin ores together. They used the bronze to make hard, sharp swords, spearheads and axe heads.

THE BRITISH ISLES AND THE BEAKER PEOPLE

The technology and customs of the Beaker People may have originated in Spain, a region rich in metals, before spreading through Europe. Beaker sites are found in both Great Britain and Ireland.

Pottery had been made in Britain since the fifth millennium BC. However the beakers of the early Bronze Age belong to a different tradition, which is also found in Spain and the Rhineland region of Europe. The beakers, probably used for drinking mead, are thought to have been symbols of wealth and power.

NORTH SEA

IRELAND

IRISH SEA

GREAT BRITAIN

Areas of concentration

Beaker Extent

ENGLISH CHANNEL

WHO WERE THE BEAKER PEOPLE?

At about the time that metals first appeared in the British Isles, there was a change in the way in which the dead were buried. Personal possessions were now often placed in single graves, along with pottery containers called beakers. These burial customs began to spread to the British Isles from mainland Europe.

We now know that new invaders or traders arrived and displaced much of the local population around this time. By this period of history there was a Europe-wide network of trading routes by land and sea.

METAL AND POTTERY   23

Celts and Romans

700 BC–AD 446

THE WORLD AT A GLANCE

ELSEWHERE IN EUROPE	ASIA	AFRICA
c.700 BC Rise of 'Celtic' cultures in Europe.	**c.660 BC** Jimmu, legendary first emperor of Japan.	**600 BC** Meroë in Nubia (Sudan) becomes a powerful city.
509 BC Rome expels kings and becomes a republic.	**c.563 BC** Birth of religious teacher Gautama Siddhartha (the Buddha) in Nepal.	**c.500 BC** Bantu-speaking peoples start to spread out from West Africa.
432 BC The Parthenon temple is built in Athens, golden age for Greece.	**550 BC** Cyrus the Great founds the Persian empire.	**c.450 BC** Rise of Nok civilisation in Nigeria, iron working, terracotta heads.
52 BC Romans finally defeat the Gauls (Celtic tribes living in France).	**334 BC** Alexander the Great begins the Greek invasion of Western Asia.	**c.400 BC** Phoenician city of Carthage, North Africa, at height of power.
27 BC Rome becomes an empire under the rule of Augustus.	**322 BC** The Mauryan empire is founded in India.	**331 BC** Greeks found city of Alexandria, Egypt.
AD 9 Germanic tribes under Arminius (Hermann) defeat the Romans.	**221 BC** Chinese empire unites under Qin Shi Huangdi.	**AD 44** Romans now rule North Africa from Egypt to Morocco.
AD 285 The Roman empire splits into two halves, east and west.	**c.AD 30** Possible date for the crucifixion of Jesus Christ in Jerusalem.	**AD 50** Kingdom of Axum, in Ethiopia, rises to power.
AD 410 Visigoth warriors sack the city of Rome.	**AD 132** Jews rebel against Roman rule and are finally defeated in AD 135.	**AD 429** The Vandals, a Germanic people, found kingdom in North Africa.

"Iron swords are drawn – for the tribe or for the empire?"

NORTH AMERICA	SOUTH AMERICA	OCEANIA
c.500 BC Picture writing (hieroglyphs) at Monte Albán, Mexico.	**c.700 BC** Rise of the Parácas civilisation in Peru.	**c.700 BC** Pacific trade in obsidian, a black stone used to make weapons.
c.310 BC Chiefdoms in America's eastern woodlands – the Hopewell culture.	**c.400 BC** The great temples of Chavín de Huantar, Peru.	**c.300 BC** Polynesian settlement of Ellice Islands (Tuvalu).
c.100 BC The Hohokam people of the American South irrigate their crops.	**c.200 BC** Rise of the Nazca civilisation in Peru.	**c.200 BC** Later burials at Aboriginal site of Roonka Flat, Australia
c.AD 1 North Pacific coastal villages, carving and building in cedarwood.	**c.200 BC** Nazca people scratch ceremonial lines across the desert, Peru.	**c.200 BC** Polynesians reach the Marquesas Islands.
c.AD 1 Villages being built in the American Southwest.	**c.200 BC** Decline of the Chavín civilisation.	**c.AD 1** Large increase in the Aboriginal population of Australia.
c.AD 1 Possible date for first Arawak settlement of the Caribbean islands.	**c.AD 1** The Moche people of northern Peru, gold working and pottery.	**c.AD 150** Egyptian geographer Ptolemy suggests 'unknown southern land' – perhaps Australia.
c.AD 50 The city of Teotihuacán is built in Mexico, massive pyramids.	**c.AD 100** Growth of the city of Tiwanaku, near Lake Titicaca.	**c.AD 400** Polynesians reach Easter Island, in the eastern South Pacific.
c.AD 300 Height of the Maya civilisation in Mexico, great cities.	**c.AD 400** Powerful chiefdom on Marajó island at mouth of the River Amazon.	**c.AD 400** Polynesians reach the Hawaiian Islands, in the Central Pacific.

Masters of Iron

Copper and bronze continued to be used for making tools, weapons and jewellery. However a new metal was soon being worked in Europe. Iron-working had first been mastered in western Asia, between about 2700–1300 BC. By about 800 BC, smiths were also hammering glowing bars of iron across the British Isles.

IRON AGE PEOPLES

Many Europeans peoples became expert at working the new metal. Sometimes we refer to these peoples as 'Celts', named after a people the Greeks referred to as Keltoi. In reality, these Celts were many different peoples. However through trade and travel many of them did come to share technologies, customs and religious beliefs. Some spoke similar langauges. 'Celtic' cultures may have spread up the Atlantic coasts or from central Europe

and the Alps. Some southern Celts raided Italy, Greece and Turkey. The three main groups of northern and western Celts were the Gauls of France, the Britons of Great Britain and the Gaels of Ireland. They lived as many separate tribal groups.

BRITONS AND GAELS
'Celtic' cultures reached Britain and Ireland by contact with the European mainland, rather than by any big invasions. These were the names of tribal groups living in Britain and Ireland in the later Iron Age, as recorded by the Romans.

GREAT BRITAIN

Caledonians

NORTH SEA

Venicontes
Robogdii
Novantae
Selgovae
Votadini
Erdini Darini
Nagnatae Voluntii
Brigantes
Auteni Eblanii
Parisi
GAELS Cauci
BRITONS
Gangani Manapi
Deceangli
Cornovii
Coritani
Usdiae Coriondi IRISH SEA
Ordovices
Iceni
Iverni Brigantes
Trinovantes
Vellabori
Catuvellauni
Demetae Dobunni
IRELAND
Silures
Atrebates Cantiaci
Durotriges
Dumnonii
ENGLISH CHANNEL

c.800 BC
Rise of Iron Age cultures known as Halstatt, after an Austrian site.

c.500–450 BC
Rise of Iron Age cultures known as La Tène, after a Swiss site.

⬇ The Celts were brilliant metal workers who often decorated their work with birds, animals and interlacing patterns. Bronze mirrors such as these were used after 100 BC by the peoples living in what is now southern England.

SMITHS AND FORGES

Iron was much harder and tougher than copper or bronze. It proved ideal for making swords and spears, or hammers and axes. Some people believed iron was magical, and horseshoes are still a symbol of good fortune. The blacksmith's forge was at the centre of Celtic village life.

CELTIC SOCIETY

The ancient Celts never saw themselves as one people and were rarely united. Celtic tribes were ruled by kings and by queens, too, for women held considerable power. Warriors came from noble families and prided themselves on being brave, heroic fighters and skilled hunters. They loved feasting and drinking. Both British and Gaelic tribes fought endlessly amongst themselves, quarrelling and raiding each others' cattle. The poorer members of the tribe were farmers, toiling on the land, raising animals and cutting the hay. They served as charioteers and fort-builders. Prisoners of war and lawbreakers were treated as slaves.

↑ *The Celts wove their clothes from linen and wool and wore cloaks fastened at the shoulder.*

↑ *The ancient Celts were famed for their love of gold and jewellery. Nobles wore splendid brooches, rings, armbands and torcs (ornate metal collars).*

200s–100 BC
Close contact between southeastern Britons and continent.

c.70 BC
Hoard of gold torcs, dating from c. 70 BC, found in Snettisham, Norfolk, between 1948 and 1973.

POTTERY MAKERS

In some regions of Britain, Iron Age peoples made pottery from coils or slabs of clay mixed with sand. This was fired in a pit or under a bonfire. Pots shaped on a wheel did not appear until 75 BC, in southeast England.

CELTIC LANGUAGES

Most of the languages spoken today in lands from Western Europe to northern India share a common origin. They are called Indo-European. Some languages still spoken in modern times came down to us from the ancient Celts. The language of the Britons turned into Welsh, Cornish and Breton (spoken in Brittany, France). The language of the Gaels gave us Irish, Scottish Gaelic and Manx (spoken on the Isle of Man). In Britain, no fewer than six rivers are called Avon. Why? It is simply a Celtic word for 'river'.

◄ Celtic potters made all sorts of items including jugs, storage jars, bowls, funeral urns and loom weights. Many items were beautifully decorated.

◄ This ancient white horse design is carved into the chalk at Uffington, Oxfordshire, England. Its date is uncertain. By the Iron Age, horses had become very important. The Celts mostly rode small, stocky ponies, but probably bred larger, more powerful horses too.

c.600 BC
First settlement at Colchester, Essex England.

c.325 BC
First documented reference to the name British ('Pretanic') Isles.

The Celts at Home

Forts had been built in the British Isles before the Iron Age. They were large enclosures protected by earthworks and walls, and were sited on hilltops and headlands. They often enclosed dwellings that were occupied in peacetime as well as war. New enclosures were raised by the Celts. Within Tre'r Ceiri hillfort in North Wales, the walls of 150 huts built in about 200 BC can still be seen today. Farming villages were often built on less protected lowlands, wherever the soil was good. In Ireland and Scotland, some villages were built on artifical islands in lakes. Towns in the 'Belgic' style of the continent were built at St Albans and Colchester.

ROUND HOUSES

Royal enclosures may have included large, rectangular halls, but most ordinary people in the western lands of the Celts lived in round huts that were about 15 metres across. The roofs were cone-shaped with a heavy thatch. The walls were normally built of timber and wattle-and-daub (interlaced sticks covered in clay). Stone was used in areas where timber was scarce.

On the floor
Floors were of beaten earth or slabs. They could be strewn with sweet-smelling rushes or grasses.

c.100 BC
Lake village at Glastonbury, Somerset, England.
Beautifully decorated hand mirrors become popular.

c.90 BC
First British coins, southern England.

↓ *Inside the Celtic roundhouse, smoke drifted up to the rafters from the central hearth. The timber posts may have been carved with ornate decorations. People slept on the ground in the cubicles, beneath warm animal skins.*

Livestock
Farm animals were kept in pens or even in the same huts as the villagers. They included sheep, goats, pigs, cattle and horses.

The loom
Looms (weaving frames) stood in most huts, for each household would produce its own cloth.

Compartments
Each hut was really one single room, but the inside edge of the wall was divided into separate cubicles, used for storage of weapons and supplies or for sleeping.

The hearth
A wood fire in the centre of the hut was used for cooking and heating.

CELTIC FOOD

A big cauldron steamed over each hearth and the Celts were famous for enjoying their food. They might eat beef, mutton or pork, cheese or buttermilk. Bread and porridge were made from wheat, barley, rye or oats. Hunting and fishing provided boar, venison (deer meat) or salmon. Southern Europeans were amazed by the large amounts of alcohol drunk by Celtic men and women – imported wine, home-brewed ale and mead, a drink made from honey.

Apples

Wild boar

Honey

Nuts

c.700 BC
Royal fort of Emain Macha, northern Ireland.

c.450 BC
First Iron Age phase of Maiden Castle, Dorset, England. South Barrule hillfort, Isle of Man.

Warrior Heroes

The Celts were famed as fighters through most of Europe. Far to the south of the British Isles, Celtic warrior bands were storming into Rome and Greece between 387 and 279 BC. Celtic tribes did take part in large pitched battles, but they preferred single combat, where champions from each army came out to fight each other. They belonged to an age that admired individual bravery more than organisation or discipline. In the royal halls, warriors would boast of their exploits and drink to their dead companions.

➡ *Maiden Castle in Dorset, England, was already an important site during the New Stone Age. From about 450 BC, it was a major hillfort and the capital of a Celtic tribe called the Durotriges.*

Timber defences
Heavy timbers were used to build fences and gates, the last line of defence against invaders.

High earthworks
The banks were staggered so that it was impossible to launch a direct attack on the gates. The fort was finally taken by the Romans.

RATHS, DUNS AND BROCHS

Some forts were large defended settlements, but others were smaller and built more like castles. The remains of stone 'duns' may still be seen in Scotland and royal 'raths' in Ireland. The Picts, ancient inhabitants of northeastern Scotland who adopted the Celtic way of life, built 'brochs' – big stone towers that could be used as shelter in wartime.

The settlement
The settled area covered 18 hectares. Finds here have included Iron Age pots, sickles, combs made of bone and the skeletons of warriors who died in battle.

c.300 BC
Celts in mainland Europe probably invent chain mail.

c.250 BC
War chariots introduced to the British Isles.

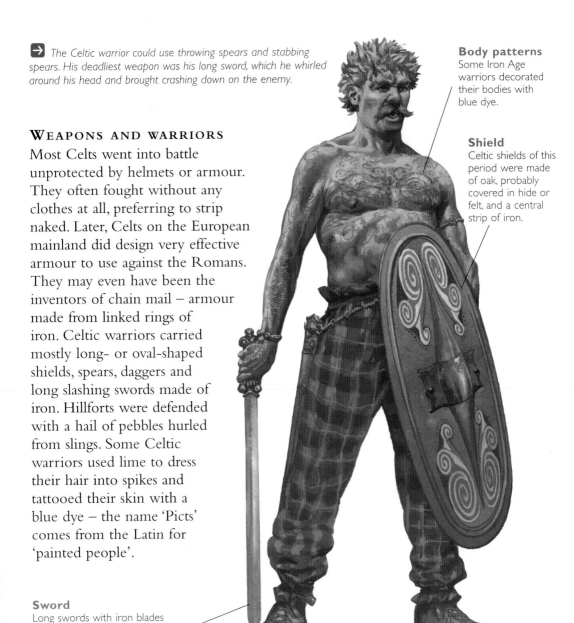

→ *The Celtic warrior could use throwing spears and stabbing spears. His deadliest weapon was his long sword, which he whirled around his head and brought crashing down on the enemy.*

WEAPONS AND WARRIORS

Most Celts went into battle unprotected by helmets or armour. They often fought without any clothes at all, preferring to strip naked. Later, Celts on the European mainland did design very effective armour to use against the Romans. They may even have been the inventors of chain mail – armour made from linked rings of iron. Celtic warriors carried mostly long- or oval-shaped shields, spears, daggers and long slashing swords made of iron. Hillforts were defended with a hail of pebbles hurled from slings. Some Celtic warriors used lime to dress their hair into spikes and tattooed their skin with a blue dye – the name 'Picts' comes from the Latin for 'painted people'.

Body patterns
Some Iron Age warriors decorated their bodies with blue dye.

Shield
Celtic shields of this period were made of oak, probably covered in hide or felt, and a central strip of iron.

Sword
Long swords with iron blades were used in battle. The hilt was usually beautifully decorated.

200 BC
Druidism already an ancient tradition amongst the Celts.

c.150 BC
The Isle of Anglesey, North Wales, is the centre of druidism in Britain.

Druids and Mistletoe

The landscape was sacred to the ancient Celts, with holy mountains, mysterious woods and magical waters. Offerings were thrown into lakes and left by springs and wells. In parts of Ireland, Scotland and Cornwall today, it is still believed to be lucky to tie ribbons to trees near certain springs. Groves of sacred trees formed places of worship. There were important religious enclosures called nemetons, although we do not know how they were used. Birds, snakes, fish and animals such as boars and stags were believed to have magic powers. The priests were called druids. They also served as teachers, healers, law–makers and envoys.

Hen-dŷ head,
Anglesey

⬆ *The Celts made many sculptures of human heads in stone or wood. Some were double or triple heads. Celts believed that the human soul lived inside the head. Celtic warriors cut off the heads of their enemies and displayed them in halls and shrines. This custom may be the origin of the pumpkin and turnip heads people place in their windows at Hallowe'en.*

THE FIRES OF BELTAIN

Celtic festivals were held throughout the year. On Beltain, 1 May, the dark hills were ablaze with bonfires. Lughnasa, for two weeks after 1 August, was a harvest festival in honour of Lugh. At Samhain, on the eve of 1 November, spirits from the other world were believed to walk the Earth. Imbolc, on 1 February, honoured the powerful goddess known as Brigit or Brigantia.

The goddess
Brigantia

c.AD 50
First evidence of the Celtic calendar – a bronze plate from Gaul.

c.AD 500s
Druidism finally dies out in British Isles.

GODS AND MYSTERIES

The oldest form of worship in the British Isles honoured the Earth Mother, bringer of fertility to the land. She was still honoured by the ancient Celts, under various names. They also believed in other gods and goddesses. Some belonged to a particular tribe or place. Irish gods included the Dagda, or supreme god, the goddess Dana, the shining Lugh, Nuada of the Silver Hand, Morrigan, the terrifying raven goddess. Gods of the British Celts included a giant called Bran the Blessed, the powerful warrior Gwydion, Llew of the Strong Hand and the goddess Arianrhod. The Celts believed in other worlds, too, home of gods and the dead.

Sometimes these were described as a happy island beneath the setting sun, sometimes as a mysterious fairy-world beneath the ground.

➡ *Cernunnos, was one of the most important Iron Age gods. He was worshipped throughout the Celtic world and is often shown surrounded by sacred animals. Later, Christians identified him with the devil.*

A MURDER MYSTERY

In 1984 a body was discovered in Lindow Moss, Cheshire, England. It had been preserved beneath the bog for over 1900 years. The dead man wore an armband of fox fur. His stomach contained traces of burnt bread and mistletoe pollen. He had been hit over the head with an axe, strangled with a rope and cut across the throat. His hands were well cared for, so this was no warrior or labourer. Archaeologists have guessed that he was a druid who was sacrificed to the gods.

Sacrifice of Lindow Man

DRUIDS AND MISTLETOE 35

Roman Invasion

After about 100 BC, the Celts in mainland Europe came under attack from German and Central European warriors. From Italy, too, Roman armies marched northwards to conquer the Gauls. In August 55 BC the Roman general Julius Caesar landed near Deal, in Kent, with 10,000 troops. He met with furious resistance, but returned the following year with at least 30,000 foot soldiers and 2000 cavalry. This time they crossed the River Thames and invaded the tribal lands of the Catuvellauni, Belgic Celts who had settled around St Albans. The Britons of southeast England were forced to pay tribute to Rome, and Caesar withdrew.

Aquila
Each legion had an eagle standard. This was carried at parades and served as a rallying point in battle. The standard bearer defended the eagle with his life.

Animal skins
Standard bearers wore animal skins over their helmets, with the upper jaw resting on the helmet.

Armour
Shirts of mail armour provided protection.

← *The aquilifer (standard bearer) carrying an eagle standard. Each legion had an eagle standard. Units of cavalry and auxiliaries carried standards of other animals.*

JULIUS CAESAR
The conqueror of the Gauls and southern Britons was one of the most brilliant generals the world has known. Born in about 100 BC, his military campaigns made him the most powerful man in Rome. He made many enemies and was stabbed to death in 44 BC.

⬆ A Roman warship. The war fleet of 54 BC was much bigger than the previous invasion. It included 28 warships and hundreds of other ships to carry troops, horses, weapons, equipment and stores.

⬆ These coins are marked 'Cunobelin'. They show the wealth of the Catuvellauni just before the Roman conquest.

THE CONQUEST BEGINS

In the years following Caesar's death, the Romans found out more about Britain. They heard of rich prizes, such as tin mines. They sent merchants to spy, who reported that the Catuvellauni were growing powerful under a new king called Cunobelinus. Then in AD 41, Cunobelinus died. Some rival British kingdoms called for the Romans to teach the Catuvellauni a lesson. In AD 42 the emperor Claudius raised an army that was 40,000 strong. It aimed to bring the whole of Britain under Roman rule.

BRITONS ATTACKED

Roman troops, under general Aulus Plautius, landed in Kent in AD 43. They defeated two sons of Cunobelinus – Caratacus and Togodumnus. The biggest battle was fought by the River Medway, where the Romans broke through the massed tribes. Advancing into Essex, the Romans captured Camulodunum (Colchester). It was there that the emperor Claudius, on a fortnight's visit, took surrender of 11 tribes.

CARATACUS THE REBEL

Eleven British rulers immediately allied themselves with the Roman invaders. However Caratacus waged a fierce guerrilla campaign. Defeated, he sought refuge with Cartimandua, queen of the Brigantes, but she handed him over to the Romans. He was taken to Rome in chains, but in the end he was pardoned. He died in AD 52.

THE ROMAN EMPIRE AD 43

The Roman invasion of AD 43 brought Britain into a vast empire that stretched from Spain into Western Asia, and southwards into North Africa. Its capital was Rome. Britain marked the northern limits of Roman rule. The Romans never conquered the far north of Scotland and Ireland too remained free.

BRITAIN

GERMANY

Extent of Roman Empire AD 43

FRANCE

SPAIN

Rome
ITALY

TURKEY

GREECE

SYRIA

MEDITERRANEAN SEA

NORTH AFRICA

EGYPT

AD 51
Caratacus taken to Rome as a prisoner.

AD 60
An uprising against the Romans, lead by Boudicca, queen of the Iceni, begins in East Anglia.

RESISTING THE INVADERS

Many tribes tried to resist the Romans. It took about four years for the invaders to finally gain control over southern England, and another 30 years for them to conquer all of the West Country and the mountains and valleys of Wales. The battle for Yorkshire and the remainder of northern England was still underway in AD 70, when a tribe called the Brigantes rose in rebellion.

⬇ *The Britons fought bravely, but the Roman troops were better equipped, better trained and highly disciplined. The Romans had experience of fighting in many parts of their empire.*

⬇ *The Romans sometimes used elephants to trample the enemy in battle. The emperor had some brought to Britain to impress the natives.*

ROMAN INVASION **39**

AD 61
Boudicca sacks Colchester, St Albans and London.

AD 70
The Romans attack the Brigantes tribe in Yorkshire.

THE ATTACK ON MONA

As the Romans advanced, many Britons fled into Wales. The island of Mona (Anglesey) was a holy centre of the druids, and must have been a major centre of resistance. The Romans attacked in AD 60. As they crossed the water, druids cursed them, women dressed in black screamed abuse and warriors hurled spears. The Romans slaughtered them and burned down the sacred groves of oak trees.

Boudicca's rebellion was savage and many Roman citizens died in the flames of London. The revenge of the legions was merciless. About 80,000 British warriors were killed and Boudicca committed suicide by taking poison.

AD 84
The Romans defeat the Caledonian tribes at
Mons Graupius.

AD 70
The Romans mine gold in Wales.

REBELS AND CONQUERORS

Just as the Romans were attacking Mona, they
had to march back to southeastern Britain where
a rebellion was breaking out. It was led by
Boudicca, queen of the Iceni. When her husband,
Prasutagas, died, the Romans had broken their
word by annexing his kingdom and had wronged
his family. The tribes joined Boudicca. Colchester
and London were destroyed. Eventually the
Romans caught up with the rebels and massacred
them. Boudicca took her own life. By the AD 70s
the Romans had control of the north and in
AD 84 they defeated the tribes of what is now
southern Scotland at Mons Graupius, near
Inverurie. Calgacus, the defeated leader, said
bitterly, 'They make a wilderness and call it peace'.

The Iron Legions

Once the native resistance had been broken, the Romans imposed their government on the island of Britain. The limits of their rule were marked by the Irish Sea to the west and by a series of defences to the north. The farthest of these was the Antonine Wall, built in AD 142, but this was later abandoned in favour of the earlier Hadrian's Wall, built in AD 122. Large forts were built across Britain. Roman rule was maintained through the second century AD by the iron grip of its army, which was highly mobile and ruthlessly efficient.

BRITANNIA
(GREAT BRITAIN)

MARE
ORIENTALE
(NORTH SEA)

MARE
HIBERNIAE
(IRISH SEA)

Luguvalium
Carlisle

Eboracum
York

Segontium
Caernarfon

Deva
Chester

Lindum
Lincoln

Ratae
Leicester

Camoludunum
Colchester

Glevum
Gloucester Verulamium
St Albans

Isca Silurum
Caerleon

Londinium
London

Venta Belgarum
Winchester

Dubris
Dover

Isca Dumnoniorum
Exeter

MARE AUSTRUM
(ENGLISH CHANNEL)

ROMAN BRITAIN

The new Roman province was called Britannia. London soon outgrew Colchester as the most important town. Important bases for the legions were built at Chester and York in northern England, and Caerleon in South Wales. After about AD 213, Britannia was divided into two regions – Upper and Lower.

↑ *When storming a hill fort, Roman soldiers would form a close unit, crouching with shields covering their heads and their sides. This formation was called a 'testudo', or tortoise. Hillforts were also attacked with huge catapults.*

THE ROMAN ARMY

When the Britons were called to arms, their organisation suffered from tribal rivalries and lack of military planning. In contrast, the Roman army was completely professional. It was organised into legions, military units that at the time of the conquest numbered about 5500 troops each. Each legion was divided into ten sections called cohorts. The backbone of the legion was formed by 59 middle-ranking officers called centurions. Support troops who were not Roman citizens were known as auxiliaries.

← *Horses were used by officers and by separate cavalry units. These were armed with long swords and spears.*

Throwing spear
The legionary's spear was a weighted javelin, made of wood and iron.

Marching baggage
The legionary marched with a heavy bundle slung over his shoulder. It included all sorts of digging tools, buckets and clattering tins as well as his basic food rations – biscuits, cheese and bacon.

Hand-fighting
The legionary carried a short sword in a scabbard and also a dagger.

Armour
Caesar's legions wore armour of mail, but by the time of Claudius, Roman foot soldiers wore armour made of metal plates.

Sandals
Sandals were made from leather and the soles were studded with iron for the long marches.

A SOLDIER'S LIFE

The Roman legionary was a paid, professional soldier. Recruits were given very hard training. They learned parade-ground drill and battle formations. They were forced to march very long distances. They were taught how to fight with swords and throw javelins, how to pitch camp and dig defences. Punishments for disobedience were harsh. At the time of the conquest of Britain, legionaries were not allowed to marry whilst in service. After 25 years, however, they could retire. Many then settled around military camps and towns, often marrying a British woman and raising a family.

Shield
Roman shields at this time were rectangular. They were made of wood, leather and linen, with a boss (central stud) of iron or bronze.

← *The Roman legionary was soldier, builder, engineer and labourer all in one.*

HADRIAN'S WALL

Hadrian's Wall stretched from the Solway Firth in the west to the river Tyne in the east, a distance of 177 kilometres. Much of it still stands today, and offers us a fascinating glimpse of military life on the Roman frontier at the time of the wall's construction in AD 122, The wall took its from the emperor Hadrian (AD 76–138). The wall served several purposes. It divided the rebellious Caledonians (the tribes from the far north of Britain) from the tribes to the south. It provided a route for rapid movement of troops and supplies, and traded goods.

LETTERS FROM THE WALL

Life on Hadrian's Wall was hard for the Roman legionaries and the foreign auxiliaries stationed there. Winters were cold, duties were dull or sometimes dangerous, always exhausting. Archaeologists have found orders for supplies, accounts, requests for leave, and even letters from home saying that the underpants and socks requested have been sent.

A Roman patrol brings in two Picts ('painted people') from beyond the wall, for questioning.

THE IRON LEGIONS   **45**

AD 43
Roman legions build the first proper roads in Britain.

AD 45
Pottery imported from Gaul (Roman France).

All Roads Lead to Rome

The Romans did not conquer Britain just for the glory, or simply to protect their territories in mainland Europe. They wanted to make a profit. The island had precious metal ores, fertile lands for farming and a large labour force. It could also provide a new market for goods produced in Italy or Gaul. Imports into Britain included pottery from Gaul and wine from southern Europe and the Rhineland. Exports included woollen cloaks, lead, silver, the black stone called jet, oysters and hunting dogs.

ROMAN MONEY

Coins of gold, silver and brass became common throughout Britain. There was now a single currency, or money system, across a vast area of Europe, Western Asia and North Africa.

▶ A coin of the emperor Constantine (c.AD 274–337).

AD 49
Lead and silver being mined in southwest England.

AD 50
The Roman town of Londinium (London) is founded on the River Thames.

SHIPS AND CARGOES

Creaking, square-sailed wooden ships carried cargoes and merchants across the choppy waters of the North Sea and the English Channel. London, on the River Thames, became Britain's biggest port.

▶ Roman ships followed coastlines whenever possible.

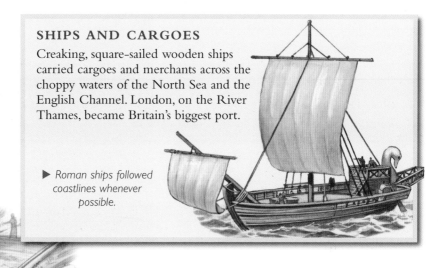

THE GROWING TOWNS

Celtic life had mostly been based in the country, but Roman life was centred on towns with about 5000 inhabitants. The Romans rebuilt many of the old British settlements with straight streets and drainage. They built large town halls, law courts, markets, shops, bakeries, restaurants and bars, even public toilets. Smaller towns grew up around military camps and forts, or wherever there was a need to trade.

◀ Layers of broken flint and crushed stone were laid as foundations. The surface was generally of gravel, but sometimes paved. The roads were built by the army using troops or slaves as labour.

ROMAN ROADS

Most roads were made using whichever stone was available locally. The route was carefully surveyed and forest was cleared well back from the verges, to prevent ambush.

AD 75
A splendid palace is built at Fishbourne, near Chichester, England.

AD 78
Aquae Sulis (Bath) already famous for its warm springs.

Roman Peace

British rebels were sold into slavery, but local rulers and nobles who supported Rome prospered. Many of them adopted Roman ways and dress. They learned to speak Latin, the language of Rome. Roman rule was often harsh, but it did bring a period of peace to large areas of Europe.

⬆ *The baths at Aquae Sulis (Bath) had changing rooms and lockers, hot baths, warm baths and cold baths – but no soap. Bathers oiled their bodies and then scraped themselves clean.*

BRITISH AND ROMAN

Romans who stayed in Britain for more than a few years were influenced in turn by the Celts. Although Romans worshipped their own gods and goddesses, they were also prepared to honour many of the Celtic gods.

When the Romans built luxurious new public baths at Bath, in western England, these were dedicated both to the Celtic goddess Sulis and the Roman goddess Minerva.

c.AD 90
A Roman theatre is built at Canterbury, Kent.

c.AD 90
Large town houses being built in Britain for the first time.

LIVING IN STYLE

Large country houses called villas were built for important Roman officials or for local British rulers who remained loyal to Rome. They were surrounded by large farm estates. Over the years, villas became more and more luxurious, with under-floor central heating, baths and dining rooms where visitors from Rome would be entertained with lavish banquets.

Roofs
Roofs were wooden framed and covered with tiles of baked clay.

 The most impressive Roman villas were built in the AD *200s and 300s.*

Roman dining
Guests ate lying down on couches around a low central table.

In the kitchen
Cooks prepared dishes with food from the villa farm. Hunting in the forests provided wild game. Roman food was highly spiced.

Serving the master
The villa was kept running by a large team of slaves and servants.

Gardens
Walkways with columns and statues passed through gardens of shrubs, herbs and fruit trees.

ROMAN PEACE **49**

AD 60
Town built at Corinium (Cirencester).

AD 78
Founding of Venta Silurum (Caerwent)
and the town at Lindum (Lincoln).

Roman Towns

The Romans built towns, often on the sites of the former tribal capitals of the Britons. Smaller towns and villages grew up around crossroads, along rivers and by the sea. The Romans who moved into these towns were officials, lawyers, traders or craftworkers. They were soon joined by those Britons who could afford to take up the Roman way of life.

LONDINIUM (LONDON)

Sited on the banks of the river Thames, London was ideally sited for trade with the rest of the empire. A long, wooden bridge was built across the river. London became a great centre of trade and was the biggest city in the province. At its peak it had a population of about 45,000. An army fort was built, a huge town hall, or basilica, a market place, or forum, and temples.

AD 79
Rebuilding of St Albans.

AD 140
Forum and town hall built at Venta
Icenorum (Caistor).

ROMAN ENGINEERING

The Romans were great engineers.
Their towns were supplied with fresh
water by aqueducts (water channels)
and pipes made of lead and timber.
Towns had drains and sewers.

⬆ The biggest towns in Britannia, such as
Londinium, served as military bases.

AD 280
Start of Saxon raids on southern and eastern Britain.

AD 287
Carausius rules Britain independently.

The Fall of Rome

The mighty empire of Rome began to look less powerful after AD 200. There were bitter civil wars and struggles for power. In AD 286 the empire was divided into an eastern and western part. Britain was in the west, and so was still ruled from Rome. However in AD 287 Carausius, commander of the Roman fleet in Britain, declared himself ruler of Britain. He was murdered by a fellow rebel, Allectus, in AD 293. Rome regained control in AD 297, but not for long. Frontier defences were now being breached all around the empire.

← *A beacon blazes on top of a lighthouse as Roman ships patrol the English Channel.*

AD 297
Rule from Rome is restored in Britain.

AD 306
Constantine the Great is declared Roman emperor
at York.

⬇ A Germanic people, the
Saxons, sailed across the
North Sea to attack Roman
Britain and test its defences.

THE TROUBLED EMPIRE

The entire Roman empire was
increasingly in crisis. Germanic
tribes were under attack from
Asiatic invaders in the east and
were soon being pushed into
western Europe. Germanic
warriors poured into Roman
territories in Gaul (modern
France), Spain, southeastern
Europe and Italy itself. As Roman
troops were deployed to meet
these threats, Britain itself lay open
to attack.

INVADERS CHALLENGE ROME

Roman Britain now came under attack
from all sides. In the far north the Picts
overran Hadrian's Wall and advanced south.
Western shores and shipping were under
attack from the Gaels, the unconquered
Celts of Ireland. The English Channel was
plagued by pirates. Southern England and
East Anglia were attacked by a people from
Germany, the Saxons. From about AD 280
Romans built a chain of massive stone forts
to defend southeastern coasts, which
became known as the Saxon Shore.

THE FALL OF ROME 53

THE MILDENHALL TREASURE

In 1946 it was officially reported that four years earlier a Roman treasure hoard had been ploughed up at Mildenhall in Suffolk, England. The pieces discovered were made of solid silver and dated from about AD 350. They may have originally been imported from Roman North Africa. They included spoons, splendid dishes, plates and wine goblets – 34 pieces in all. In the days before banks and safes, people stored their wealth as precious metals. In times of war they would bury them at a secret spot, to prevent them falling into enemy hands. Hoards like this one suggest that by the 300s, Roman Britain was no longer a peaceful or secure place to live.

▲ This splendid dish from the Mildenhall treasure hoard is now in the British Museum, in London.

MAGNUS MAXIMUS

Magnus Maximus was a Spanish-born commander of the Roman troops in Britain. He made treaties with Celtic peoples such as the Votadini and Dumnonii to take on defending Britain against the Picts and Gaels. In AD 383 he marched with his troops to Rome and seized the throne. He was killed five years later. His memory survives in the folklore of Wales, where he is known as Macsen.

➔ In AD 410 Alaric, leader of a Germanic people called the Western Goths, sacked the city of Rome itself.

THE EMPIRE FALLS

Between AD 401 and 410, Roman troops were withdrawn from Britain as Germanic tribes crossed the River Rhine and poured into Gaul. Within the empire there were revolts and uprisings, and more attempts to seize local power. The economy collapsed. In AD 410, Rome itself was sacked by northern invaders called Goths. The emperor Honorius declared that from now on, the Britons would have to defend themselves. In AD 446 British leaders made one last appeal to Rome, but it was hopeless. It took just 30 more years for the Roman empire in Western Europe to come to an end. Rome had ruled Britain for nearly 400 years. It had changed the history of the island forever, with its language, its law, its towns and roads, its technology and its religion. Rome was never forgotten.

Anderitum (modern Pevensey, in Sussex) was the site of a stone fort built by the Romans to defend Britain from attacks by Saxons. It probably dates from about AD 343 and was re-fortified in the Middle Ages. Other forts already built on the 'Saxon shore' included Brancaster, Burgh Castle, Walton Castle, Bradwell, Reculver, Richborough, Dover, Lympne and Portchester.

Raiders and Settlers

AD 446–1066

ELSEWHERE IN EUROPE

AD 476
End of the Roman empire in western Europe.

c.AD 500
Migrations of Slavs begin, to east, west and south of their homeland in eastern Europe.

AD 529
Justinian, emperor of East Rome, or Byzantium (now Istanbul), draws up laws.

AD 711
Muslim Moors (Arabs and Berbers) invade Spain from North Africa.

AD 732
Charles Martel, ruler of the Franks, drives Arab invaders from France.

AD 800
Charlemagne, ruler of the Franks, is crowned emperor in Rome.

AD 912
The Viking warlord Rollo becomes Duke of Normandy in France.

AD 962
King Otto I of Germany becomes Holy Roman Emperor.

ASIA

AD 531
The Sassanid empire expands in Persia (Iran) under Chrosroes I.

AD 535
Collapse of the Gupta empire in India.

AD 552
The Buddhist faith reaches Japan from China.

AD 570
Muhammad the Prophet, founder of Islam, is born in Mecca, Arabia.

AD 610
A Grand Canal links China's two greatest rivers, the Huang He and the Chang Jiang.

AD 618
China is ruled by the Tang emperors, a golden age of arts and science.

AD 786
Harun al-Rashid is Caliph (ruler) of Baghdad and head of a vast empire.

AD 802
The Angkor kingdom is founded by Khmer rulers in Cambodia.

AFRICA

AD 500
Bantu-speaking migrants arrive in southern Africa.

AD 531
A Christian Church is founded in Ethiopia, North Africa.

AD 600
Rise of the powerful gold-producing kingdom of Ghana, in West Africa.

AD 641
Arabs invade Egypt, beginning their conquest of North Africa.

AD 750
Trade across the Sahara Desert between North and West Africa.

AD 900
Rise of Swahili culture on the coast of East Africa.

AD 969
Foundation of the city of Cairo, on the River Nile in Egypt.

c.1000
First settlement at Great Zimbabwe.

"Monks take refuge as bands of warriors invade the island."

NORTH AMERICA

AD 500
Teotihuacán city in central Mexico has a population of about 200,000.

AD 700
Temple mounds built in the valley of the Mississippi river.

AD 700
Cahokia, the first town in the region now taken up by the United States.

AD 700
Hohokam, Anasazi and Mogollon peoples in the southwest.

AD 800
The 'Dorset' culture amongst Inuit hunters of Canada and Greenland.

AD 950
The Toltecs found the city of Tula in central Mexico.

1000
Vikings try to found settlements in Labrador and Newfoundland.

1050
The Anasazi build defensive settlements in the southwest.

SOUTH AMERICA

AD 500
Tiwanaku city, near Lake Titicaca, has a population of 40–100,000.

AD 600
The great Gateway of the Sun is raised at Tiwanaku.

AD 700
The Andean city state of Wari becomes very powerful.

AD 700
The decline of the Moche culture in northern Peru.

AD 750
The Nazca civilisation of southern Peru comes to an end.

AD 800
The Chimú city of Chan Chan, northern Peru, covers an area of 15 sq km.

AD 900
The Chimú empire at the height of its power in northern Peru.

1000
The city of Wari is abandoned.

OCEANIA

c.500
Polynesians settle in the southern Cook Islands.

c.AD 700
Easter islanders raise platforms of large stone blocks.

c.AD 800
Earliest evidence for Polynesian hand clubs made of wood and whalebone.

c.AD 850
The Maoris, a Polynesian people, settle New Zealand coasts.

c.AD 850
Maoris begin to hunt large flightless birds such as the moa.

c.AD 900
Aborigines mining rock for axes, Mount Isa, bartering routes across Australia.

c.1000
Last phase of Pacific settlement by Polynesian seafarers.

c.1000
Easter Islanders begin to raise huge heads of carved stone.

Sign of the Cross

One of the new eastern religions that appeared in Britain towards the end of the Roman period was Christianity. Its founder, Jesus Christ, had been put to death by the Roman rulers of Jerusalem in about AD 30. Christians believed that there was just one God, and that Jesus was his son. They taught people that they should love their enemies.

CHRISTIANITY SPREADS

At first the Romans punished the Christians for believing that their God was more powerful than the emperor. Even so, the new faith spread quickly, among both Romans and Britons, rich and poor alike.

Jesus Christ was pictured in this floor mosaic found at a Roman villa in Hinton St Mary, Dorset, England. It dates from the early years of Christianity in Britain. The symbols in the background are the Greek letters Chi and Rho, the first two letters of the name 'Christ'.

c.AD 313
Christians given full rights of worship in Roman empire.

c.AD 390
St Ninian (Nynia) founds church in southern Scotland.

CHRISTIANS AND PAGANS

In Britain, a Christian legionary called Albanus (St Alban) was executed in about AD 300. However the emperor Constantine made Christianity legal in AD 313 and himself became a Christian. The new faith spread among both Romans and Britons. As the ages passed, the old Celtic beliefs only survived as country customs. The word 'pagan', meaning non-believer, originally came from the Latin word for 'countryside'.

⬇ Christian burial grounds and chapels date from the fourth century AD. Finds have included silver chalices, the cups used during Christian worship. Lead tanks have been discovered, too, which held the water in which new Christians were baptised.

Silver chalice

⬅ Constantine, son of emperor Constantius, addressing troops in York. In AD 306 the legions serving in York proclaimed their backing for Constantine, who had been a successful soldier. He succeeded his father as emperor and became known as Constantine the Great. Constantine made Christianity legal, and in AD 324 it became the official religion of the empire.

THE CELTIC CHURCH

After the Romans left Britain, raids by non-Christian Saxons increased in southern and eastern Britain. Christianity spread most rapidly in the west, in Wales and Cornwall. Many place names in these areas today begin with 'Llan–' or 'Lan–'. A 'llan' was a religious enclosure, where monks would teach people about the life of Christ, farm the land and care for the sick. A type of Christianity grew in Celtic lands that was rather different from that of Rome. It was influenced by the teachings of a British monk called Pelagius. He believed that people were basically good, that they were not born sinful. He also attacked wealth and privilege. It was AD 664 before the Celtic and Roman Churches finally came together.

← Jesus Christ, like many condemned to death by the Romans, had been crucified – left to die on a wooden cross. The cross eventually became the most common symbol of Christianity. Early and medieval Celtic crosses were beautifully carved in stone and often formed a 'wheel' design, which became popular once more in modern times. This cross is at Iona, in Scotland, a Christian site since AD 563.

AD 574
Rome orders conversion of Anglo-Saxons.
Mission postponed to AD 597.

AD 601
Death of St David (Dewi Sant) South Wales.

THE AGE OF SAINTS

St Patrick (c.AD 385–460) was born in western Britain. Kidnapped by pirates, he escaped to Ireland and later studied in Gaul. In about AD 432 he went back to Ireland, probably to Armagh, to spread the Christian message.

St Ninian or Nynia (c.AD 390) was a Briton born near the Solway Firth. He studied in Rome, became a bishop and founded a church in what is now Wigtownshire, Scotland. He converted the southern Picts to Christianity.

St David or Dewi Sant (c.AD 520–601) was born in southwest Wales. He founded religious centres in South Wales and the West of England and became Bishop at Menevia (St David's).

⬆ St Patrick was made a bishop at the age of 45. He was probably sent back to Ireland by Pope Celestine I.

➡ Monks of the early Celtic Church lived in beehive-shaped cells called clocháns. This style of building has been adapted to a rectangular stone chapel on the Dingle peninsula in Ireland. The Gallarus Oratory (chapel of prayer) may be 1400 years old.

AD 430
Possible date for rule of Ambrosius (Emrys)
over Britons.

AD 448
Vortigern asks Hengist and Horsa to help him fight
the Picts.

The Age of Arthur

The thousand years between the fall of Rome and the start of modern European history are known as the Middle Ages. After Rome withdrew from Britain, the country was divided between local rulers. Many of them still tried to follow the Roman – and Christian – way of life. However trade was disrupted by war and grass grew through cracked pavements as Roman towns and villas fell into disrepair.

AD 455
Hengist and Horsa attack Vortigern. Horsa is killed.

AD 456
Hengist and his son Aesc defeat Britons in Kent.

⬅ *Dragons were used as emblems (left) by the Britons after the Roman withdrawal. Dragons, originally an Asian design, were used on some Roman cavalry standards and may have appeared on the standard of Magnus Maximus. A red dragon remains the emblem of Wales today.*

⬅ *Legend has it that Arthur was born at Tintagel, on the northern coast of Cornwall. This cliff-top site was inhabited in Roman times and by AD 500 had a Christian monastery. It also has the ruins of a castle from 500 years later.*

TALES OF ARTHUR

It cannot be proved that Arthur or Artorius, one of the most famous names in British history, existed at all. However many clues suggest that he was indeed a historical figure. If so, he was probably of noble birth, a British Celt and a Christian who followed the Roman way of life.

Arthur would have been a war leader or general rather than a king. He would have led a band of armoured, mounted warriors that could assist local defence groups, moving at speed to meet invading Saxons or Picts. He is linked with a great victory at somewhere called Mount Badon in about AD 516 and is said to have been killed at the battle of Camlan in AD 537.

During the later Middle Ages, tales about Arthur spread far and wide. Many of them mixed him up with ancient Celtic gods and heroes. He became a king in shining armour, famous for his bravery. Stories about Arthur and his companions were told in France, Germany and Italy.

AD 495
Saxons under Cerdic invade Wessex
(central Southern England).

AD 516
Possible date for Battle of Mount Badon.
Britons halt West Saxon advance.

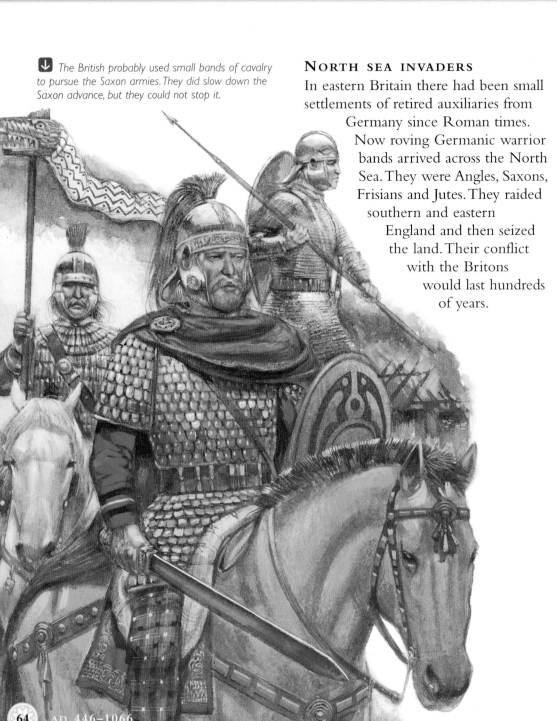

⬇ *The British probably used small bands of cavalry to pursue the Saxon armies. They did slow down the Saxon advance, but they could not stop it.*

NORTH SEA INVADERS

In eastern Britain there had been small settlements of retired auxiliaries from Germany since Roman times. Now roving Germanic warrior bands arrived across the North Sea. They were Angles, Saxons, Frisians and Jutes. They raided southern and eastern England and then seized the land. Their conflict with the Britons would last hundreds of years.

AD 539
Supposed date for battle of Camlan and death of Arthur.

AD 547
Ida founds the Saxon kingdom of Bernicia at Bamburgh, Northumberland.

BATTLING FOR BRITAIN

We know little of the kings and armies who defended Britain against the new invaders. Emrys or Ambrosius seems to have been a very powerful ruler in about AD 430, possibly later. In AD 449 another king called Vortigern invited two Jutes called Hengist and Horsa to help him fight the Picts, in return for land. By AD 455 they had turned against Vortigern and were waging war on the Britons.

⬅️ ➡️ *The Saxons from Germany were just some of the people who tried to invade Britannia as Roman power declined.*

Saxon settler

Saxon war chief

ANCIENT TALES

The first mention of Arthur in literature comes in a series of fantastic tales, which were written down in Wales later in the Middle Ages. They had been passed down over the ages by word of mouth. Some are tales of ancient Celtic gods and the underworld, of severed heads and magical animals. Others refer to Magnus Maximus (Macsen), the age of Arthur and the Christian period. Today this group of tales is known as the *Mabinogion*.

THE AGE OF ARTHUR **65**

Saxon Swords

The early Middle Ages were troubled times in Western Europe. Historians used to call this period the 'Dark Ages', because it seemed that the light of Roman civilisation had been put out forever. This name was never really fair, for the period also saw beautiful arts and crafts, great poetry and scholarship in the new monasteries. However this was often a violent age. Invasions by Slavs and Huns in eastern and central Europe were pushing the Germanic peoples ever westwards, where they carved out new kingdoms for themselves in the ruins of the Roman empire.

➡ *Anglo-Saxon warriors of the AD 400s and 500s might be armed with a battle axe, a long sword, a spear, or a long knife called a sax. They wore woollen tunics over trousers and carried round shields. Chieftains wore helmets and shirts of mail.*

GERMANIC INVASIONS

The invaders came from the lands now occupied by Germany, Denmark and the Netherlands. They crossed the North Sea and English Channel in wooden boats and fought their way westwards.

- Frisians and Jutes
- Angles and Saxons
- Franks

IRELAND

NORTH SEA

DENMARK

BRITAIN

Jutes

Frisians

GERMANY

Franks

Angles

ENGLISH CHANNEL

Saxons

THE DAY OF WODEN

The newcomers brought with them worship of the ancient Germanic gods. These survive in English names for days of the week. Tuesday is named after Tiw, god of war. Wednesday is the day of Woden, the chief god. Thursday is the day of Thor, god of thunder. Friday is from Frigg, goddess of love.

BRITONS AND SAXONS

The Anglo-Saxon invaders killed and enslaved many native Britons. Some fled westwards into Wales and Cornwall, or escaped to lands across the Channel that the Britons had already settled, a region known as Brittany. The Britons believed that the Angles and Saxons were savages. These peoples had never experienced Roman civilisation, nor were they Christians. In reality the two peoples shared similar European origins. They both lived in small kingdoms and depended on farming and fishing. They used similar technology and both were fine craftworkers.

← *Woden, also known as Wotan or Odin, rode an eight-legged horse.*

SAXON SWORDS   67

AD 625
Probable date of the Sutton Hoo burial in East Anglia.

AD 625
First Anglo-Saxon coins to be minted in England.

ANGLO-SAXON LANDS

Modern names for counties and regions of England
recall the first advances of the Anglo-Saxons. Essex
comes from East Seaxe, land of the East Saxons. Sussex
come from Suth Seaxe, land of the South Saxons. East
Anglia was East Engle, the eastern territory of the
Angles. By AD 550 the Anglo-Saxons controlled
large areas of eastern and southern Britain.
The Britons still ruled in the west and
much of the north.

THATCH AND TIMBER

The Anglo-Saxons built small,
compact farming villages in the lands
they conquered. Many Anglo-Saxon
place names are found on the map
of England today, containing
elements such as '-stead', '-ham',
'-ing', '-ford', '-ton', '-stow',
'-wich' or -'wick'. Houses
were rectangular, with walls of
timber planks and pitched
roofs covered in a heavy
thatch. These were surrounded
by a fenced yard. In some
areas, huts seem to have been
raised over sunken pits. which
may have been boarded over.

➡️ An Anglo-Saxon farmstead was
surrounded by a few large fields cleared from
the forest. Within these, farmers worked their
own strips for cultivation and harvest.

AD 642
Penda of Mercia kills Oswald of Northumbria
at Maserfeld.

AD 655
Penda of Mercia killed by Oswiu of Northumbria
at Battle of the Winwaed.

A ROYAL SHIP BURIAL

In 1939 a grave was discovered at Sutton Hoo, near Woodbridge in Suffolk, England. It was a royal burial, probably that of Raedwald, a ruler of East Anglia who died in about AD 625. He was buried in a ship beneath a mound of earth. His ship was 27 metres long and was rowed by 40 oars. Inside a wooden chamber in the boat was a rich treasure hoard. There were buckles and fasteners of shining gold, a jewel-covered purse containing 37 gold coins. There was a musical instrument called a lyre. There was a sword, a shield and the remains of a splendid helmet made of iron and bronze.

The ornate Sutton Hoo helmet shows the influence of Roman styles on European design 200 years after the collapse of the Roman empire.

C.AD 500
The founding of the kingdom of Dál Riada by
Fergus Mór.

AD 574
Colmcille crowns Aedán MacGabráin High King
of Dál Riada.

The Making of Scotland

Scotland takes its name from a people whom the Romans called Scoti. These 'Scots' were Gaels who sailed from northern Ireland to raid Britain's western coasts and islands as the Roman empire collapsed. By AD 500 they had founded a kingdom called Dál Riada on the Scottish mainland. For many years the Scots battled with the Picts, who still controlled the lands of the northeast, around Aberdeen.

⬇ For hundreds of years after the Picts first built brochs, they used these round towers for shelter when attacked by enemies. This is Don Carloway Broch on the Isle of Lewis.

AD 604
Strathclyde and Dál Riada defeated by Angles at Degsástan.

AD 642
Owain of Strathclyde defeats Dál Riada at Strathcarron.

Columba arrived on the Scottish island of Iona with a handful of companions. He converted many people to the Christian faith.

IONA AND COLMCILLE

Colmcille, or Columba, was born in AD 521, into a noble Irish family. In the old days he would probably have been a druid, but instead he was an enthusiastic Christian. In AD 563 he set up a monastery and centre of learning on the island of Iona, in the Hebrides. He and his monks travelled through Scotland, founding churches and preaching Christianity to the northern Picts. It was another monk from Iona, Aidan, who set up a monastery at Lindisfarne, in Northumbria, in about AD 635.

c.AD 650
Dál Riada loses its territories in
northern Ireland.

AD 685
Picts stop northern advance of Angles at
Nechtansmere.

DÁL RIADA

The new kingdom of Dál Riada
included part of northern Ireland, islands
such as Iona, and the Argyll region of
the Scottish mainland. By about AD 650
the Scots had lost their lands back in
Ireland. Cut off from their homeland,
the dialect of Irish that they spoke
gradually developed into the Gaelic
language still spoken today in the
islands and highlands of Scotland.

⬆ This beautiful wooden box, the Monymusk
Reliquary, is decorated with gilt and silver. It was made
in the 600s or 700s and is said to have contained the
remains of Colmcille (Columba).

⬅ Picts were
one of four
groups of people
living in Scotland
at this time.

BATTLE FOR THE LOWLANDS

The Angles who had founded Bernicia
(later part of Northumbria) soon
pushed further northwards, into the
Scottish Lowlands. The Britons living
in the Lowlands were under pressure
from all sides. They made an alliance
with the Scots to fight the Angles, but
were defeated at the battle of Degsástan
(perhaps near Jedburgh) in AD 603. The
Angles now controlled the Lothian
region – eastern Scotland below the
Firth of Forth. This left the Britons of
the Lowlands isolated in their kingdom
of Strathclyde. Their lands to the south
were also being overrun by Angles and
they were soon cut off from their
fellow Britons in Wales.

THE KINGDOM OF ALBA

In AD 685 the Picts halted the northward advance of the Angles with a desperate battle at Nechtansmere, Dunnichen. But it was not until AD 843 that northern Scotland finally became united. That was when a ruler of the Scots called Kenneth MacAlpin ('mac' meaning 'son of') joined his kingdom with that of the Picts. The centre of the Christian Church in Scotland now moved eastwards from Iona to Dunkeld, in Perthshire. The new kingdom was called Alba and it linked most of the region lying to the north of the Firth of Forth and the River Clyde. It was one of the most important kingdoms in the Celtic world and formed the chief building block of the future kingdom of Scotland. Alba rarely knew peace, for it was under constant attack by Anglo-Saxons from the south and by Scandinavians around its coasts.

THE STONE OF DESTINY

A ceremonial slab of sandstone was brought by the Scots from Ireland to Iona. From there it was taken to Dunstaffinage and later to Scone, near Perth. This 'Stone of Destiny' was used at the coronation of the kings of Alba and of united Scotland. In 1297 the English King Edward I stole the stone and took it south to London. There it stayed until 1950, when it was reclaimed by four Scottish students. The stone was recovered in Arbroath and returned to England. However in 1996 it was officially installed in Edinburgh Castle.

⬆ Kenneth I succeeded his father Alpin as King of the Scots in AD 841. Two years later he united the lands of the Scots and the Picts. He died in AD 858.

c.AD 540
The voyages of Brendan around North
Atlantic coasts.

c.AD 550
Start of the age of the monasteries in Ireland.

Across the Irish Sea

As Roman power declined and finally vanished, Irish ships raided the western coasts of Britain. Irish settlements were founded in West Wales and in Scotland. Whilst Angles and Saxons were streaming into eastern Britain, trade prospered in the west, around the Irish Sea. Merchants and monks sailed between Ireland, Scotland, Wales, Cornwall, Brittany and southwestern Europe. Ireland was entering one of the greatest ages in its history.

⬇ *An Irish raiding party clambers ashore on the west coast of Britain, looking for cattle, slaves and plunder.*

THE VOYAGE OF BRENDAN

Brendan, or Brandan, was born in Tralee, in County Kerry, in AD 484. A Christian saint, he is said to have founded Clonfert monastery in Galway in AD 561. Tales about him were written down later in the Middle Ages, describing his sea voyages. Brendan seems to have been a navigator who sailed the North Atlantic Ocean and knew its eastern coasts. A description of the 'mouth of hell' suggests that he may have seen volcanic eruptions off the coast of Iceland.

CHILDREN OF NIALL

The greatest ruler of the Gaels at the end of the Roman era was Níall Naoi-Ghiallach (Níall of the Nine Hostages). He became High King of Ireland at the end of the fourth century AD and was renowned for carrying out raids on Britain and Gaul. He was the founder of the O'Neill dynasty, which remained a powerful force in Ireland throughout the Middle Ages and beyond.

c.AD 650
The Book of Durrow, start of the golden age of
Celtic Christian art.

AD 697
Synod of Birr discusses Christian treatment of
women and children.

▼ The Tara brooch is made of
gilded bronze and silver and is
decorated with glass and amber. It
probably dates from about AD 700.

OGHAM SCRIPT

A kind of alphabet made up of criss-
cross lines was carved on Irish stones
from about AD 300. It is called ogham.
Ogham fell out of use as Christian
monks in the 600s and 700s introduced
the letters of the Roman alphabet.

▼ The Book of Kells may
have been produced on
the Island of Iona, but
finished in Ireland.

ART OF THE MONKS

Christian monasteries in Ireland
became great centres of learning.
They also held great political
influence. Important monasteries grew
up at Clonmacnoise in County Offaly
and Clonard in County Meath. Derry,
Durrow and Kells were linked with the
church at Iona. Armagh was another
great Christian centre. The Irish
monasteries inspired beautiful works of
art and craft. In the Book of Kells,
produced before AD 800, religious texts
are decorated with elaborate patterns,
animal designs and pictures.

c.AD 700
Fine metal working, such as the Tara brooch and Ardagh chalice.

c.AD 800
The Book of Kells, the masterpiece of Celtic Christian art.

KINGS, LORDS AND PEASANTS

Irish society was divided into three classes. At the bottom were the commoners. These included some slaves, serfs (labourers who were not allowed to leave the land) and freemen who owned their farms. Life for poor people was very hard. They lived largely on a diet of porridge and oatcakes. Hunger and disease were common. Labourers toiled on the land. Commoners had to declare their loyalty to the lords and the lords to the kings. There were many minor kings, but real power lay with the regional kings of Ulster, Meath, Munster, Leinster and Connaught. A High King was based at the ancient royal site of Tara, but rarely ruled all Ireland because of the endless wars between Ireland's royal families.

⬆ This chalice, a cup used during Christian worship, was dug up at Ardagh, in County Limerick, in 1868. It is one of the finest pieces of metal working produced in Europe during the early Middle Ages. It is made of silver and gilt bronze, with a central stud of rock crystal. It dates from about AD 700.

AD 577
West Britons defeated by Wessex at the Battle
of Dyrham.

AD 600
Earliest known Welsh poetry, the *Gododdin*.

The Making of Wales

The advancing Angles and Saxons
gradually conquered the lands of the
Britons. After the Battle of Dyrham in AD 577
the Britons of Devon and Cornwall were cut
off from the Britons to the north. However
independent kingdoms survived in the
far west. The Saxons called these
Britons 'Welsh', meaning
'foreign'. The western Britons
began to call themselves
'Cymry', meaning
'compatriots'.

WELSH RULERS
Houses of Gwynedd, Powys and Dyfed

✦ Rhodri Mawr ('the Great')	AD 844–878
✦ Anarawd	AD 878–916
✦ Hywel Dda ('the Good')	AD 915–950
✦ Iago ab Idwal	AD 950–979
✦ Hywel ab Ieuaf	AD 979–985
✦ Cadwallon II	AD 985–986
✦ Maredudd ap Owain	AD 986–999
✦ Cynan ap Hywel	AD 999–1008
✦ Llywelyn ap Seisyll	1018–1023
✦ Iago ap Idwal ap Meurig	1023–1039

⬆ *At the courts
of the Welsh kings,
harpists praised rulers
for their wisdom and
bravery, or lamented
their defeat by the
Anglo-Saxons.*

AD 607
The battle of Chester. Aefelfrith of Northumbria defeats the Britons.

AD 635
The West Britons start to call themselves *Cymry* – the Welsh.

THE OLD NORTH

In Welsh history, the lands of the northern Britons are known as the Old North. This region was divided into several kingdoms. They included Elmet (around the hills of the Pennines), Rheged (Cumbria), Manaw Gododdin (around Edinburgh) and the kingdom of Strathclyde. All but the last were invaded by the Angles. An Anglo-Saxon victory at Chester, in AD 615, drove a wedge between Wales and the Old North. Links between the two were finally broken after AD 654.

"MEN WENT TO CATRAETH..."

Welsh poetry has a very long history. Some of the earliest and finest verse was written down later in the Middle Ages. The story of the *Gododdin* comes from the Old North and is dated to about AD 600. It describes a British war band that sets out, perhaps from Edinburgh, to attack the Angles at Catraeth (today's Catterick, in Yorkshire). The war band suffers a terrible defeat.

⬇ *This tombstone records the death of King Cadfan of Gwynedd in AD 625. The words are written in Latin and his name is made Roman (Catamanus). The words mean 'King Cadfan, wisest and most renowned of all kings'.*

AD 784
Offa's Dyke marks the eastern border of Wales.

AD 844
Rhodri Mawr becomes king of Gwynedd and extends its power.

KING OFFA

In AD 784, Saxon King Offa ordered that a great dyke be built between his kingdom of Mercia in the English midlands and Wales. The dyke acted as a defence against Welsh attacks.

▲ This penny coin, made from silver, is decorated with King Offa's portrait and his name.

WELSH KINGDOMS

Even when Wales was cut off by the Anglo-Saxons, its merchants and monks could still sail to Ireland, Cornwall, Brittany and beyond. Wales was made up of rival kingdoms. Gwynedd was in North Wales. This kingdom became the most powerful under the rule of Rhodri Mawr ('the Great'), who died in AD 877. In southwest Wales, an area settled by Irish invaders, was the kingdom of Dyfed. It later joined with Ceredigion to make a kingdom called Deheubarth. The royal house of Powys in mid–Wales was said to have been founded by Vortigern. Gwent and other small kingdoms of southeast Wales joined together to form Morgannwg (Glamorgan).

WEST OF OFFA'S DYKE

During the early Middle Ages, Wales was made up of several smaller kingdoms, each with its own ruler. These rulers were constantly fighting each other, trying to conquer the rest of Wales.

Gwynedd

Offa's Dyke

IRISH SEA

Powys

Ceredigion

WALES (CYMRU)

Dyfed

Morgannwg

THE LAWS OF HYWEL

Hywel ap ('son of') Cadell was a grandson of Rhodri Mawr. He came to rule most of Wales and made peace with the Anglo-Saxons. In AD 928 he went on a pilgrimage to Rome. Hywel is famed as a law-maker, for it was in his reign that the ancient laws of Wales were written down. The laws deal with property, murder, theft and the rights of women. They describe compensation for crimes, oath-taking and the part played by witnesses. Welsh law was carried out by trained judges and remained in use for over 500 years. Hywel died in AD 950 and is remembered as Hywel Dda ('the Good').

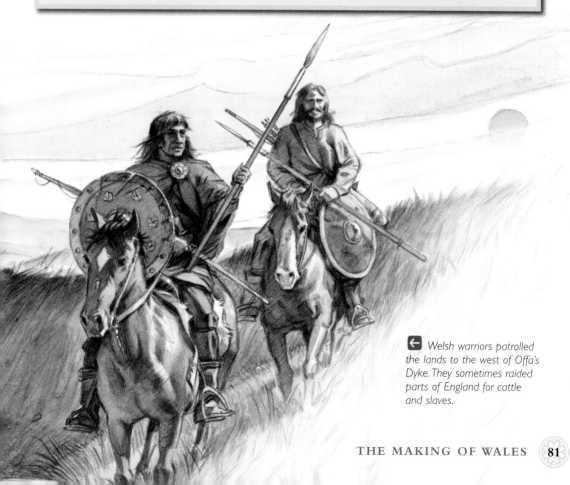

Welsh warriors patrolled the lands to the west of Offa's Dyke. They sometimes raided parts of England for cattle and slaves.

AD 597
Augustine becomes first Archbishop of Canterbury.

AD 634
Oswald becomes king of Northumbria, introduces Celtic Christianity.

The Making of England

Anglo-saxon kings such as Offa of Mercia held great power. They constantly attacked neighbouring kingdoms in their search for wealth and more land. Kings demanded personal loyalty and support from their lords, who were called thanes. Many of the peasants were conquered Britons. They included free men called ceorls, as well as serfs and thralls (slaves). Anglo-Saxon merchants traded across the English Channel, the North Sea and the Baltic.

➜ *Most Anglo-Saxons lived by farming. They laboured on the land of the thane, ploughing, harvesting, and raising sheep and pigs. They cleared the oak forest for new land.*

AD 664
Synod of Whitby unites Roman and Celtic Churches in England.

AD 698
The *Lindisfarne Gospels* produced by monks in Northumbria.

ANGLO-SAXON KINGDOMS

Kent, Sussex and Essex ruled the southeast. Wessex, in the southwest, grew more and more powerful. Mercia, occupying the English Midlands, was the biggest kingdom. The kingdoms of Deira and Bernicia united as Northumbria, taking in all northern England and Lothian.

CELTS

Northumbria

NORTH SEA

ANGLO-SAXONS

East Anglia

Mercia

CELTS

Essex

Kent

Wessex

Sussex

CELTS

ENGLISH CHANNEL

BEOWULF AND THE MONSTER

In about AD 700 an exciting tale was told and retold in the halls of the Anglo-Saxon kings. It was written down in the Old English language of the Anglo-Saxons. It took the form of a long poem about a monster called Grendel, which terrorises the Danes until they are saved by a hero called Beowulf. The verse is alliterative, which means that it plays on repeated sounds.

CHRISTIAN ENGLAND

In AD 597 St Augustine and 40 of his monks arrived from Rome with a mission – to convert the Anglo-Saxons to Christianity. King Ethelbert of Kent, who had a Christian wife, became a Christian too. England's first cathedral was built at Canterbury. In Northumbria, however, the Roman teachings clashed with the Celtic version of Christianity, as preached by the monks of Lindisfarne. In AD 664, a meeting, or synod, was held at Whitby. Here the Celtic Church agreed to recognise the Roman Church.

AD 735
York becomes an archbishopric.

AD 757
Offa makes Mercia the most powerful
Anglo-Saxon kingdom.

BEDE'S HISTORY

Bede or Baeda was born in about AD 673 at Monkwearmouth,
in Tyne and Wear. He became a monk at Jarrow in AD 703
and studied Latin, Greek, Hebrew, medicine and astronomy.
In AD 731 he wrote *The Ecclesiastical History of the English
People* in Latin. It was translated into Anglo-Saxon and still
serves as a very useful guide to early English history. Bede
was buried at Jarrow in AD 735 and his remains were later
moved to Durham.

As Christians, the Anglo-
Saxons built many fine churches
of timber and stone. This
example, dating from AD 960, is
St Mary's Church at Breamore, in
Hampshire. It is a large church
built largely of round flints, but
originally these would have been
plastered over.

Viking Raids

In AD 793 the monastery of Lindisfarne was ransacked and burnt down. A few years later the island of Iona came under attack and its monks were slaughtered. The raiders were known as Northmen or Danes. They are often called Vikings, from an Old Norse word meaning 'sea raiders'. Vikings came from the lands of Scandinavia – Denmark, Norway and Sweden. No sight in Europe was feared more than the sails of their ships coming over the horizon.

GREENLAND

ICELAND

NORWAY
SWEDEN

IRELAND

CANADA

BRITAIN
NORMANDY
FRANCE
DENMARK
GERMANY

RUSSIA

NEWFOUNDLAND
- Viking homeland
- Viking settlements
- Viking routes

SPAIN

ITALY

BYZANTINE
EMPIRE

THE VIKING WORLD

The Vikings were Germanic peoples who originated from the lands we call Scandinavia. They were fearless seafarers, warriors, pirates, farmers, merchants and explorers, who formed settlements over a vast area of the world, from North America to Russia.

LANDS IN PERIL

Soon no region of the British Isles was safe from the Vikings. They raided along all English Channel and North Sea coasts. They attacked villages and towns in Wales, Scotland, Ireland and the Isle of Man. They sailed along the coasts of Germany, the Netherlands, France and Spain. Vikings travelled east into Russia and down to the Middle East. They sailed west, settling Iceland and Greenland. They even reached North America.

↑ *Viking longships were sleek, wooden vessels about 18 metres long. They had a single sail and could speed through the waves. The oars were manned by a crew of 30 or more.*

Jorvik to Dublin

During the 800s, many areas of the British Isles were permanently settled by Vikings. They included the isles of the Shetlands, Orkneys, and Hebrides and the northern and western coasts of the Scottish mainland. The Vikings invaded the Isle of Man and occupied the northern Irish coast. After the 830s the Vikings founded settlements at Dublin and other places in southern Ireland, too. Dublin Vikings later married into the royal family of Gwynedd, in North Wales. In England, Vikings captured York, which they called Jorvik, in AD 867. Three years later they invaded East Anglia and killed King Edmund. Their next prize was the Midland kingdom of Mercia.

Vikings settled from Scotland in the north of Europe to Sicily in the south. Everywhere they went they founded new villages and towns. Sometimes they fought for land from local peoples, and sometimes they lived peacefully alongside them.

IN A VIKING TOWN

A typical Viking settlement in the British Isles was built around quays on a coast or river bank. Moored at the jetties there might be a *knarr*, a broad-beamed merchant ship. A small four-oared *færing* might be seen rowing in from a day's fishing, followed by squawking gulls. Buildings were rectangular and normally made of wattle and daub or oak planks. In the northern islands, stone and turf were common building materials.

AD 850
Viking settlements on Isle of Man.

AD 850
Viking raiders over-winter in England for the
first time.

BLACKSMITHS AND WOODCARVERS

Viking settlements included smithies, where sparks flew as the blacksmith forged swords and spears on the anvil and repaired iron tools for the farm. Metalworkers and jewellers produced finer craft, working with gold, silver, pewter (an alloy of lead and tin), with black jet and yellow amber. The Vikings carved wood, stone and whale bone, often using intricate designs of animals. Vikings often formed a business fellowship called a *felag*, which was rather like a company. The members, who might be craft workers, merchants or mercenaries, put up money and shared the risks and the profits of the enterprise.

Hair
Viking men wore their hair long or tied back.

Plaits and scarves
Women's hair was worn long. It was tidied with a comb made of horn or bone before being plaited or covered by a scarf.

Dress
Viking women wore a shift of linen or wool covered by a long woollen tunic with shoulder straps fastened by brooches.

Tunic
Men wore a knee-length long-sleeved tunic over trousers. Cloaks would be worn against the cold.

➡ *Fragments of Viking clothing have been discovered by archaeologists at York, including boots, shoes and socks.*

AD 851
Norwegian and Danish Vikings battle for control of Dublin.

AD 867
The Vikings take York (Jorvik), which becomes their chief settlement in England.

THE VIKING LONGHOUSE

Viking farmers often settled on remote shores, far from towns such as Jorvik and Dublin. In places such as the Orkney Islands they built longhouses, from timber or stone. When these materials were in short supply, turf was used to cover the roof. The growing grass kept the warmth in and the rain out. The longhouse was built around a central hearth and provided sleeping and living quarters, storage for food, tools and weapons, and stabling for livestock.

Walls made of logs

Animals were kept in the longhouse

Loom for weaving cloth

Meat was smoked to preserve it

AD 914
New wave of Viking attacks on Ireland.

AD 950
Death of Erik Bloodaxe, last Viking king of Jorvik (York).

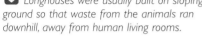 *Longhouses were usually built on sloping ground so that waste from the animals ran downhill, away from human living rooms.*

Wooden rafters

Turf (earth with growing grass) roof

THE TYNWALD

Vikings passed laws and settled disputes at a public assembly called a *Thing*. The Isle of Man assembly met at a grassy mound called the Tynwald. This is still the name of the Manx parliament today. It claims to be the world's oldest legislative (law-making) assembly with an uninterrupted history. Viking assemblies were attended by all free men, but not by women or slaves.

▲ *A Viking chieftain rides to the assembly. Here there would be discussion about new laws and judgements to be passed.*

Outside lavatory

AD 829
Egbert of Wessex becomes overlord of the
Anglo-Saxon kingdoms.

AD 866
The Grand Army of 'Danes' arrives in England.

Alfred and the Danes

The Scandinavian conquest of East Anglia, Mercia and Northumbria was carried out by a Grand Army of Danes. This was an alliance of warriors recruited in AD 866 from many different Viking settlements. Their chief enemy was Wessex, in southern England, for in AD 829 King Egbert of Wessex had become overlord of all the other Anglo-Saxon kingdoms. In AD 871, Egbert's grandson, Alfred, came to the throne. If the Danes conquered Wessex, all England would be in their grasp.

THE DANELAW
The Vikings' permanent settlements in England were known as the Danelaw. The relentless advance of the 'Danes' was first reversed by Alfred of Wessex.

NORTH SEA

IRISH SEA

DANES

ANGLO-SAXONS

Wessex

ENGLISH CHANNEL

⬇ A statue of Alfred stands in Winchester, Hampshire.

ALFRED FIGHTS BACK
A great army of Danes descended on Wessex again in the winter of AD 876. Alfred took refuge at Athelney, in the marshes of Somerset. He then fought back and defeated the Danes in AD 878. They gave up the lands of southern Mercia and their leader Guthrum agreed to become a Christian – but Alfred had to recognise the rule of Danelaw to the north.

D 871
Alfred becomes the king of Wessex.

AD 879
Treaty of Wedmore. Alfred recognizes the Danelaw.

DANEGELD

Shortly after Alfred became king of Wessex, his army was defeated by the Danes. Alfred could think of only one solution – bribery. He paid the Danes money to leave Wessex alone. They did – but only for four years. A later king adopted the same policy. Ethelred II, who came to the throne in AD 978, brought in a tax called Danegeld ('Dane money') to keep the Danes out of the south. Needless to say, they kept coming back for more. The name Ethelred means 'wise counsel' or 'good advice'. He of course became known as 'Redeless' – meaning 'ill-advised'.

◀ In the 700 and 800s, the Anglo-Saxons began to produce large numbers of silver pennies and other coins. Many of these found their way back to Scandinavia. Viking settlements minted their own coinage as well.

← King Alfred is named on this jewelled ornament found at Athelney.

← After the Vikings invaded England, King Alfred and his soldiers hid in the Athelney Marshes, Somerset. In AD 886 the Vikings agreed to a peace treaty, which meant that southwest England was ruled by the Anglo-Saxons.

ALFRED AND THE DANES 93

AD 926
Athelstan brings the Britons of Cornwall under
Anglo-Saxon rule.

AD 991
Danes win Battle of Maldon. Payment of Danegeld
by Ethelred.

➡ *Alfred learned many lessons from
the Vikings. One was the importance of
ships in warfare. He was the first English
ruler to build a fleet. He also reorganised
the fyrd, the Anglo-Saxon peasant army.*

ALFRED'S LEGACY

Alfred proved to be a wise ruler.
He encouraged learning and wrote
down the laws of England. In the
890s he planned a new type of
stronghold called a *burh* and built
many of these to hold back the
Danes. His lands grew wealthy
from trade. Alfred's daughter,
Ethelflæd of Mercia, fought the
Danes in battle and Alfred's good
work was continued by his sucessors
Edward the Elder, Athelstan and
Edgar. However peace broke down
after AD 979 and Ethelred II
provoked a major Danish invasion by
the Danish king Svein 'Forkbeard'.

1016
Battle of Ashingdon. England under Danish rule.

1042
Witan appoints Edward the Confessor as English king.

↓ Cnut I reigned from 1016–1035. He was a Christian king, and once, to display his piety, stood on a beach and attempted to turn back the tide. Of course he could not – he was simply trying to demonstrate that his power was insignificant compared to God's.

ENGLAND UNITES

After many battles and treaties, in 1016 England came under the rule of Svein's son, Cnut I (Knut or Canute). He married Ethelred II's widow, Emma, and went on to reign over Denmark and parts of Sweden and Norway as well. The appointment of Anglo-Saxon kings had to be approved by a council of nobles, called the Witan. In 1042 the Witan chose Edward, the son of Cnut I and Emma. The ruler of a united England, he was a devout Christian and is remembered in history as 'the Confessor'. He founded Westminster Abbey near the growing city of London.

RULERS OF WESSEX AND ENGLAND
Houses of Cerdic and Denmark

✤ Egbert	AD 802–839	✤ Eadwig	AD 955–959
✤ Ethelwulf	AD 839–855	✤ Edgar	AD 959–975
✤ Ethelbald	AD 855–860	✤ Edward 'the Martyr'	AD 975–978
✤ Ethelbert	AD 860–866	✤ Ethelred II 'the Redeless'	AD 978–1016
✤ Ethelred I	AD 866–871	✤ Edmund 'Ironside'	AD 1016
✤ Alfred	AD 871–899	✤ Cnut I	1016–1035
✤ Edward 'the Elder'	AD 900–924	✤ Harold I 'Harefoot'	1037–1040
✤ Athelstan	AD 924–939	✤ Cnut II 'Harthacnut'	1040–1042
✤ Edmund I	AD 939–946	✤ Edward 'the Confessor'	1042–1066
✤ Eadred	AD 946–955	✤ Harold II	1066

AD 866
High King Áed Finlliath drives Vikings from
northern coast.

AD 919
Vikings defeat the Irish at the Battle of Dublin.

Bloodshed at Clontarf

The Viking attacks on Ireland came in several waves. At first, in the 800s, the Scandinavians – mostly from Norway – came to plunder. Later they built permanent camps and then settlements and towns. The Vikings met fierce resistance from the Irish kings and often from the monks, too. After AD 914 there was another great wave of Viking invasions, and in AD 919 King Niall Glúndub, along with many lords of Ireland's most powerful family, the O'Neills, were killed at the Battle of Dublin.

VIKING TOWNS IN IRELAND

The Vikings' chief town was Dublin, but there were also settlements at Strangford, Carlingford, Limerick, Waterford, Wexford, Cork and Youghal. The Irish Vikings were known as Ostmen ('men from the east').

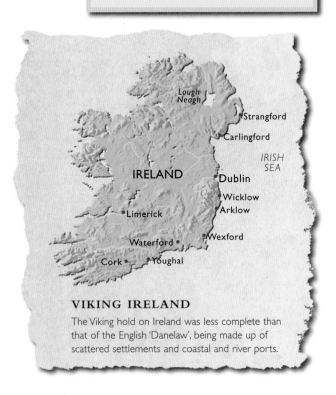

VIKING IRELAND

The Viking hold on Ireland was less complete than that of the English 'Danelaw', being made up of scattered settlements and coastal and river ports.

OSTMEN AND IRISH

In these times of trouble, tall, round towers were built at many Irish monasteries, such as Glendalough in the Wicklow mountains. They served as beacons, bell towers and refuges from Viking invaders. Sometimes, however, the invaders joined forces with one Irish king to fight another. The Vikings had a great effect on Irish life. They influenced Irish arts and crafts and encouraged long-distance trade. They also taught the Irish their boat-building and sailing skills.

➔ Brian Boru, born in AD 926, was a ruthless fighter who spent as much time battling with other Irish kings as with the Ostmen.

HIGH KINGS OF IRELAND	
House of Níall of the Nine Hostages (Tara)	
✤ Máel Sechnaill I	AD 842–862
✤ Áed Findliath	AD 862–879
✤ Flann Sinna	AD 879–916
✤ Níall Glúundub	AD 916–919
✤ Donnchad Donn	AD 919–944
✤ Congalach Cnogba	AD 944–956
✤ Domnall ua Néill	AD 956–980
✤ Máel Sechnaill II	AD 980–1002
✤ Brian Boru	1002–1014
✤ Máel Sechnaill II	1014–1022

BRIAN BORU, HIGH KING

During the 900s, the royal family of Munster, the Eóganacht, lost pride of place to a dynasty from North Munster, called the Dál Cais. Their king, Cennétig, died in AD 951. One of his sons was called Brian Bóruma, or Boru ('Brian of the Tribute'). By AD 976 Brian had gained control of Munster. By AD 984 he was king of Leinster and by 1002 he ruled all Ireland as High King, going on to conquer the Vikings' settlements.

AD 999
Leinster-Viking alliance defeated at battle of
Glenn Máma.

1002
Brian Boru rules all Ireland as High King.

THE BATTLE OF CLONTARF

The people of Leinster had never been happy with the rule of Brian Boru, and he soon faced revolt on many sides. Brian's son was sent to subdue Leinster in 1013. Leinster allied with the Dublin Vikings and in the spring of 1014 there was a fierce battle at Clontarf, to the northeast of Dublin. The ageing High King's forces won the day, but he was murdered after the battle. Clontarf marked the end of Viking power in Ireland. The *Ostmen* who remained gradually took on Irish ways and language.

← *The battle of Clontarf was brutal and bloody, even by the standards of the day.*

1014
Death of Brian Boru. Máel Sechnaill II regains
High Kingship.

1022
Power of the Irish High Kings fragments.

IRELAND FRAGMENTS

With the death of Brian Boru, the office of High King passed back to Máel Sechnaill II of the Uí Néill, who had been High King before Brian rose to power. He died in 1022. After that, real power passed back to the kings of the provinces. It was they who laid down the law and taxed the people heavily in order to fight the endless wars they waged upon their rivals.

This beautiful crozier or staff belonged to the abbot of Clonmacnoise in the 1100s. In the century after Clontarf, the powerful Irish Church was reformed by Rome.

THE RAVEN STANDARD

A key figure at the Battle of Clontarf was Sigurd Hlodvirsson, the Earl of Orkney. He had a flag with a picture of a raven on it. Sigurd believed that whoever carried this flag was sure of victory for his army – but would die himself. In 1014 Sigurd carried his flag at the Battle of Clontarf. He died – and his army lost the battle.

After Sigurd Hlodvirsson lost the Battle of Clontarf, Viking power in Ireland began to decline.

BLOODSHED AT CLONTARF   99

1018
Battle of Carham. Malcom II defeats Northumbrians.

1034
Duncan I becomes king of all Scotland.

Macbeth's Scotland

In 1018 Macolm II, King of Alba, marched southwards across the River Tweed and defeated the Northumbrians at the battle of Carham. Lothian was now in Scottish hands. In 1034 another piece of the jigsaw puzzle fell into place when King Duncan of Strathclyde, (the kingdom of the Britons in the southwest) inherited the throne of Alba. The kingdom of Scotland had now been created and within it were Scots, Britons and Angles. However Norwegian Vikings still held on to the northern and western fringes of the kingdom, and the southern border would be fought over for hundreds of years.

STRUGGLES FOR POWER

The lands of Scotland may have been united under the rule of Duncan I, but all around the throne there were old scores to settle and quarrels betwen rival groups or factions. One faction was led by Macbeth, the Mórmaer (chief) of Moray who married Gruoch, granddaughter of Kenneth III. He defeated and killed Duncan in 1040 and banished Duncan's sons, Malcolm and Donald Bán, from the kingdom.

↑ Duncan's son Malcolm avenged his father's murder, killing Macbeth at Lumphanan in 1057.

1039
Duncan I launches attack on the English city of Durham.

1040
Macbeth kills Duncan I and seizes throne.

↓ *The island of Skye is part of Gaelic Scotland, but the strong Norse presence there is confirmed by many place names and by hoards of coins.*

MACBETH'S SCOTLAND

Scotland was fashioned out of four smaller kingdoms – Dál Riada, Pictland, Strathclyde and Lothian. Its southern borders were constantly shifting.

NORSE LANDS

Dál Riada

Pictland

ALBA (SCOTLAND)

NORTH SEA

Strathclyde

Lothian

IRISH SEA

ENGLAND

NORSE AND GAELIC

In the Hebrides, the old Gaelic way of life was now mixed with the Norse. A group of independent chieftains arose, part Scots and part Norwegian. They sailed in longships and answered to no king. It was not until the 1100s, when Somerled, ancestor of the Macdonald clan, gained control of the islands, that the Viking way of life finally began to disappear. But even then, the islanders were a law to themselves.

1045
Duncan's father, Crínán, fails in revolt against Macbeth.

1057
Malcolm Canmore kills Macbeth.

RULERS OF ALBA AND SCOTLAND
House of MacAlpin

Ruler	Reign
✦ Kenneth I MacAlpin	AD 843–858
✦ Donald I	AD 858–862
✦ Constantine I	AD 862–877
✦ Aed	AD 877–878
✦ Eochaid and Giric	AD 878–889
✦ Donald II	AD 889–900
✦ Constantine II	AD 900–943
✦ Malcom I	AD 943–954
✦ Indulf	AD 954–962
✦ Dubh	AD 963–966
✦ Culen	AD 966–971
✦ Kenneth II	AD 971–995
✦ Constantine III	AD 995–997
✦ Kenneth III	AD 997–1005
✦ Malcolm II	1005–1034
✦ Duncan I	1034–1040
✦ Macbeth	1040–1057
✦ Lulach	1057–1058
✦ Malcolm III 'Canmore'	1058–1093

MALCOLM CANMORE

Malcolm III came to the Scottish throne in the following year. He was nicknamed Canmore, from the Gaelic *Ceann Mor*, which could mean either 'big head' or 'great chief'! He built a new palace at Dunfermline, which was now the Scottish capital. Malcolm's long reign was marked by endless wars south of the border, with Cnut I and the kings of England that followed him. He was killed at Alnwick in 1093.

DEATH AND REVENGE

The famous play *Macbeth* was written in England by William Shakespeare hundreds of years after the real Macbeth ruled Scotland. In the play, Macbeth is a murderous villain, driven by personal ambition. In reality, Macbeth may have been no more villainous than many other kings of his day. His motives for killing Duncan were probably part of a family feud. Macbeth went on a Christian pilgrimage to Rome and Scotland prospered under his rule. However Duncan's son, Malcolm, supported by his uncle Earl Siward of Northumbria, returned to kill Macbeth in 1057.

MARGARET, QUEEN AND SAINT

Malcolm Canmore's first wife was Ingiborg, the widow of a powerful Norse leader called Thorfinn, Earl of Orkney (the son of Sigurd Hlodvirsson who died at Clontarf). She died and in about 1070 there was another royal wedding, at Dunfermline. The bride was 24 year-old Margaret, daughter of an exiled claimant to the English throne, called Edward the Ætheling. Born in Hungary, Margaret brought the customs of mainland Europe to the Scottish court. Her palace shone with gold and silver, but she was a careful manager of finances. She founded many monasteries and was later made a saint.

▶ *Under Margaret's influence, Roman forms of Christian worship replaced traditions of the Celtic Church that had survived in Scotland.*

⬇ *Dunfermline Abbey was built by King David I in 1072, in honour of his mother Margaret.*

Castles and Knights

1066–1509

THE WORLD AT A GLANCE

ELSEWHERE IN EUROPE

1220
King Frederick II of Sicily and Germany becomes Holy Roman Emperor.

1226
Louis IX (St Louis) comes to the throne in France.

1237
Mongol armies invade East and Central Europe (to 1241).

1378
A split in the Roman Church, with one Pope in Rome and another in Avignon, France.

1453
Turks capture Constantinople (Istanbul). End of the Byzantine empire.

1462
Lorenzo de' Medici rules over splendid court at Florence, Italy.

1480
Ivan the Great, first Tsar of Russia, expels the Mongols and unites his country.

1492
Christians finally reconquer all of Muslim Spain, rule of Ferdinand and Isabella.

ASIA

1096
European Crusaders attack Muslims in the Near East and found Christian kingdoms.

1170
The Hindu Srivijaya kingdom rules Java, Southeast Asia.

1190
Temujin (Genghis Khan) starts to create the Mongol empire.

1192
Yoritomo Minamoto becomes first Shogun (military dictator) in Japan.

1206
The Islamic Sultanate rules in Delhi, India.

1271
Mongol ruler Kublai Khan becomes the emperor of China.

1368
Ming emperors rule China, capital at Nanjing.

1405
Death of Timur the Lame (or Tamberlaine), Tatar ruler of a vast Asian empire.

AFRICA

1200
The rise of the state of Mali in West Africa.

1200
Rise of Hausa city-states in northern Nigeria and Kanem-Bornu in Lake Chad region.

1250
Rise of the Benin empire in southern Nigerian forests.

1250
High stone enclosures built at Great Zimbabwe, in southeast Africa.

1300
Founding of the Kongo kingdom in southern Central Africa.

1400
Chinese, Arab and Indian traders along East Africa's Swahili Coast.

1400
Fine heads made from bronze in the Benin empire.

1450
Height of Songhai power in southern Sahara, university at Timbuktu.

"The peasant toils, the king rules – and God is in His heaven..."

NORTH AMERICA

1100
Thule culture of the American Arctic, based on whaling.

1150
The Anasazi people settle Mesa Verde in the southwest.

1170
Collapse of Toltec rule in Mexico, period of wars and strife.

1300
The Maya people return to power in Mexico, with capital at Mayapán.

1345
Aztecs build the great city of Tenochtitlan on the modern site of Mexico City.

1428
The Aztec empire expands and becomes very powerful.

1492
Christopher Columbus, in the service of Spain, lands in the Caribbean.

1493
The Spanish settle on the Caribbean island of Hispaniola.

SOUTH AMERICA

1100
The city of Cuzco, Peru, is founded by the first Inca emperor.

1370
The Chimú empire expands in northern Peru.

1450
The founding of the Inca town of Machu Picchu, high in the Andes.

1470
The Incas conquer the Chimú empire.

1492
The Incas conquer northern Chile.

1493
The Treaty of Tordesillas. Spain and Portugal divide up the Americas.

1498
The Inca empire is at its greatest extent under ruler Wayna Qapaq.

1500
The Portuguese claim Brazil.

OCEANIA

1100
Increased farming and irrigation begins on the Hawaiian islands.

1200
Powerful chiefdoms grow up in Polynesia.

1200
The Tu'i Tonga dynasty rules the Tongan Islands and part of Samoa.

1200
Large numbers of stone platforms and houses built in the Society Islands.

1250
Funeral of the Melanesian ruler Roy Mata on the island of Retoka.

c.1280
Ancestors of the Maori settle in New Zealand.

1350
Classic Maori period begins on New Zealand, large fortresses.

1400s
Malay fishermen camp on shores of northern Australia.

1064
Harold swears to support William of Normandy.

1066
Harold II chosen as King of England. King Harald III of Norway defeated at Stamford Bridge.

Hastings 1066

In the summer of 1066 a large fleet assembled along the French coast. Its commander was William, Duke of Normandy. Ships wallowed at anchor in choppy seas, waiting for the northerly wind to turn. Norman lords galloped to and fro on horseback. Carts trundled along the beach loaded with spears, swords, arrows and axes, iron helmets, shields and coats of mail. This would be the last major invasion of England in the Middle Ages.

CLAIMS FOR THE THRONE

Harold of Wessex was the son of a powerful Anglo-Saxon earl called Godwin. In January 1066 the Witan named Harold as King of England, but their decision was challenged at once. Edward the Ætheling, nephew of Edward the Confessor, claimed the throne. So did Harold's own brother, Tostig. A third claimant was King Harald III of Norway, known as 'Hardraade, the Ruthless'. The fourth was William of Normandy. William swore that in 1064 Harold had made a solemn vow to support the Norman claim.

1066
Norman invasion. Harold II defeated at Battle of Hastings.

1067
William I starts to build the Tower of London.

↓ *Anglo-Saxon England was defeated at the Battle of Hastings, in Sussex, in 1066. The battle began in King Harold's favour. However he was killed by a stray arrow and the day was won by the Norman invaders.*

WHO WERE THE NORMANS?

The Anglo-Saxon kings were not the only ones who attempted buy off the Vikings. In AD 911 Charles 'the Simple', King of France, offered a Viking warlord called Rollo part of northern France in a desperate bid to win peace. It became called Normandy ('land of the Northmen'). Rollo became a duke and married Giselle, a French princess. Like their Viking ancestors, Norman warlords stormed their way around Europe. They invaded the Italian island of Sicily in 1060.

ONE BATTLE TOO MANY

Harold II's troops were waiting for the Normans when word came that Harald III of Norway had joined forces with Tostig. Harold marched northwards at speed. He defeated and killed them both at Stamford Bridge, near York. Just three days later, Norman troops landed in Sussex. Harold had to march his exhausted army south again. On 14 October 1066, the two great armies clashed at Senlac Hill, near Hastings. All day, wave after wave of Normans broke against the Anglo-Saxon shields. Harold's men stood firm but, scenting victory, they broke rank too soon. The victory belonged to William – 'the Conqueror'.

This tapestry of wool on a linen backing has a 70-metre long 'strip' format, which tells the story of the Noman invasion of England. It can still be seen today in Bayeux, Normandy.

The Tower of London was added to over the ages. It played a central role in English history, with many famous prisoners being locked up in its dungeons.

1070
Rebellion in East Anglia by Hereward 'the Wake'.

1087
War with France, William I dies after he falls from horse.

THE CONQUEST

On Christmas Day 1066, William I was crowned king in Westminster Abbey. Within months of his coronation, William ordered the building of a new fortification by the River Thames, in London. Its great keep, or stronghold, was the White Tower. This became the centre of the Tower of London.

Within two years most of England was under his control. Revolts led by Edward the Ætheling and an Anglo-Saxon lord called Hereward the Wake ('the Watchful') were crushed.

THE DOMESDAY BOOK

Exactly 19 years after his coronation, William I announced that all the lands in England south of the rivers Ribble and Tees (and excluding the cities of London and Winchester) were to be registered in a great book. From 1086 onwards, royal officials travelled from one estate to another. They wrote down the details of buildings, land and resources, so that they could be taxed.

RULERS OF ENGLAND

House of Normandy

✤ William I 'the Conqueror'	1066–1087
✤ William II 'Rufus'	1087–1100
✤ Henry I 'Beauclerk'	1100–1135
✤ Stephen	1135–1154

1066
The Norman Channel Islands come under the
English crown.

1072
William I of England leads army into Scotland.

The Mailed Fist

The Norman kings of England and their successors wanted to be recognised as overlords of all the British Isles. Their fleets sailed north and their armies were soon battling with the Scots. Norman warlords were given territories on the Welsh borders (the 'Marches'), and stormed into North and South Wales. Within 100 years, their great castles of stone could be seen in Ireland, too.

Braided hair
Norman ladies often wore their hair in plaits. Heads were sometimes covered with a short veil, secured by a circlet of silver or gold.

Cloak
A long woollen cloak was worn for warmth, fastened across the front by a cord.

Girdle
A cord or jewelled belt was worn around the waist.

Flowing dress
A long-sleeved shift was covered by a long tunic called a bliaut, which was laced at the side.

Norman lady

Supplies
Weapons and equipment had to be carried with the troops. Food and grain could be seized by force along the way.

THE NORMANS IN SCOTLAND

After repeated Scottish invasions of his new kingdom, William I marched into Lothian at the head of a large army in 1071, but he made peace with Malcolm Canmore at Abernethy. In 1092 the Normans took Cumbria from the Scots, but a full-scale invasion of Scotland never occurred. Norman settlers did arrive, bringing their ways to the Lowlands and to the Scottish court. Later Scottish kings, including Robert Bruce and the Stewarts, were of Norman descent.

1092
Normans build castle at Pembroke in South Wales.

1094
'Marcher' Lordships established in the Welsh borders.
Norman invasion of North Wales.

STRONGBOW'S IRELAND

In Ireland, warring between provincial kings gave a chance for Norman descendants to invade. In 1166 Dermot MacMurrough, King of Leinster, appealed to Henry II of England for help. He had lost his lands in the wars between Ireland's provincial kings. Henry authorised Norman lords to carry on this fight independently. In 1169, Richard fitz Gilbert de Clare, Earl of Pembroke, agreed to help Dermot in return for land. De Clare, half Norman and half Welsh, was known as 'Strongbow'. His invasion of Ireland was successful – too much so for Henry II, who was jealous of Strongbow's new-found power. The English king and his army arrived in Ireland in 1171.

➡ *Dermot, the Irish ruler of Leinster, needed the support of Strongbow (right). In return he offered him the hand of his daughter, Aoife, and succession to the throne of Leinster.*

Metal in motion
The mounted knight was the key to Norman success.

Horse power
The Normans used highly mobile forces to control their conquests.

⬅ *The Norman invasion did not stop at the borders of England.*

1097
Normans defeat Donald III of Scotland.

1100
William II of England is killed, possibly murdered, in the New Forest.

Wooden watchtower

WALES AND THE MARCHES

The Norman kings did not intend to rule Wales directly, but they wished to control it. As early as 1067, William I gave land on the borders to William Fitzosbern, Roger Montgomery and Hugh d'Avranches. These 'Marcher Lords' were a law to themselves. They launched savage raids into North Wales in the 1080s. By the 1090s Norman warlords were gaining control of large areas of South and West Wales. They met fierce resistance, but this was a period when the Welsh kingdoms were at war with each other. The Normans were defeated in 1096 at Gelli Carnant, Gwent, but they kept their foothold in Wales.

Motte
The motte was an area of raised earth.

1106
Henry I of England defeats and imprisons his brother
Robert in Normandy.

1166
Dermot MacMurrough of Leinster invites Normans
into Ireland.

GWENLLIAN GOES TO WAR

Gwenllian was the daughter of Gruffudd ap Cynan,
ruler of Gwynedd in North Wales. She married
another Grufudd, son of Rhys ap Tewdwr, ruler of
Deheubarth. In 1136 her husband went to meet her
father, to plan a rising against the Normans in South
Wales. While he was away, Gwenllian led a
warrior band to storm Kidwelly Castle.
They were beaten back and defeated
by Maurice de Londres. Gwenllian
was captured and executed.

Palisade
A wooden palisade
surrounded the bailey, which
was the enclosure where
people and livestock lived.

⬆ At first the Normans built
simple 'motte and bailey' castles.
Each had a wooden tower, standing
on a tall earth mound called a
'motte' and an enclosed area called
a 'bailey'. Both were surrounded
by fences and ditches.

Ditch
A ditch was dug
around the motte for
extra defence.
Sometimes this was
filled with water to
become a moat.

1086
Population of two million in area surveyed by the Domesday Book.

1191
First record of windmills being used for grinding wheat.

The Feudal System

The division of society into classes of serfs, free men, nobles and rulers had started earlier in the Middle Ages. The Normans were the first to enforce this 'feudal' system rigidly. The king was at the top, ruling by the will of God. He parcelled out land to his lords in return for their support. The land was worked by free men and serfs (or 'villeins'), who provided the nobles with food and served in their armies. In return, the poor were, in theory at least, protected by their lord.

Field use
One field might be for oats and another for wheat. The third might lie 'fallow' (uncultivated) and be grazed by cattle. Field use changed from year to year so that the goodness in the soil was not all used up.

The feudal economy was based on land and services rather than money. It only worked if people stayed on the land. Villeins were not allowed to leave their village and were forced to work on their lord's estates.

1200s
Rapid growth of towns and cities.

1300s
Feudal system begins to be replaced by a money-based economy.

OATHS OF LOYALTY

The feudal system was a series of two-way contracts, reinforced by oaths of loyalty. The loyalty was not to a nation, but to a noble or royal family. A lord could even insist that 'his' people take up arms against their own countrymen. The feudal system crossed national borders. Europe's ruling classes were allied with each other, rather than with the peasants who worked for them. If a king from one royal family married the princess of another, the lands they ruled might be joined together, regardless of public opinion or geography.

⬆ Kings of the Middle Ages held extreme power over their subjects. Every royal document was marked with a personal badge called a seal, pressed into soft wax. This one belonged to Henry III of England.

Windmill
Windmills, originally an Asian invention, were first built in Britain during the 1190s. They were mounted on an upright post, and could be turned so that the sails caught the wind. They were used for grinding grain into flour.

Harrow
A harrow was a spiked frame used for preparing the soil, ready for the seeds to be scattered by the sower.

1300s
Rise of a middle class made up of merchants and craft producers.

1300s
Cloth production moves out of towns, water power needed for fulling. Spinning wheels introduced.

WOMEN IN THE MIDDLE AGES

In the medieval (Middle Ages) period, most women in Europe had few rights. Strict vows bound together man and wife, just as society was bound by oaths of feudal loyalty. It was the men who held real power and wealth. Despite this, many women were strong characters and became widely respected in their own right. There were powerful queens and noblewomen, abbesses and nuns, scholars and poets, and able working women in every village. In the later Middle Ages, poets began to sing the praises of women, but in a very idealised way.

▲ Women may have been honoured in medieval poetry but in reality had hard lives. Many died in childbirth.

c.1330
The *Luttrell Psalter* includes illustrations of everyday English life.

1349
Ordinance of Labourers tries to limit English wages.

RICH AND POOR

The Norman lords who had supported William I during the invasion of England profited hugely. They were rather like the lottery winners of today, only their new-found wealth was based on land rather than money. This created problems for kings that followed, for there were now many very powerful lords who could challenge their rule. At the other end of the scale were the villeins. They had to labour on the lord's land for, say, three days a week. They also had to pay taxes and supply farm produce to the lord. The Church too demanded one-tenth (a 'tithe') of their harvested crops.

← *A knight and his squire ride through the busy streets of a medieval town. The feudal system ensured that the upper classes had great powers within their own domain.*

1100
Death of William II of England, called 'Rufus'.

1135
Stephen is crowned English king. Start of civil war.

Is Might Right?

In the days of William the Conqueror, life was short and violent. The road to kingship was not through election or consent. It was often through murder and battle. Even the laws reflected the belief that 'might is right'. A legal dispute might be settled by an official fight – 'trial by combat' – or by making the accused grasp a red hot bar of iron – 'trial by ordeal'. God, it was believed, would punish the guilty and protect the innocent.

A KING'S NIGHTMARES

In 1100, William II of England was killed in a hunting accident in the New Forest. Or was it murder? Nobody knew for sure. Six years later his successor, Henry I, imprisoned his own brother for 28 years. A series of pictures drawn in the 1140s shows Henry I haunted by royal nightmares. Haughty bishops, armed knights and angry peasants all protest by his bedside.

THE FIGHTING EMPRESS

When Henry I's son was drowned at sea in 1120, he named his daughter Matilda as his heir. She lived in Germany at that time, for she had been betrothed (engaged to be married) at the age of just seven to the Emperor Henry V. She had married him in 1114, aged twelve. Widowed in 1125, Matilda soon remarried another very powerful but younger man, Geoffrey of Anjou. She fought desperately for the English throne until 1148.

▼ Matilda flees from Oxford. She was unpopular with the English people. At one time she captured Stephen, but was never crowned queen.

A TIME OF TERROR

Henry I did manage to keep order in the land, but after his death in 1135, there was chaos. Before his chosen heir, Matilda, arrived back in England, the throne was seized by Stephen, a grandson of William I. There followed 13 years of war between the two. It was a terrible period for the common people, as lord fought lord and armies looted the land.

THE CHURCH IN CONTROL

The Roman Church was very powerful. Popes believed that as God's representatives they had the right to control European politics. Quarrels between kings and the Church became common. In 1170 supporters of Henry II of England murdered Thomas Becket, the Archbishop of Canterbury.

⬆ *Armed might invades the peace of Canterbury Cathedral in 1170. Four knights have burst in to murder English archbishop Thomas Becket while he prays.*

TRIAL BY JURY

A fairer legal system was brought in by Henry II of England during the 1100s. Punishments for crimes were still often brutal, but now courts were held around the country in the king's name. Juries were called to decide guilt or innocence. In those days, juries were not independent members of the public but people who may have known the accused or witnessed the crime.

RISE OF THE BARONS

In 1215, English barons forced King John to agree to recognise their legal rights. The agreement was known as Magna Carta ('the great charter'). The barons did not need protection, but at least the law was now recognised as more important than the word of kings and queens.

← At Runnymede, near the River Thames, King John signed the Magna Carta as demanded by his rebellious barons.

Magna Carta

A SUMMONS TO PARLIAMENT

Magna Carta may have been one of the first moves towards social justice, but its immediate effect was to make the warring barons even more powerful. When Henry III of England came to the throne in 1216, he was only a child. In 1258 he was forced to hand over power to the barons. Their leader was Simon de Montfort, Earl of Leicester and brother-in-law of the king. He imprisoned Henry III at Lewes, Sussex, in 1264. The next year de Montfort called a great council, or 'parliament'. Each county sent a knight and each town sent a burgess (leading citizen). De Montfort was killed in 1265, but parliaments were again summoned by later kings. By 1352 parliament had two sections or 'chambers'. The House of Lords was for the nobles and the bishops, while the House of Commons was for knights and burgesses.

IS MIGHT RIGHT? 121

The Angevin Empire

Although Matilda failed to win the throne of England, her son was crowned King Henry II in 1154. His royal line is sometimes called Plantagenet, named after the sprig of broom (in Old French, *plante genêt*) that his father Geoffrey wore in his cap. Henry II ruled over a huge area of western Europe called the Angevin (Anjou) empire.

SCOTLAND

NORTH SEA

IRELAND

WALES

ENGLAND

London

THE ANGEVIN EMPIRE

The patchwork of territories claimed by Henry II made England a major European power.

Acquisitions by marriage with Eleanor

- under direct rule
- owing allegiance

other acquisitions 1169–72

control by marriage of Geoffrey with Constance of Brittany

unsuccessfully claimed

Kingdom of France

inherited through Henry's father
- under direct rule
- owing allegiance

ENGLISH CHANNEL

Normandy

Paris

Brittany   Anjou   FRANCE

Poitou   Bourges

Aquitaine

Bordeaux

Gascony   Toulouse

Béarne

⬆ *The lute, a musical instrument of Arab origin, was widely played in western Europe in the Middle Ages. Musicians performed at court and poets and singers travelled from one castle to another.*

1154
Henry II is crowned first Plantagenet king of England.

c.1167
Students start to study at Oxford.

ROYAL LANDS

Henry II's lands stretched from the sunny vineyards of Bordeaux in southwest France, to the rainy Scottish borders. He had inherited Anjou from his father and gained Poitou, Aquitaine and Gascony on marrying Eleanor of Aquitaine. Henry also claimed to be overlord of Brittany, Wales, Scotland and Ireland.

ELEANOR OF AQUITAINE

Eleanor of Aquitaine was one of the most remarkable women in medieval Europe. She was born in about 1122. She became Duchess of Aquitaine in 1135, when she married the heir to the French throne. He was crowned Louis VII two years later. Eleanor was unconventional and beautiful. She and a troop of women, dressed as classical warriors, joined the Second Crusade (one of the wars between Christians and Muslims in the Near East). After her marriage was annulled (cancelled) in 1152, Eleanor married young Henry of Anjou, who became King Henry II of England. Their love soon turned sour and when Henry was unfaithful she supported his sons in rebellion against him. She was imprisoned from 1174 until the death of Henry in 1189. She died in 1204.

→ *Eleanor's court in Poitou attracted poets, musicians and scholars from all over Europe.*

1198
Richard I 'Cœur de Lion' dies from a crossbow wound.

1205
England loses Normandy to France.

THE EMPIRE UNRAVELS

Henry II of England was energetic and fiery-tempered. He was a very able ruler, but he quarrelled bitterly with his wife and with his sons. They rebelled against him and the great empire began to break up. Royal power lessened under Stephen and John, but the struggle to control France would continue for hundreds of years.

WHICH LANGUAGE?

The English spoken today began to take shape in medieval England. It grew out of several languages. The court used French, while scholars and the Church used Latin. Most ordinary people spoke dialects of English. Other languages spoken in the British Isles at this time included Cornish, Welsh, Scots Gaelic, Irish and Norse.

Henry III's beautiful tomb still survives and is admired by visitors at Westminster Abbey today.

RULERS OF ENGLAND

House of Anjou (Plantagenet)

✤ Henry II 'Curtmantle'	1154–1189
✤ Richard I 'Cœur de Lion'	1189–1199
✤ John 'Lackland'	1199–1216
✤ Henry III 'of Winchester'	1216–1272
✤ Edward I 'Longshanks'	1272–1307
✤ Edward II	1307–1327
✤ Edward III 'of Windsor'	1327–1377
✤ Richard II	1377–1399

A LONG REIGN

Henry III was the son of King John. After coming to the throne as a child in 1216, he ruled England for 56 years. The country prospered, but he was not popular. Despite raising taxes to pay for wars against France, his armies won few victories.

SCHOLARS AND INVENTORS

Under Plantagenet rule in England, few people could read or write. Some children were taught in church schools or were tutored by monks or nuns. University students may have been studying at Oxford as early as 1167, and Cambridge University was founded in 1215. One scholar who studied at Oxford and Paris was Roger Bacon (*c*.1214–1292). He was a scientist who predicted the use of flying machines and telescopes. At this time all sorts of exciting new inventions were arriving in Britain from abroad, including gunpowder, clocks and spectacles.

Boar's head

MEDIEVAL FOOD

The common people of Britain ate coarse bread of rye or barley, cheese and buttermilk, 'pottages' (thick soups or stews of vegetables), pickled herrings and bacon. In the great halls of the feudal lords, splendid banquets would be served, sometimes made up of 20 or more courses. These included fine wheaten bread, roast boar, venison, mutton, geese, swan or peacock. All sorts of pies and custards and dishes were served, sometimes dyed in brilliant colours or served with precious spices imported from Asia.

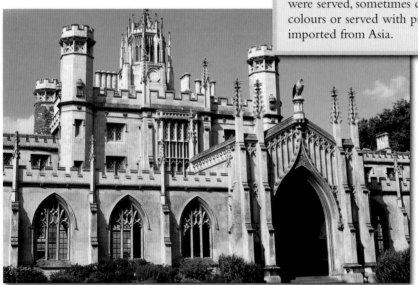

◄ *From the 13th century onwards, Cambridge University became one of the great centres of European scholarship. This is St John's College, Cambridge, founded in 1511.*

THE ANGEVIN EMPIRE 125

The Crusades

I n 1075 the city of Jerusalem was captured from its Christian rulers by Turkish Muslims. Twenty years later, Pope Urban II appealed to all Christian knights to launch a holy war, or Crusade. Its aim was to recapture Jerusalem and the 'Holy Land'. The First Crusade began in 1096 and Jerusalem was taken after three long years.

The Crusaders built huge castles to defend their lands against the much larger Muslim armies. The biggest castles could house up to 2000 soldiers as well as servants and horses. In the port of Acre the Crusaders had constructed a vast underground fortress.

1096
The First Crusade leaves Europe for the Holy Land.

1099
Crusaders capture Jerusalem, massacre 40,000 Jews and Muslims. Christian kingdom founded at Jerusalem.

Jews, christians and muslims

By now, most of Europe was Christian. The Moors (Muslim Berbers and Arabs) had conquered much of Spain, but were under constant attack by Christian armies from the north. Their ancestors had been expelled from Jerusalem by the Romans in AD 70. In Moorish Spain, Muslims, Christians and Jews lived peaceably together. However in most of Christendom, religious hatred against Muslims and Jews ran rife. Jews were persecuted terribly in England and in 1290 they were expelled by Edward I.

Religious wars

There were several further Crusades between 1096 and 1270. These shameful wars poisoned relations between Christianity and Islam into modern times. Religious motives soon gave way to looting and land-grabbing. Muslims were not the only enemy. In 1204, Crusaders turned aside to sack the Christian city of Constantinople. In 1208 a Crusade was launched against Christians in southern France, who differed from Rome in their beliefs. German Crusaders invaded Poland and the Baltic lands in the 1200s.

THE CRUSADES **127**

1148
The Second Crusade fails to capture Damascus
in Syria.

1189
The Third Crusade is launched, Richard I
pledges support.

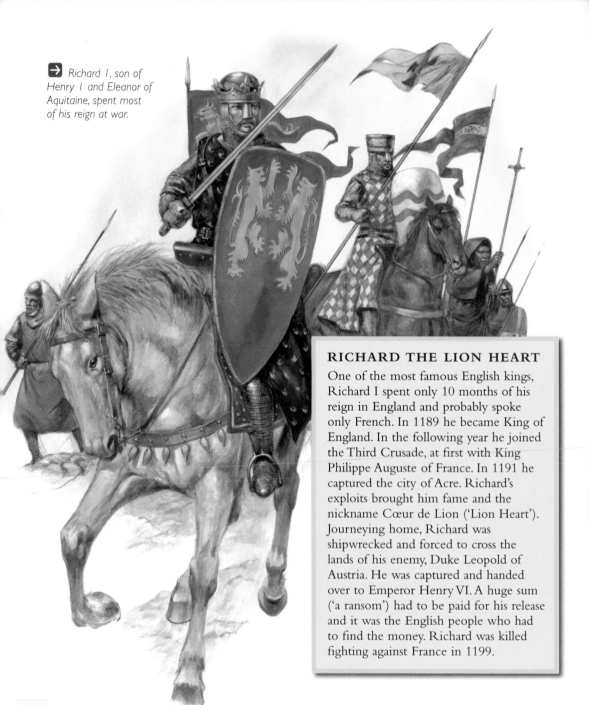

➜ Richard I, son of
Henry I and Eleanor of
Aquitaine, spent most
of his reign at war.

RICHARD THE LION HEART

One of the most famous English kings,
Richard I spent only 10 months of his
reign in England and probably spoke
only French. In 1189 he became King of
England. In the following year he joined
the Third Crusade, at first with King
Philippe Auguste of France. In 1191 he
captured the city of Acre. Richard's
exploits brought him fame and the
nickname Cœur de Lion ('Lion Heart').
Journeying home, Richard was
shipwrecked and forced to cross the
lands of his enemy, Duke Leopold of
Austria. He was captured and handed
over to Emperor Henry VI. A huge sum
('a ransom') had to be paid for his release
and it was the English people who had
to find the money. Richard was killed
fighting against France in 1199.

1202
Crusaders attack the Christian city of
Constantinople.

1291
The fall of Acre, end of crusading against the Saracens.

The Crusader
Crusaders were
armed with swords,
lances, axes and
maces. Their armour
varied over the years.
Chain mail gave way
to solid plate armour.

Saracen armour
Muslim troops either wore
tunics that were padded or
sewn with metal plates, or
coats of mail.

CRUSADERS AND SARACENS
Crusaders came from all over Europe,
including the British Isles. Some joined
international 'orders', such as the
Knights of St John (founded in 1099),
or the Knights Templar (1119). The
Muslim soldiers of the 'Holy Land'
were called Saracens and included
Arabs, Turks and Kurds. Their most
famous leader was Salah-ed-din Yussuf
('Saladin', 1137–1193). He earned the
respect of many Crusaders. Contact
with Arab civilisation opened the eyes
of many Europeans to the wider world.

Saracen weapons
The Saracens had swords of the
finest steel, spears and round
shields. Archers fired arrows
from small bows while riding.

Fighting in the dry heat and
dust of the Near East, when
weighed down with armour and
weapons, was often an ordeal.
Although the Crusades were
meant to be 'holy' wars, the
citizens of besieged towns were
often slaughtered without mercy.
The Crusades left a bitterness
between Christianity and Islam
that still affects the politics of
southwest Asia today.

THE CRUSADES   129

Knights in Armour

In the 700s, a simple invention had reached Europe from Asia – stirrups. They supported the legs of a horseback rider and made it possible for mounted soldiers to charge the enemy really hard, without falling. By Norman times, horse soldiers called knights had become the most important part of most armies. Even lords and kings had to learn how to be good knights. In the 1100s and 1200s, almost every battlefield shook to the thundering hooves of great war-horses leading a cavalry charge.

THE AGE OF CHIVALRY

In the high Middle Ages, knights developed a code of behaviour, called 'chivalry'. It was based on Christian virtues. A knight vowed to protect the weak, honour women, keep his word and respect his enemies. These ideas were admired by many later generations, but they were only ever an ideal. Battles may have had strict rules, but they were still brutal affairs. Respect was certainly not extended to peasants or to enemy foot soldiers, who were slaughtered without mercy.

1200s
Horses protected with padded or mail coats called trappers.

1292
Statute of Arms lays down rules for English tournaments.

 Knights would also engage in foot combat wearing full plate armour. Skill and speed were more important than strength.

HERALDRY

In a tournament or a battle, it was hard to tell one armoured knight from another. Knights began to use personal badges or emblems, which were displayed on surcoats (tunics worn over armour), on shields and standards. These emblems were passed down from one generation of a family to another. They became known as coats-of-arms and can still be seen carved on castle stones or coloured in the stained glass of old churches. The rules for drawing up coats-of-arms are known as heraldry.

▲ Heraldic design and colouring followed strict rules. It used various geometric patterns as well as emblems such as the fleur-de-lys ('lily flower', above right).

The Age of Castles

Fortresses had been built in Britain in Roman times. After the Normans invaded England in 1066, powerful kings and lords began to build new kinds of fortresses, called castles. Castles served as homes, as well as military bases and centres of government. They were used to control conquered lands and show off the power of their owner. Kings and lords sometimes owned several castles and moved from one to the other during the year.

Stonemason

Wooden scaffolding

1100s
Castle defences centred on massive stone towers called keeps.

1180s
Castles built with square wall towers.

⬇ The best place to build a castle was on top of a hill. A hilltop position gave good views over the surrounding countryside, and made it harder for an enemy to launch a surprise attack. Sometimes a castle was built on the banks of a river or lake, and its waters were used to create a moat.

Wheel for haulage

Architect

1220s
Castles built with round wall towers.

1224
Bedford Castle in England is captured. Its garrison is hanged.

LIFE IN A CASTLE

The centre of activity in the castle was the Great Hall. This was where banquets and important meetings were held. In the kitchens, meat sizzled on spits in front of the fire. The bedrooms and the main living room (called a 'solar') were often cold and draughty. Fresh reeds were strewn on the stone floors, as there were no carpets. There were rooms for the servants, guard rooms and stables.

➡ Castles were built with rings of defences and were hard to attack. They were garrisoned by footsoldiers, archers and men-at-arms.

KING OF THE CASTLES

Beaumaris Castle is on the Isle of Anglesey, in Wales. Work on it began in April 1295 and cost a fortune. It employed no fewer than 2000 labourers, 200 stonemasons and 400 quarrymen. Beaumaris was the last in a powerful chain of castles built by King Edward I of England to secure his conquest of North Wales. He was the greatest castle builder of his day.

◀ Stonemasons and carpenters were recruited from all over the kingdom of England.

Arrow loops
Archers could shoot arrows through loops – narrow slits in the castle walls.

Outer walls
Thick stone walls were fireproof and hard to knock down.

1266
Kenilworth Castle in England withstands siege for
six months.

1290s
Concentric castles, built with rings of walls and
towers.

Battlements
The walls were topped by battlements. These
walk-ways were defended by stone blocks
called merlons and firing gaps called crenels.

Machicolations
Chutes overhung the
outer walls, for
dropping missiles on
the enemy.

Gatehouse
A strong gate called a
portcullis could be
dropped to seal off the
entrance to the castle.

To the Glory of God

In later medieval Europe, the Christian faith was part of everday life. It was expressed in the great stone cathedrals and abbeys that were raised all over the British Isles in the Middle Ages. Building styles changed over the years. Some cathedrals had massive, awe-inspiring towers. Others were graceful, with tall spires pointing to heaven. Inside, gold glittered in candle light and coloured ('stained') glass windows glowed like precious gems.

➡️ *Durham Cathedral, towering above the River Wear in the northeast of England, was started by the Normans in 1093. It contains the tombs of St Cuthbert and Bede. During the Middle Ages the bishops of Durham were as warlike as any barons and had great political power.*

↓ *In the Middle Ages, the language of the Roman Church was Latin, which few ordinary people could understand. Most were unable to read either. Stained glass windows were an ideal way of telling worshippers stories from the Bible or the lives of the saints.*

LETTERS OF GOLD

Before the days of printing, books had to be copied out by hand. The work was often done in monasteries. The pages were made of vellum (animal skin) and decorated with elaborate letter designs and small pictures, called 'illuminations'. Books were such rare and precious objects that they were often chained to the shelf.

▶ *Illuminated letters were decorated with coloured paint and gold leaf. They were works of art in themselves.*

1063
Death of Gruffudd ap Llywelyn, having briefly
united Wales.

1164
Founding of Strata Florida abbey (Ystrad Fflur).

The Welsh Princes

Wales in the 1100s and 1200s was a rural land, with few large towns. People farmed and hunted, travelling by narrow tracks through the mountain passes, which were guarded by castles built by the Welsh rulers. They also endowed (funded) great monasteries such as Strata Florida (Ystrad Fflur) in the Teifi valley and Llanfaes, on Anglesey. There was a rich tradition of music, and a great gathering of poets (an *eisteddfod*) was held at Cardigan in 1176.

← *Rhys ap Gruffudd ('the Lord Rhys' of Deheubarth) weakened Norman power in South Wales during the chaotic reign of King Stephen in England.*

WHO HOLDS POWER?

Under rulers such as Rhys ap Gruffudd in the south and Owain Gwynedd in the north, Norman power in Wales declined. The Marcher Lords still held the borders, however, and the English kings regarded themselves as overlords of the Welsh. The division of Wales into separate kingdoms played into the hands of the English. In 1157 Madog ap Maredudd of Powys helped King Henry II of England invade Wales, in order to weaken his rivals in Gwynedd.

THE GREAT LLYWELYN

In 1170 three sons of Owain Gwynedd fought each other at Pentraeth, on Anglesey, for the throne of Gwynedd. Hywel was defeated by Rhodri and Dafydd and the kingdom was divided. By 1194 all Gwynedd had come under the rule of Llywelyn ap Iorwerth, 'the Great'. Llywelyn married Joan or Siwan, daughter of King John of England, but the two rulers later became enemies. Llywelyn was the most powerful ruler in medieval Wales, a strong supporter of the Church and the law.

⬆ *Llywelyn the Great fought against rival princes and forced them to swear loyalty to him and his son.*

THE LAST PRINCE

Llywelyn was succeeded by his younger son, Dafydd, but he died in the sixth year of his reign. He was to be followed by his nephews Llywelyn and Owain, but the former seized the throne for himself and gained control of all Wales. Llywelyn II ap Gruffudd was recognised as Prince of Wales by the English in 1267. However he would be the last Welsh prince. He quarrelled with King Edward I and after long wars, was killed in a skirmish with English troops near Cilmeri. His severed head was displayed in London.

⬅ *Llywelyn II's death near Cilmeri in 1282 marked the end of Welsh independence. He is remembered in Wales as 'The Last Prince'.*

RULERS IN WALES

✤ Gruffudd ap Llywelyn 1039–1063

✤ Bleddyn ap Cynfyn 1063–1075

✤ Trahaearn ap Caradog 1075–1081

✤ Gruffudd ap Cynan 1081–1137

✤ Owain Gwynedd 1137–1170

✤ Dafydd ap Owain Gwynedd 1170–1194

✤ Llywelyn 'Fawr' ('the Great') 1194–1240

✤ Dafydd ap Llywelyn 1240–1246

✤ Llywelyn ap Gruffudd 1246–1282

GERALD OF WALES

Gerald de Barri was born in about 1146. His ancestry was part Norman, part Welsh. Gerald became a talented writer in Latin and a great churchman. In 1188 he travelled through Wales with Archbishop Baldwin, and his *Journey Through Wales* and *Description of Wales* give us lively and good-humoured pictures of Wales in the high Middle Ages. He died in 1223 and has gone down in history as Giraldus Cambriensis, or Gerald of Wales.

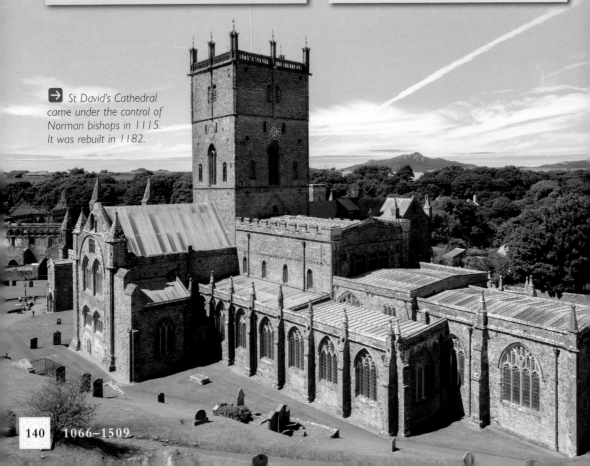

➡ *St David's Cathedral came under the control of Norman bishops in 1115. It was rebuilt in 1182.*

1267
English recognise Llywelyn ap Gruffudd as Prince of Wales.

1283
Llywelyn ap Gruffudd killed in skirmish with English, Cilmeri.

THE CONQUEST

King Edward I of England was now the undisputed ruler of Wales. His castles ringed the land. English criminal laws replaced Welsh ones and the Statute of Rhuddlan (1284) divided Wales into counties, along English lines. In 1301 Edward I's son (the later Edward II) was declared Prince of Wales, and ever since then the title has been held by the eldest son of the English monarch.

Edward I's Welsh castles were designed with strong 'curtain' walls and tall look-out towers. Many were also surrounded by deep moats filled with water. Conwy Castle is one of the great fortresses of medieval Europe.

1174
William I of Scotland forced to recognise English king as overlord.

1264
Norwegian invasion defeated at Largs.

Scottish Freedom

In the 1100s, Scotland saw great changes. Norman families gained Scottish lands. Three sons of Queen Margaret ruled the country in turn – Edgar, Alexander I and the great David I. Many fine churches and abbeys were built during their reigns, and around them developed prosperous 'burghs' (large towns). Peasants lived in small farming villages called 'touns'.

RULERS OF SCOTLAND

♣ Donald III Bán	1093–1097
♣ Duncan II	1094
♣ Edgar	1097–1107
♣ Alexander I 'the Fierce'	1107–1124
♣ David I 'the Saint'	1124–1153
♣ Malcolm IV 'the Maiden'	1153–1165
♣ William I 'the Lion'	1165–1214
♣ Alexander II	1214–1229
♣ Alexander III	1249–1286
♣ Margaret 'Maid of Norway'	1286–1290
♣ Throne disputed	1290–1292
♣ John (Balliol)	1292–1296
♣ Edward I of England	1296–1306

House of Bruce

♣ Robert I Bruce	1306–1329
♣ David II	1329–1371
♣ Edward Balliol	1306 & 1333–1336

SCOTLAND STANDS FIRM

In 1174, William I of Scotland was captured by English troops and forced to recognise Henry II as his overlord. It was an act never forgotten by the English – or the Scots. Alexander III, who came to the throne as a boy, had another old enemy to deal with – Norway. The Norwegians invaded in 1263, but were forced to withdraw and finally lost their mainland and island territories.

1296
Edward I of England defeats John Balliol at Dunbar.

1297
William Wallace defeats English army at Stirling Bridge.

SCOTLAND FALLS

Tragedy now struck the Scots. In 1286 Alexander III fell from his horse and was killed. Four years later his successor, the young girl Margaret of Norway, also died. Who should reign next, was unclear. The Scots turned to Edward I of England for advice.

His candidate was John Balliol, a distant descendant of David I. Edward I thought he could control his chosen man, but instead Balliol turned and made an historic alliance with France. Edward I stormed into Scotland in 1296 and defeated Balliol at Dunbar.

WAR OF INDEPENDENCE

Resistance to English rule was fierce. Its champion was William Wallace, who defeated an English army at Stirling Bridge, but was himself defeated at Falkirk in 1298. Captured in 1305, Wallace was horribly executed in London. Parts of his body were sent to Newcastle, Berwick, Stirling and Perth.

← *William Wallace blocked the northern advance of English forces at Stirling Bridge in 1297 and became Edward I's most hated foe.*

Legend has it that Robert Bruce was inspired to keep fighting the English by watching a spider try time after time to rebuild its web. At last it succeeded. Bannockburn was the turning point, although the war continued for another 14 years.

ROBERT BRUCE

The fight was taken up by Robert Bruce (who had stabbed his chief rival, John Comyn, to death). Robert was crowned king by the Scots in 1306. Edward I died in the following year and at Bannockburn, on 24 June 1314, Bruce turned the tide and defeated 20,000 troops of Edward II. The English finally recognised Scotland's independence in 1328.

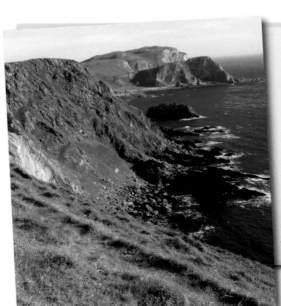

LORDS OF THE ISLES

In the Highlands and Western Isles, the old Gaelic way of life continued. Here, first loyalty was to the chief of the clan (a group sharing descent from a common ancestor). The lands of Clans Dugall, Donald and Ruairi became known as the Lordship of the Isles. The first Lord of the Isles was John of Islay of Clan Donald, who died in 1387. The Lordship was in constant conflict with the Scottish kingdom and was brought to an end in 1493.

◀ *The Mull of Oa, Islay.*

➡ *Arbroath Abbey was founded in 1178. Its abbot, Bernard de Linton, drafted the Declaration for Robert Bruce.*

1175
Treaty of Windsor. Rory O'Connor recognises
Henry II as overlord.

1210
Irish kings submit to King John of England.

The Pale and Beyond

The word 'pale' means fence or enclosure. In medieval Ireland it came to mean the area of the country that was directly controlled by the kings of England. It lay in the east of the country, around Dublin. Within the Pale, English language, laws, fashions, architecture and customs became normal. The Pale was settled not just by English royal officials, but by merchants and labourers too, from across the Irish Sea.

THE STATUTES OF KILKENNY

From the early days of English rule in Ireland, the official policy was one of separation and apartness. In 1366 the English, under Prince Lionel of Clarence, called a parliament at Kilkenny and passed a wide range of statutes (laws). According to these, English colonists were not allowed to marry into Irish families, or to adopt Irish dress or customs. They were not to speak Irish or use the ancient Irish legal system, known as Brehon Law.

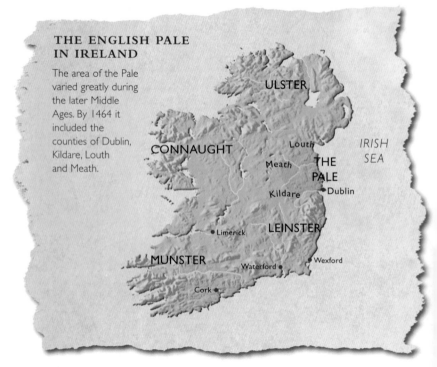

THE ENGLISH PALE IN IRELAND

The area of the Pale varied greatly during the later Middle Ages. By 1464 it included the counties of Dublin, Kildare, Louth and Meath.

ULSTER

CONNAUGHT

Louth

Meath

THE PALE

IRISH SEA

Kildare

Dublin

Limerick

LEINSTER

MUNSTER

Waterford

Wexford

Cork

➡ *The Breac Maedhóc is a bronze shrine from Drumlane, County Kavan. Its figures show the Gaels of Ireland in the 1100s. The men have long hair and beards and wear long cloaks. The women wear their hair in ringlets.*

THREE WORLDS, ONE LAND

Beyond the Pale, lay the lands of two other groups – the Irish-speaking Gaels and the powerful, independent Norman families who had seized Irish land. Over the years, many of the latter adopted Irish ways. The English kings, however, firmly believed that civilisation ended 'beyond the Pale'. This phrase is still sometimes used today to describe unacceptable or uncouth behaviour. From time to time the English attempted to expand their rule by founding colonies beyond the Pale. These were English settlements protected by soldiers.

➡ *The Abbey of the Holy Cross at Thurles. Founded by Donald O'Brien, King of Thomond, in 1169, it was rebuilt by the wife of King John of England, Isabella of Angoulême, around 1233.*

THE PALE AND BEYOND 147

➡️ *These stone carved tombs represent two of Ireland's most powerful families at the close of the Middle Ages. They may be seen in St Canice's Cathedral, Kilkenny. They belong to Piers Butler, Earl of Ossory and Ormond, and his wife Lady Margaret Fitzgerald.*

BARLEY FOR THE TAKING

When Henry II of England landed in Ireland in 1171, his chief aim had been to make sure that 'Strongbow' and his adventurers did not set up a Norman kingdom in Ireland to rival his own. As the years went by, the English found another reason for staying in Ireland. The lush, green pastures and fields of ripe barley were a valuable economic resource. Grain from Irish estates could be exported to England or mainland Europe for rich rewards.

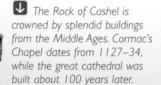
⬇️ *The Rock of Cashel is crowned by splendid buildings from the Middle Ages. Cormac's Chapel dates from 1127–34, while the great cathedral was built about 100 years later.*

Kilcrea Friary, in County Cork, was founded by Cormac Laidir MacCarthaigh, Lord of Muskerry, in about 1465.

KERN AND GALLOGLASS

Ireland saw wave after wave of English invasion. John came in 1185 as prince and again in 1210 as king. Richard II arrived in 1394–1395 and again in 1399. There were long battles between the old Norman families and amongst the Irish kings. By recognising the English kings, some Irish royal families managed to survive and even thrive in this changing world. The poor peasants experienced endless warfare. All sides used roving bands of troops who would fight for anyone who paid and fed them. These mercenaries included Norman men-at-arms, Irish footsoldiers called kerns and Scottish adventurers called galloglass, meaning 'foreign (ie Scottish) Gaels'.

The Hard Life

O n 14 April 1360 the weather was so foul and bitter that many horseback riders were reported to have died of cold, frozen to death in their saddles. There were few comforts in the Middle Ages. Castles were draughty and stank of sewage from the cesspit or the moat. People rarely bathed and disease was common. Many women never survived childbirth and children often died when young.

"OUR DAILY BREAD"

While the nobles ate fine wheaten bread, the poor ate crusts of coarse rye. Rye crops were sometimes spoiled by a fungus disease called ergot. People who ate flour made from mouldy rye became sick and saw strange visions. Country people preserved their own food, salting fish and smoking bacon. They ate eggs and caught hares and waterfowl. If the harvests failed and prices rose, then people starved.

Eggs and milk

Rye bread

Hare

▲ Food supply was seasonal and depended on good harvests. Famine was common.

THE BLACK DEATH

In August 1348 a new disease appeared at the port of Weymouth, in the southwest of England. It was known as the Pestilence, later as the Black Death. This terrible plague, spread by rats and their fleas, had already devastated Central Asia and Europe. Soon it was raging across England, Wales, Scotland and Ireland. The Black Death took various forms. One poisoned the bloodstream and caused horrid swellings and boils on the body. Another affected the lungs and could be passed on by coughing and sneezing.

← *The sick were sometimes cared for by nuns. The Black Death killed many carers as well as the patients. Soon, plague victims were being buried in mass graves and there were no priests left to pray for their souls.*

SINNERS AND LEPERS

Natural disasters and illnesses were often believed to be punishments sent by God, because of human sinfulness. One of the most feared diseases was leprosy, which causes lumps, discoloured patches and ulcers to form on the body. Fingers and toes would sometimes become numb and fall off. Sufferers (lepers) were banned from public places and were only allowed to watch church services through a slit in the wall.

MEDIEVAL MEDICINE

Medical knowledge had grown little since the days of the Romans. Surgeons could mend bones and monks grew herbs to make medicines. Some of these cures worked, but many didn't. One common treatment was bleeding – taking blood from the patient.

→ *Leprosy was an infectious disease. Lepers had to carry a wooden clapper, to warn people that they were coming along the road.*

THE HARD LIFE **151**

THE FEAR OF DEATH

The worst plague years were 1348–49. However, the dreadful 'pestilence' returned in 1361, 1369 and 1390. No doctors understood the cause of the disease or how it was passed on. They blamed bad smells or warm air rather than rats and fleas. Many people believed that the disease was God's punishment for sinful behaviour. Some predicted the end of the world. In many European countries people called 'flagellants' paraded through the streets carrying holy images and whipping themselves, in order to atone for their sins.

⬆ Many Europeans responded to the widespread deaths by becoming more religious. Flagellants (people who deliberately whipped themselves) marched through many towns.

A LABOUR SHORTAGE

In the years 1347 to 1351, the plague may have killed 75 million people in Asia and Europe. Many villages in the British Isles lost half to two-thirds of their population. In some there were no survivors at all. There was a great shortage of labour, so workers now found that they could demand high wages. In 1349 and 1351 the English government passed harsh laws in a desperate bid to keep wages at the same level.

⬆ Edward III tried to address the the labour shortage by passing the Statute of Labourers law in 1351, which tried to fix peasants' wages at their pre-plague level. But eventually the labour force rebelled against opressive measure.

THE PEASANTS' REVOLT

Taxes on all citizens, regardless of their income, were introduced after 1377. These 'poll taxes' made life wretched for the poor. In 1381, 20,000 peasants from Kent and Essex, led by Wat Tyler and a priest called John Ball, stormed London. They burned the palace of John of Gaunt, Duke of Lancaster. They killed the Archbishop, captured the Tower of London and freed the prisoners. The rising was savagely suppressed.

King Richard II, aged only 14, rode out to make peace. However the rebels were betrayed, attacked and killed.

The Hundred Years War

The period we know as the Hundred Years War was a long drawn out, bloody struggle between England and France. It took place across the muddy battlefields of northern France and Flanders (in what is now Belgium). It was never really one war, but a series of raids, battles, campaigns and treaties. Nor did it last 100 years, but from 1337 until 1453.

← Edward 'the Black Prince', was the eldest son of Edward III. His nickname came from the colour of his armour. Edward was a brilliant soldier who made a name for himself when he was only 16, at the Battle of Crécy. In 1356 he won a great victory at Poitiers. He died in 1376.

WHO RULES FRANCE?

King Edward III of England was related to the French royal family and in 1337 he claimed the throne of France as his own. England had fought for its lands in France ever since the days of the Normans and the Angevin empire. What was more, France was now a close ally of Scotland, England's enemy. The result was a war that cost Edward III's subjects dearly. They had to pay for it with taxes, loss of trade – and their lives.

In October 1415, Henry V found his route blocked by a huge French army (foreground) at the village of Agincourt. His 6000 troops were sick with dysentery and greatly outnumbered, but he won a great victory. The French knights became bogged down in mud, while flight after flight of arrows whistled through the air.

THE GAME OF CHESS

The English were not alone in their attacks on the French kings. At times they were allied with the Bretons of the northwest, at times with powerful barons from Burgundy, in the east. At first the English achieved some great victories. At Poitiers in 1356 the French king, Jean II ('the Good'), was captured. Three years later, the Treaty of Brétigny offered Edward III one-third of France if he gave up his claims to the throne.

WEAPONS AND TACTICS

For campaign after campaign, the English raided and plundered northern France. Long columns of battle-weary knights, waggons, footsoldiers and archers trailed across the countryside. Some carried new-fangled handguns, others hauled early cannon. When it came to pitched battles, England's great strength lay in its use of archers, armed with deadly longbows. They could fire up to 12 arrows a minute.

◀ The crossbow was more accurate than the longbow, but slower to reload.

THE HUNDRED YEARS WAR   155

THE TABLES ARE TURNED

Peace did not last. When Henry V came to the throne of England, he led his army back across the Channel and was victorious. In 1420 the Treaty of Troyes made him heir to the French throne – but within two years he was dead. French fortunes now began to turn. Their knights were inspired by a peasant girl called Joan of Arc. She claimed that voices of the saints had called her to free her homeland. The English accused her of witchcraft and burned her alive in 1431. However by 1453 France had regained most of the English-occupied lands.

↑ *French fortunes improved in 1429. Joan of Arc (or Jeanne d'Arc) rode out with the French army to break the siege of the city of Orleans, and succeeded in nine days.*

"DEAR KATE"

In Shakespeare's play *Henry V*, she is called 'dear Kate'. 'Kate' was Catherine de Valois, daughter of Charles VI of France. In 1420 she married Henry V of England, at the height of his success, but her husband became sick while away at the wars and died in 1422. Nine years later, Catherine secretly married a handsome young Welsh courtier. His name was Owain Tudur or Tudor, and it was their grandson, Henry VII, who founded the most famous dynasty in English history.

◀ *Catherine de Valois married Henry V at Troyes. She was crowned Queen of England and gave birth to a son, the future Henry VI, in 1421. Her eldest son by Owain Tudor was Edmund, Earl of Richmond, and he was father to Henry VII, the first Tudor monarch.*

1420
The *Treaty of Troyes*. Henry V becomes heir to the French throne.

1453
English defeat at Castillon, end of the 100 Years War.

↓ One of the major battles of the Hundred Years War was fought at Crécy in 1346. English soldiers defeated a much larger French army, killing almost half the French soldiers. During the battle, the English army used gunpowder and cannons.

↓ Deadly weapons called caltrops were used in the Hundred Years War. A caltrop was a star-shaped piece of metal. These were scattered along the ground in front of an attacking army. They stopped both horses and footsoldiers in their tracks.

The Welsh Rise Up

Wales was changing under English rule. Towns had already been developing in the days of the Welsh princes. Now, new shire or county towns controlled all local trade, and they prospered. In the Welsh heartlands, the new towns took the form of colonies, settled by incomers from England, France or Flanders. Welsh citizens were sometimes forcibly removed to other settlements.

↑ *Harlech Castle, completed by King Edward I of England in 1289, was besieged and captured by Owain Glyndŵr's rebels in the spring of 1404. It remained in Welsh hands until 1409.*

POET OF LOVE AND NATURE

Dafydd ap Gwilym is believed by many to be the greatest writer in the Welsh language. He was born in the parish of Llanbadarn Fawr, near Aberystwyth, and wrote his masterpieces between 1320 and 1370. He broke with traditional Welsh verse forms and was influenced by French literature. Dafydd wrote light-hearted and joyful poems, many of them about his sweethearts, Morfudd and Dyddgu. He wrote about nature, too, describing the grace of a seagull's flight in a way that still seems very modern today.

▲ *Love and life in 14th century Wales is described in the poems of Dafydd ap Gwilym.*

TROUBLED TIMES

Many Welsh people protested against the taxes and laws brought in by the English. An uprising began in 1294, led by Madog ap Llywelyn, but it was put down in 1295. In 1317 there was a revolt in South Wales, led by Llywelyn Bren. Perhaps the greatest danger to English rule came from Owain Lawgoch, grandson of Llywelyn Fawr. He fought as a mercenary for the French, who called him Yvain de Galles. He planned to reconquer Wales with French help, but was murdered by a secret agent in 1378.

A SPARK CATCHES FIRE

In 1400, Lord Grey of Ruthin, a personal friend of the English king, Henry IV, siezed some land from his neighbour in the Marches of northeast Wales. Owain Glyndŵr was a middle-aged Welsh nobleman of royal descent. He appealed to the English parliament for justice, but they reacted with contempt, declaring the Welsh to be 'barefoot rascals'. A simple land dispute became a full-scale national uprising. Owain was supported by all ranks of Welsh society, including monks and bishops. Welsh labourers and students returned from England to join him.

➔ *Owain Glyndŵr had studied law in London and fought with the English army, but he now became leader of a Welsh uprising. He summoned Welsh parliaments at Machynlleth and Dolgellau.*

MASTERS OF THE LONGBOW

Welsh archers are said to have been the first to develop the longbow. Unlike the shorter Norman bow, it was the full height of a man. It was normally made of yew and had a pull of about 40 kilograms. Arrows were about 78 centimetres long, made of ash with long metal tips. Goose-feather flights made them spin as they flew through the air. They could even pierce armour. The English used companies of Welsh archers to devastating effect during the Hundred Years War with France.

THE LONG FIGHT

Owain Glyndŵr was acclaimed the true Prince of Wales and by 1401 most of his country had joined the uprising. Castles were captured from the English and towns were sacked. Owain planned to join forces with rebel English barons Henry Percy ('Hotspur') and Edmund Mortimer, but they were defeated at Shrewsbury in 1403. In 1404 Owain was at the height of his power, having taken Harlech, Aberystwyth and Cardiff. In that year he held a parliament at Machynlleth.

← *The longbow was a deadly weapon in the hands of Welsh archers.*

1408
English start to regain control of Wales.

1413
The end of the Welsh uprising, English rule restored.

A FINAL MYSTERY

In 1405 the French sailed to the support of the Welsh, but were defeated. The war became a guerrilla campaign and resistance continued until 1413. Glyndŵr however had vanished. Had he gone into hiding? Was he already dead? Many Welsh people believed the myth that he was sleeping in the hills, and would return to lead them one day.

Castles remained the focus of warfare in the 1400s. By 1408 the English were regaining control over Wales. The countryside lay ravaged by their armies and many castles were recaptured.

1399
Henry IV, son of John of Gaunt, is first
Lancastrian king.

1453
Henry VI suffers from mental illness.

Wars of the Roses

As battle-hardened soldiers returned from the French wars, many entered the service of powerful English lords. Their job was to bully peasants for payment of taxes, or to fight in private armies. There was no shortage of work for them. For 30 years, from 1455 until 1485, there were civil wars as rival branches of the royal family fought for the throne of England.

LANCASTER AND YORK

The Houses of Lancaster and York were both descended from Edward III. Their rivalry came to a head when a Lancastrian king, Henry VI, became too mentally ill to rule. In 1454, Richard, Duke of York, was appointed Protector. When Henry VI got better, Richard would not give up his new-found power, and went to war. Henry VI was defeated at St Albans in 1455, but then Richard was killed at Wakefield in 1460.

Lancaster

York

 A red rose stood for the House of Lancaster. A white rose was the badge of the House of York. When Henry VII came to the throne, he combined both designs in a red-and-white 'Tudor rose'.

ENGLISH KINGS

House of Lancaster	House of York	House of Tudor
✤ Henry IV 1399–1413	✤ Edward IV 1461–1470 & 1471–1483	✤ Henry VII 1485–1509
✤ Henry V 1413–1422		
✤ Henry VI 1422–1461 & 1470–1471	✤ Edward V 1483	
	✤ Richard III 1483–1485	

1454
Richard, Duke of York appointed Protector.

1455
Battle of St Albans. Wars of the Roses begin.

WARWICK 'THE KINGMAKER'

The most powerful man in England at this time was not the weak king, but Richard Neville, Earl of Warwick. It was he who had Richard's son proclaimed Edward IV in 1461, the first Yorkist king. Henry VI was imprisoned and exiled. Later, Warwick fell out with Edward and brought Henry VI back to the throne. No wonder he was remembered in history as the 'kingmaker'. Edward returned to seek revenge. Warwick was killed in battle and Henry was murdered in the Tower of London in 1471.

A NEW POWERFUL KING

Edward IV was a brave fighter, a clever army commander and a good politician. He became king in 1461. Edward liked food, drink and pretty women. He was also ruthless in his search for power and he gave orders for Henry VI to be murdered. When he suspected his brother of plotting against him, he ordered him to be drowned. Edward died in 1483.

 Edward IV won his first battle in 1416 when he was 18. Nobles fighting with him against Henry VI agreed he should be the next king.

Printing press

THE AGE OF PRINTING

In 1471 an Englishman called William Caxton travelled to the German city of Cologne. There he learned about a new technology that had been invented in China and developed in Germany and the Netherlands. It was called printing, and it would change the world. Caxton set up his own printing press at Westminster in 1476 and produced about 100 titles.

◀ Famous books published by Caxton at Westminster include Le Morte d'Arthur and Geoffrey Chaucer's Canterbury Tales.

THE MARCH TO BOSWORTH

Edward IV died in 1483. His heir, Edward V, was too young to rule for himself, so he and his young brother were left in the care of their uncle, Richard of Gloucester. They went to live in the Tower of London, but mysteriously, were never seen again. Gloucester was crowned Richard III in the same year, at the request of parliament. He did not rule for long. In 1485 the Earl of Richmond, a Lancastrian, landed in Wales. His name was Henry Tudor and he defeated and killed Richard III at the battle of Bosworth, near Leicester.

WHO MURDERED THE PRINCES?

Did Richard III murder the princes in the Tower? He had every reason to. Skeletons were found in the Tower in 1674 and buried in Westminster Abbey. However some historians believe that Richard III was not such a villain as he is often made out to be. Might Henry VII have been the true murderer?

Henry VII married Elizabeth of York and united the houses of Lancaster and York. The Wars of the Roses had ended.

Richard III was killed at the battle of Bosworth in 1485. His body was taken to Leicester, where it was discovered in 2012.

A NEW DYNASTY BEGINS

Henry VII founded a new ruling family. Henry Tudor was the son of a Welsh lord, Edmund Tudor, and an English noblewoman, Lady Margaret Beaufort. He had a weak claim to be king but he brought peace to England, and an end to the Wars of the Roses. When he died in 1509, England was richer and calmer than it had been for hundreds of years.

palaces and players

1509–1714

THE WORLD AT A GLANCE

ELSEWHERE IN EUROPE

1512
Michelangelo completes painting of the Sistine Chapel, in Rome.

1517
German monk Martin Luther starts the Protestant Reformation.

1571
Naval Battle of Lepanto, Christian fleet led by Venice defeats the Turks.

1618
Religious strife in the Holy Roman Empire leads to the Thirty Years War.

1643
Louis XIV the 'Sun King' becomes ruler of France.

1648
Spain recognises independence of the Netherlands, art and trade flourish.

1701
Frederick I becomes first King of Prussia, in east Germany.

1703
Peter the Great, Tsar of Russia, builds new capital at St Petersburg.

ASIA

1526
Babur defeats Delhi and founds the Moghul empire in northern India.

1566
The Ottoman (Turkish) empire is at its greatest extent.

1581
The Russians begin their conquest of Siberia (northeast Asia).

1587
Abbas I 'the Great' rules Persia, a golden age of arts and crafts.

1603
Tokugawa Ieyasu becomes Shogun, brings all Japan under his rule.

1619
The Dutch found colonial empire in the East Indies, based at Djakarta.

1644
Manchurian emperors now rule China: the Qing dynasty.

1707
The death of Emperor Aurangzeb, decline of Moghuls, power in India.

AFRICA

1546
Songhai destroys the empire of Mali in West Africa.

1517
Egypt is conquered by the Turks and becomes part of the Ottoman empire.

1575
Portuguese found Luanda and settle the coast of Angola.

1578
Moroccans defeat Portuguese in North Africa.

1600
The Oyo state is at the height of its power in Nigeria.

1632
Emperor Fasilidas closes Ethiopia to foreigners.

1662
Portuguese defeat the kingdom of Kongo, southern Central Africa.

1700
Rise of Ashanti power in Ghana, West Africa.

"New faiths, new nations and faraway lands..."

NORTH AMERICA

1510
First African slaves begin to arrive in North America.

1519
Spanish begin conquest of Aztec empire in Mexico.

1570
Northeast Native Americans form an alliance, the Iroquois Confederacy.

1607
English found a permanent settlement at Jamestown, Virginia.

1608
French colonists found a settlement at Québec, in Canada.

1625
Dutch settle New Amsterdam (later New York City).

1684
French explore the Mississippi region and claim Louisiana.

1692
Port Royal, Jamaica, a notorious pirate haven, is destroyed by an earthquake.

SOUTH AMERICA

1519
Portuguese Ferdinand Magellan explores the Strait named after him.

1532
The Spanish invade and defeat the Inca empire of Peru.

1536
The first Spanish settlement at Buenos Aires, Argentina.

1541
The Spanish found a settlement at Santiago, in Chile.

1545
Spanish develop silver mining in the Andes mountains.

1560
The Portuguese lay out sugarcane plantations in Brazil.

1620
Dutch West India Company settles Guyana, northern South America.

1667
Dutch colonists take Suriname, in northern South America.

OCEANIA

1519
Portuguese explorer Ferdinand Magellan enters the Pacific Ocean.

1521
Ferdinand Magellan claims the Philippines for Spain.

1526
Portuguese explorer Jorge de Menezes visits New Guinea.

1600
Tu'i Kanokupolu dynasty comes to power in Hawaiian islands.

1606
Dutch explorer Willem Jansz sights Cape York Peninsula, Australia.

1616
Dutch crew under Dirck Hartog lands in Western Australia.

1642
Dutch explorer Abel Tasman reaches Tasmania and New Zealand.

1643
Tasman sails to the Pacific islands of Tonga and Fiji.

1509
Henry VIII marries Catherine of Aragon (Spain).

1512
Henry VIII claims French throne. War with France.

King Harry's Days

Young Henry VIII, crowned King of England in 1509, loved to fight tournaments in gleaming armour. In 1520 he met François I of France at the Field of the Cloth of Gold, near Calais. Both sides wore the most splendid clothes imaginable. Standards fluttered in front of luxurious tents. However although royal courts still dreamed of chivalry, the period we call the Middle Ages had already slipped away.

English armies

Scottish armies

FLODDEN FIELD 1513

In 1513, while Henry VIII was away fighting in France, the Scots invaded England. They were defeated at Flodden. Ten thousand were killed, including James IV, who was married to Henry's sister Margaret.

THE EARLY TUDORS

Henry VII had been a skilful ruler, who survived false claims to the throne and rebellions over his harsh taxation. His sickly eldest son, Arthur, died young. However his second son, who became Henry VIII, was strong and energetic.

In the new Europe, nations were constantly competing for power and trade. Henry was also a cunning statesman, as was his Lord Chancellor, a bullying, arrogant churchman called Thomas Wolsey.

Henry VIII's personal life led to an historic break with the Church of Rome.

THE KING WITH SIX WIVES

The young Henry VIII cut a fine figure, but by the time of his death in 1547 he had become bloated, overweight and diseased. He married no fewer than six times. His marriages were marked by passion, political intrigue, jealousy, rage and selfishness. Henry's love for a beautiful courtier called Anne Boleyn led him to demand a divorce from Catherine of Aragon. The Pope refused and this led to a crisis that changed the direction of English history.

▲ Catherine of Aragon was the widow of Prince Arthur. Henry demanded a divorce.

▲ Henry married Anne Boleyn in 1533, but they quarrelled and she was executed in 1536.

▲ Henry married Jane Seymour the day after Anne was executed. She died in childbirth.

▲ The fourth marriage was for political reasons and Henry found Anne of Cleves too unattractive.

▲ After another divorce, Henry married Catherine Howard, but executed her too, for being unfaithful.

▲ Henry's sixth wife, Catherine Parr, was a wise queen, who survived Henry's death.

1536
Anne is executed. Henry VIII marries Jane Seymour.

1540
Henry VIII marries Anne of Cleves and
Catherine Howard.

MONEY, LAND AND SHEEP

While Henry VIII spent lavishly on court
life and on wars, ordinary people suffered
extreme hardship. The Spanish were now
mining gold and silver in the Americas, and
this upset the economy of other European
countries. Prices began to rise and rents with
them. For many years common land that had
always been used by the public for farming
and grazing, was seized by greedy landlords.
Many poor people were forced off the land,
to become beggars and outlaws. In July 1549
Robert Kett, from Wymondham in Norfolk,
led a rebellion against the enclosure of
common land for sheep pasture. Kett
attracted 16,000 supporters to his cause and
they killed 20,000 sheep as a protest. They
occupied the city of Norwich, but Kett was
captured and hanged.

▲ The Guildhall at Lavenham in Suffolk was built in
1529. Lavenham was the centre of the wool trade,
and wool was the mainstay of the English economy.

↑ Henry VIII's royal court was a place of
pleasure, but also one of political intrigue.

DIVORCE AND REBELLION

When Henry VIII demanded
something, he usually got it. Thomas
Wolsey was unable to persuade Pope
Clement VII to agree to Henry's
divorce with Catherine of Aragon, so
he was thrown out of office. In 1534
a law was passed making Henry VIII
head of the Church in England, so
that he could decide his own fate.
The arrogance of the king and his
officials led to many uprisings. In
1536–37 there was a major rebellion
in Yorkshire and Lincolnshire, called
the Pilgrimage of Grace.

A ROYAL NAVY

Henry VIII was the first king to realise that England, an island, needed a proper navy. He commissioned the building of 20 new ships, all specially designed for war, and employed full-time captains to command them. The most famous ship was the splendid *Mary Rose*, which sank in an accident after leaving harbour in Portsmouth in 1545, drowning most of the soldiers and sailors on board. An archaeological project started in 1979 recovered the ship's timbers as well as guns, bows, tools and navigational equipment.

RULERS OF ENGLAND	
House of Tudor (continued)	
✤ Henry VIII	1509–1547
✤ Edward VI	1547–1553
✤ Mary I	1553–1558
✤ Elizabeth I	1558–1603

⬇ The Mary Rose *was unstable and keeled over, allowing water to pour in through her open gun-ports (the holes through which cannon were fired). Since 2013 the wreck has been on display at Portsmouth's Mary Rose Museum.*

Clashes of Faith

In 1521, Pope Leo X had honoured Henry VIII of England with the title 'Defender of the Faith', because of his support for the Roman Church. Within 13 years, however, Henry had broken with Rome and made himself head of the Church in England. This marked the start of centuries of religious conflict in the British Isles.

← *The conflict between Henry VIII and the Roman Catholic Church eventually led to the seizure of Church properties by the state. These are the ruins of Glastonbury Abbey, in Somerset. The last abbot, Robert Whiting, was executed in 1539. Many people profited personally from the religious turmoil. It has been suggested that one of these was Whiting's steward, Thomas Horner, and that he is commemorated in the well-known nursery rhyme 'Little Jack Horner'.*

1531
English priests recognise Henry VIII as head of the Church in England.

1534
Henry VIII breaks ties with the Church of Rome.

THE PROTESTANTS

New ideas were entering the British Isles from mainland Europe during the reign of Henry VIII. They came from people who were known as Protestants, because they were protesting against the Roman 'Catholic' (meaning 'universal') Church, its teachings and its customs. Leading Protestant campaigners included a German called Martin Luther and a Frenchman called John Calvin. Their demands for reform led to this period of European history being called the Reformation.

➡ *The early Tudor period produced some beautiful church architecture. The roof of King's College Chapel, Cambridge, fans out into a delicate tracery of stone. It was completed in 1515.*

THOMAS MORE'S UTOPIA

Sir Thomas More was appointed Lord Chancellor of England in 1529. He did not want the job, but he carried it out dutifully. Although More wished to see many changes in the Roman Church, he refused to accept Henry VIII as head of the English Church. More was beheaded for treason in 1535. In 1516 More wrote a book in Latin, which compared the social problems of his day with an imagined island where there was an ideal society. The name of the book was *Utopia* – from the Greek words for 'nowhere'.

◄ *Thomas More's perfect land of Utopia was far removed from the realities of Henry VIII's England.*

AN ENGLISH CHURCH

Henry VIII broke with Rome for political reasons, rather than because of his religious beliefs. He had little sympathy for the English supporters of Martin Luther and intended the English Church to follow basic Catholic teachings. During the reign of Henry's successor, Edward VI, the Church in England did adopt Protestant policies.

DISSOLUTION OF THE MONASTERIES

The year 1535 saw Henry VIII order the closing down of Roman Catholic abbeys, monasteries and convents across England, Wales and Ireland. This act became known as the Dissolution or Suppression of the Monasteries. The properties were mostly sold off to nobles who supported the king. This raised huge amounts of money for the state. The operation was organised by Thomas Cromwell, who became Henry VIII's chief minister and was made Earl of Essex. However by 1540 Cromwell too had fallen from royal favour, and his head was chopped off at the Tower of London.

▲ Knox had a very strong character and was an influential campaigner. In an age of powerful queens, he claimed that it was against the will of God for women to be rulers.

THE SCOTTISH REFORMER

John Knox was born at Haddington, Lothian, in about 1513. He became a Catholic priest in 1540, but soon fell under the influence of the Lutheran George Wishart. Wishart was burnt for his beliefs in 1547, and Knox became a Protestant minister. He spent some time in England in the service of Edward VI and then went to Switzerland, where he studied the teachings of John Calvin. Knox returned to Scotland in 1559. Despite the efforts of the Scottish Catholics, a Protestant Church of Scotland was recognised in 1560.

 The Roman Catholic monasteries were stripped of their valuables and their precious libraries were often destroyed. The loss of the charitable services provided by monks and nuns led to hardship amongst the poor.

A Tudor Palace

In Tudor times, the River Thames was the lifeline of the growing city of London. Rowing boats called wherries carried passengers across to the south bank and sometimes a splendid royal barge could be seen, its oars dipping in the water. It would leave the royal landing stage by Whitehall Palace and beat upstream to the royal palaces at Richmond or Hampton Court, or downstream to the grand palace of Greenwich.

The Tudors moved from one palace to another during the year. Hampton Court was their favourite.

COURT AND CULTURE

In the 1500s there was a renewal of interest in learning, in the civilisations of ancient Greece and Rome, in painting and sculpture and in invention. This period, called the Renaissance or 'rebirth', began in Italy, but its influence was also felt in northern Europe. The Tudor rulers were well educated and intelligent. Artists such as the great German painter Hans Holbein the Younger came to the English court. Henry VIII and his courtiers loved music, dancing and playing royal or 'real' tennis, a version of the game that was played in an indoor court. They also loved to hunt deer in the royal parks and forests.

← *Dances at the royal courts in Tudor times included the pavane, a sequence of stately steps around the floor, and the galliard, an energetic dance that involved leaping.*

1523
Poets gather at Caerwys for an *eisteddfod*.

1536
The first Act of Union. Wales is annexed by England.

Wales Under the Tudors

Wales during the reign of the Tudors was still mostly a land of farms and villages, of windmills and water wheels. Women spun and wove their own cloth. Few towns had more than 2000 inhabitants. There was little industry, although coal was already being mined in South Wales during the reign of Elizabeth I. Ships traded with Ireland, with other parts of Great Britain, France and Spain.

NO RIVALS FOR POWER

As a member of the Tudor family, Henry VII was of Welsh descent. However he and his successors reinforced the centralised power of the monarchy and ruled Wales harshly in order to suppress any ideas of another uprising. On the borders, the powers of the Marcher Lords were removed, and in South Wales even Rhys ap Gruffudd, whose grandfather Rhys ap Thomas had helped put Henry VII on the throne, was executed on trumped up charges of treason in 1531 by Henry VIII, who wanted his rich estates.

⬆ *On the modern flag of Wales, the white and green derive from the family colours of the Tudors, while the red dragon is a much older emblem of the Welsh. The use of the dragon had been revived by the future Henry VII, who featured it on his battle standard at Bosworth in 1485.*

THE ACTS OF UNION

By the Acts of Union, passed in 1536 and 1542, Wales and the Marcher lordships were annexed, or taken over, by England. In doing this, Henry VIII took the first step towards creating a United Kingdom. Welsh law and Welsh customs were to be abolished. No Welsh person could hold public office unless they could speak English, a

↑ This fine map of Wales was published in 1579. It is from a work dedicated to Elizabeth I, made by Christopher Saxton.

ruling that excluded 95 percent of the population. Otherwise, Welsh citizens did now have equal rights with English citizens before the law, and were represented in the English parliament.

SCHOLARS AND BISHOPS

In 1571 Hugh Price, an expert in Church law from Brecon, founded Jesus College, in Oxford, England, for Welsh students. Over the ages it kept its special links with Wales. After 1588, students would have been able to read the Bible for the first time in the Welsh language. The brilliant translation was by William Morgan, who in 1595 became Bishop of Llandaff. Morgan's masterpiece helped to shape the Welsh language and keep it alive into modern times.

➡ *One of the finest Tudor town houses in Britain survives at Plas Mawr, in Conwy, North Wales. It was built in 1577 for a wealthy local gentleman named Robert Wynn. Robert Wynn had fought for the Tudors at the Siege of Boulogne in 1544 and also in Scotland. He owned lands at Dolwyddelan and married into the powerful Griffith family of Penrhyn.*

Servants' bedrooms
Servants slept in male and female dormitories in the attic.

The cellars
Barrels of ale and wine were stored in the basement. Robert Wynn was an importer of French wines into the port of Conwy.

Roofs and gables

The roof was supported by massive wooden beams and tiled with slate. The stepped design of the gable ends was copied from Flanders. Robert Wynn had travelled widely in Europe, in the service of a courtier named Sir Philip Hoby.

ELIZABETHAN WALES

In the second half of the 16th century, Wales was controlled by a few powerful families who found favour with the Tudors. Some were nobles at the royal court, others were lower in the social scale – squires, landowners and wealthy businessmen who built large country houses. A fair number of Welsh people formed a community in London, including merchants, lawyers, doctors, cattle drovers and servants. English became more widely spoken in Wales, but the attempt to eradicate the Welsh language by the Acts of Union failed. By 1563 Elizabeth I had signalled the intention that churches in Wales should have prayerbooks and Bibles in Welsh as well as in English.

The great chamber

The chief reception room had decorated plasterwork, showing Tudor roses and coats of arms.

Preparing food

On the ground floor was the kitchen, the pantry and the brewhouse.

1547
Somerset becomes Protector as Edward VI is still a boy.

1549
First Book of Common Prayer is printed in English.

Protestant or Catholic?

Henry VIII died in 1547. Would England become Protestant or Roman Catholic? Living through the years that followed was like riding a see-saw, as rulers swung from the one faith to the other. There were fierce struggles between powerful nobles. Many common people suffered economic hardship.

THE BOY KING

Edward VI was just 10 when he came to the throne. The son of Henry VIII and Jane Seymour, he was raised as a strict Protestant. He was very clever and learned Greek, Latin and French. His uncle Edward Seymour, Duke of Somerset, governed as Lord Protector in his place. However Somerset was overthrown and executed in 1552, to be replaced by John Dudley, Duke of Northumberland. Edward VI died from tuberculosis in 1553.

Edward VI was a sickly boy who died young.

THE GRAMMAR SCHOOLS

Now that there were no more monks as teachers, schools became more important. Many new schools were named after the Tudors, others after the rich merchants who funded them. It was mostly boys who received formal schooling. The school day lasted from six in the morning until five in the afternoon. Pupils learned to write using slates. They learned to read and did sums and were beaten if they made mistakes. A lot of the time was spent learning Latin grammar, so these were known as 'grammar schools'.

▼ *The grammar school in Stratford-upon-Avon was named after Edward VI. Its most famous pupil in Tudor times was a young lad called William Shakespeare.*

⬇ *Jane was a quiet, intelligent girl, a Protestant and a great grand-daughter of Henry VII. Against her will, she became a pawn in a deadly game of power politics.*

QUEEN FOR NINE DAYS

The Duke of Northumberland had persuaded the young king to make his daughter-in-law, Lady Jane Grey, heir to the throne of England. She was crowned queen in 1553, but within just nine days had been forced from the throne by the supporters of the rightful heir, Mary Tudor. Jane was imprisoned. After Sir Thomas Wyatt the Younger started a rebellion in her name, she was beheaded at the Tower of London in 1554, at the age of 16.

1553
Edward VI dies. Lady Jane Grey declared queen.

1553
Jane Grey is imprisoned. Mary I becomes queen.

BLOODY MARY

Mary Tudor was the daughter of Henry VIII and Catherine of Aragon. Her father had forced her to sign a document stating that his marriage to her mother had been illegal. Mary remained a very unhappy woman for most of her life. She was a Roman Catholic and in 1554 married King Philip II of Spain. He spent little

Protestant churchmen who went to their death in the years 1555–1556 included Hugh Latimer, Nicholas Ridley and Archbishop Thomas Cranmer.

more than a year in England and the marriage was very unpopular. Mary began to bring back the Catholic faith. During the last three years of her reign, 300 leading Protestants were burned alive. This earned her the nickname of 'Bloody Mary'.

PRINCESS ELIZABETH

Mary I had a young half-sister, the daughter of Henry VIII and Anne Boleyn. Princess Elizabeth loved learning as well as playing music, dancing and riding. She was raised as a Protestant and this aroused the suspicion of Mary, who imprisoned her for a time. Elizabeth had to tread very, very carefully. However when Mary died without a child, in 1558, it was Elizabeth who became the next Queen of England.

MARY AND PHILIP

Mary Tudor was determined to marry a Roman Catholic and to exclude her half-sister Elizabeth from the throne. After all, Elizabeth was the daughter of Anne Boleyn, who

▲ *Mary I of England*

had replaced Mary's own mother as queen. Mary was advised to marry Prince Philip of Spain, who became king as Philip II. It was a bad decision. Although she found him attractive, he felt nothing for this older woman other than a certain admiration. The English people wanted her to marry an Englishman, while the politicians feared that England would fall under the control of Spain. The couple had no children and Mary died in 1558.

◀ *Philip II of Spain and King Consort of England*

← *Queen Mary enters London, followed by Princess Elizabeth. As a potential rival for the throne, Elizabeth was in a difficult situation that required her to act very carefully. She grew up to be a wise and cautious ruler.*

PROTESTANT OR CATHOLIC? **185**

A Royal Stage

Elizabeth, pale-skinned with flaming red hair, was crowned Queen of England in January 1559, dressed in heavy robes of gold and ermine fur. She was 25 years old. The new queen was warmly welcomed by the people, for they longed for an end to the religious strife and struggles for power.

STATESMEN AND SPIES

During the reign of Mary I, Elizabeth had learned how to survive in a world of plots and intrigue. As a queen, she possessed all the diplomatic and political skills that Mary had lacked. She surrounded herself with cunning statesmen such as William Cecil (who became Lord Burleigh) and set up a secret service under Sir Francis Walsingham. Elizabeth, like her father, enjoyed power and would let nobody stand in her way.

➡ *Every ruler feared plots against them. Elizabeth I's trusted minister, Francis Walsingham, created Europe's first modern spy service. His well-educated agents worked to uncover traitors to the queen.*

THE VIRGIN QUEEN

Who would the new queen marry? The throne of England was a rich prize. Elizabeth kept everyone guessing, playing off one suitor against another in order to gain political advantage. In the end, she married no one. She said that she was already married – to the English people. Elizabeth I left no heir to the throne and so became known as the Virgin Queen. The newly formed North American colony of Virginia was named in her honour. The queen was probably reluctant to marry a foreign prince or king in view of the unpopularity of Mary I's marriage to Philip II of Spain. Even though Elizabeth I remained unwed, she openly favoured certain men at the royal court. These included Robert Dudley, Earl of Leicester, Christopher Hatton, and, until they quarrelled, Robert Devereux, Earl of Essex.

← Large areas of land were set aside as royal parks and forests. The queen and her courtiers would attend stag hunts, breaking off to enjoy open-air picnics and entertainments.

AT HOME AND ABROAD

The court moved around the country, making royal 'progresses'. Elizabeth's hosts had to spend a fortune on her entertainment and food. These journeys helped Elizabeth find out what was going on in her kingdom and made her aware of any local problems or needs. It also showed off her power and authority. Elizabeth I could speak Latin, French and Italian fluently, and she also knew ancient Greek and some Spanish. She spoke to foreign ambassadors directly – and often very forcibly – in protection of English trading interests.

GLORIANA

Elizabeth I ruled over a glittering court. It was like a continuous dramatic performance, in which all eyes were drawn to her. She is said to have owned over 1000 dresses. Courtiers competed for her approval and greatly feared falling from favour. Elizabeth I inspired a great poetical work by Edmund Spenser, called *The Faerie Queene*. Characters in the book, which was written between 1590 and 1596, were meant to represent virtues and vices. Elizabeth is called Gloriana, the ideal queen.

▼ Elizabeth's signature was scrawled across the page in ink, with a quill pen. The R stands for regina, which is Latin for 'queen'. The loops are intended to prevent anyone else adding an extra message to the bottom of the document.

1601
Last parliament summoned by Elizabeth I. Poor Laws, to support the poorest in society.

1603
Elizabeth I dies of pneumonia at Richmond Palace.

A PROTESTANT RULER

Elizabeth I steered England and Wales away from the Roman Catholic faith that had been restored by her sister. However this direction was not at all popular in Ireland. The English prayer book was restored by the Act of Uniformity in 1559. Elizabeth I was declared the Supreme Governor of the English Church, and public figures had to endorse this appointment under the Act of Supremacy passed in the same year. Elizabeth made her peace with France, but found a potentially dangerous enemy in Catholic Spain.

➔ Elizabeth I was much-loved, and knew how to win public approval. However when she was crossed, she showed a fierce temper.

c.1587
William Shakespeare arrives in London.

1593
Christopher Marlowe stabbed to death in a tavern brawl.

Shakespeare's Genius

Out of the taverns, theatres and royal courts of the Elizabethan age came some of the finest plays ever written. The master playwright and most brilliant poet was William Shakespeare. Born at Stratford-upon-Avon, Warwickshire, in 1564, he came to London in about 1587. In 1594 he bought a shareholding in a new company of players called the 'Lord Chamberlain's Men', whose leading actor was Richard Burbage. Shakespeare wrote witty comedies and heartbreaking tragedies, many of them based on British history.

⬆ *William Shakespeare lived until 1616. His great plays still speak directly to us today, wherever we live in the world.*

⬇ *William Shakespeare was probably born in this house in Stratford-upon-Avon in 1564.*

⬆ *William Shakespeare had a complete understanding of the theatre and was himself an experienced actor.*

POETRY, MUSIC AND ART

The late 1500s and early 1600s were a rich period for the arts in England. Several of Elizabeth I's courtiers, such as Sir Philip Sidney and Sir Walter Raleigh, were poets. The playwright Ben Jonson worked with Shakespeare in the 1590s and John Webster wrote the first of his tragedies, *The White Devil*, in 1612. The artist Nicholas Hilliard was making exquisite miniature paintings at the royal court, while Thomas Tallis and William Byrd were composing music for church and palace.

COMPANIES OF ACTORS

Actors formed theatrical companies, and the Globe theatre was home to the 'Lord Chamberlain's Men'. After 1603 they were renamed the 'King's Men'. The Globe's most famous shareholders were Richard Burbage and William Shakespeare.

KIT MARLOWE

Christopher ('Kit') Marlowe was born in 1564, the son of a shoemaker. He went to King's School, Canterbury, and studied at Cambridge. He was very intelligent but also loved drinking and brawling. He was rumoured to be an atheist, someone who does not believe in God. Marlowe wrote poetry and several great plays, including *Tamburlaine*, *The Tragical History of Dr Faustus*, *The Jew of Malta* and *Edward II*. He may have worked as a secret agent and was killed in a fight in a tavern ('pub') in 1593.

◀ *Christopher Marlowe led life to the full, but died in a drunken brawl.*

Ireland Rebels

During the early Tudor period, the most powerful people in Ireland belonged to an old Norman family, the Fitzgeralds. As Earls of Kildare, Gerald Mór (1478–1513) and Gerald Óg (1513–1534) came to control most of the country. England was happy for the Fitzgeralds to look after the royal interests in Ireland – but only so long as they did not challenge English rule.

RELIGIOUS DIVISIONS

The political divisions of Ireland were further complicated when Henry VIII broke with the Roman Church. The Irish-speaking Gaels remained faithful to Rome. Of the rest, some remained loyal to the king, but could not accept him as head of the Church. Others accepted the new order, and did well for themselves, as they profited from wealth seized from the Church. In 1534 the Fitzgeralds declared themselves for the Pope. One of them – Thomas, Lord Offaly – rose up against Henry VIII but was defeated by an English army.

← In the Gaelic west, long-haired mercenary soldiers, the 'kern', were armed with long swords and daggers. Their home villages were made up of simple thatched houses, often grouped around a fortified tower.

1593
Hugh O'Neill leads rebellion in Ulster.

1607
Flight of the Earls. Irish nobles flee to mainland Europe.

THE PIRATE QUEEN

During the 1560s, shipping off the west coast of Ireland came under attack from a fleet of pirate ships. These were based in Clew Bay, where they could hide out amongst a maze of small islands. The fleet was commanded by an Irish noble woman called Gráinne ní Mháille, or Grace O'Malley. In 1593 she negotiated a pardon from Elizabeth I, in person.

◀ *Grace O'Malley's pirate galleys attacked English and Irish ships. In 1557 she repelled an English attack on her stronghold.*

REBELLION AND FLIGHT

The most serious Irish rebellion broke out in Ulster, in 1595. It was led by Hugh O'Neill, Earl of Tyrone. In 1598 he led a victory over the English at the battle of the Yellow Ford, but was himself defeated by 1601. By the Treaty of Mellifont, signed in 1603, vast areas of land were seized from the Irish. By 1607 the Irish nobles were in despair. Many cut their losses and fled to mainland Europe – the 'Flight of the Earls'.

UNWELCOME SETTLERS

Mary I may have been a Roman Catholic, but she supported an English policy of colonization or 'plantation' in Ireland. English settlers were 'planted' in Laois and Offaly, which were now to be known as Queen's County and King's County. Under Elizabeth I, Irish colonization became a religious drive, with Protestant nobles eager to grab land from the Catholic Irish. Elizabeth I 'planted' Ulster, in the north. Most early plantation attempts failed, but they started a process that proved to be disastrous for Ireland.

⬆ *In 1607 Hugh O'Neill fled to the Netherlands, which were at that time ruled by Spain. He died in Rome in 1616.*

Stuart Scotland

The Stewart (later, Stuart) family ruled Scotland for nearly 340 years. Many of their early kings came to the throne in their childhood, and this allowed powerful Lowlands families, highland chieftains and Lords of the Isles to grasp power for themselves. There were court plots, royal murders and endless wars with the English. Scotland's closest links were with France, which kept to the 'auld alliance'.

James IV and many leading Scottish nobles were killed by the English army at Branxton, near Flodden in Northumbria, in 1513. The battle was fought not only with pikes, swords and longbows, but also with cannon.

1513
James IV killed by English at the battle of Flodden.

1538
James V marries Mary of Guise, a French Catholic.

The stewart court

The greatest of the Stewart kings was James IV, who became king in 1488. He married Margaret Tudor, sister of Henry VIII. His court attracted poets and musical composers such William Dunbar and Robert Carver. James IV built new palaces and a fleet of warships. Tragically, he was killed at the Battle of Flodden in 1513. He was the last Scottish king to speak the Gaelic language.

↑ King James IV was an energetic, wise and intelligent ruler. He was devoted to education and also licensed the first printing press in Scotland. However, his military strategy was flawed and his death at Flodden was a tragedy for Scotland.

The massacre at Flodden

When James IV marched into England with an army of 35,000 men, it was because Henry VIII of England was attacking France. James was duty bound under the terms of the Scottish–French alliance to support his ally. The battle of Flodden was disastrous for the Scots. It did not serve its purpose of diverting English troops from France, yet it killed the king and devastated the Scottish nobility.

SCOTLAND UNDER JAMES V

James V, son of James IV, was born in 1512. He was still a baby when his father was killed at Flodden. His mother was Margaret Tudor. While James V was a child, Scotland was ruled by regents who were hungry for power. The young king finally won power in his own right in 1528. He brought Scotland under his control and strengthened the alliance with France.

➡ *James V of Scotland was asked by his uncle, Henry VIII of England, to follow him in breaking with the Roman Catholic Church. James did not play Henry's game, and the two countries again went to war. The Scots were defeated at Solway Moss in 1542. James V was ill with a fever, and died two weeks later.*

MARY, QUEEN OF SCOTS

James V's widow, Mary of Guise, ruled as regent, for her daughter Mary was still a baby. A French Catholic, she soon clashed with the Protestants. The young queen was sent to the French court and raised as a Catholic. In 1558 she married the heir to the French throne, but her husband – and her mother – both died in 1560. Mary Stuart (as the family name was now spelt) returned to Scotland. In 1565 Mary married her cousin, Henry Darnley. It was a disastrous mistake.

➡ *Edinburgh's castle towers over the Scottish capital. Visitors can still see the rooms of Mary of Guise and Mary, Queen of Scots, as well as the room in which James VI was born.*

HOLYROODHOUSE

James IV and James V built a royal palace called Holyroodhouse in Edinburgh. It was here, in Queen Mary's apartments, that secretary David Rizzio was horribly murdered in 1566. His killers included William Ruthven and James Douglas, Earl of Morton.

▼ Holyroodhouse was built on the site of a medieval abbey founded by David I. The palace was repeatedly destroyed by the English. Much of it was rebuilt after the 1650s.

IMPRISONED IN ENGLAND

Darnley became involved in a plot to murder Mary's Italian secretary, and was then murdered himself. Mary then married the suspected murderer, the Earl of Bothwell. Mary was forced off the throne and imprisoned. Her baby son, James VI, became king. Mary escaped and fled to her cousin, Elizabeth I. In England, however, she was held prisoner for 19 years. Elizabeth feared that Catholics would plot to put Mary on the English throne.

➜ The life of Mary, Queen of Scots ended tragically. The English secret service uncovered a Catholic plot and claimed that Mary was involved. She was beheaded at Fotheringay Castle in February 1587.

The Spanish Armada

In May 1588 a massive invasion fleet or 'Armada' sailed from the port of Lisbon. It was made up of 130 ships fitted with 2500 guns. They carried 30,000 soldiers and sailors. The ships included large warships called galleons, armed merchant ships, galleys (which used oars as well as sails) and supply vessels. This great war fleet was bound for the English Channel.

WHY DID THE ARMADA SAIL?

Spain had become the richest and most powerful country in Europe. It was still ruled by King Philip II, former husband of Mary I of England. From 1580 he was also king of Portugal. The Netherlands too were under Spanish rule, as were vast, newly discovered regions of the Americas. When Dutch Protestants rose up against rule by Catholic Spain, English armies were sent to help them. And across the Atlantic Ocean, the English were fiercely competing with the Spanish to grab the riches of the Americas.

⬆ When the English sea captain Francis Drake carried out illegal raids on Spanish shipping in the Americas, Elizabeth I ignored complaints from Spain. In 1587 Drake set fire to the Spanish port of Cadiz. The raid was described as 'singeing the King of Spain's beard'.

DRAKE'S DRUM

This drum was beaten during the Armada crisis, when Sir Francis Drake called his crew to action on the deck of the *Revenge*.

1586
English and Dutch defeat Spanish at battle of Zutphen.

1587
Francis Drake raids Spanish port of Cadiz.

SEA DOGS FROM DEVON

Most of the great Elizabethan seafarers spoke English with strong west-country accents. Francis Drake, John Hawkyns, Humphrey Gilbert, Walter Raleigh and Richard Grenville were all from Devon, in the southwest of England. Francis Drake was a hero to the English and was knighted by Elizabeth I. To the Spanish, who called him *El Draque*, he was a common pirate.

⬇ The smaller, faster English ships defeated the mighty Spanish fleet, or Armada.

IN PLYMOUTH AND TILBURY

As the Armada approached Cornwall, naval squadrons were stationed along the Channel coast, under the command of Lord Howard of Effingham. Drake's ships lay in Plymouth harbour. An army of 20,000 men was drawn up at Tilbury, on the River Thames, as a Spanish army from the Netherlands was expected to invade the southeast. Elizabeth I rode out to speak to the troops and steady nerves.

SCATTERED BY STORMS

The English ships sailed out to meet the Armada. They had long-range guns and chased the big galleons as they wallowed in high seas, driven by westerly winds. Fighting off Portland Bill and the Isle of Wight was followed by an eight-hour sea battle off Gravelines. The Armada was badly damaged. It was now driven northwards and scattered by roaring gales.

BUILDING A FLEET

Elizabeth I's new navy was built at the royal dockyards in Chatham, Kent. The navy was still small, having only 34 ships – although merchant vessels could also be used in warfare. The old ships of the Middle Ages, which were really floating troop carriers, were replaced by new ships of oak. These were faster and less clumsy than the big Spanish galleons – sleeker and lower in the water.

▼ *The English sea captain John Hawkyns was responsible for the navy's new ship designs.*

1589
Francis Drake fails to capture port of Lisbon.

1591
Battle of Flores off the Azores. Richard Grenville
is killed.

← The Spanish fleet was
devastated by fireships – small
boats that were packed with
timber, pitch and explosives. It
was then the victim of
storms. Spanish ships were
wrecked off Norway,
blown around Scotland
and driven ashore in
Ireland. Only 70
battered ships
returned to Spain.

THE SPANISH ARMADA   **201**

1562
John Hawkyns ships slaves from Africa to the
New World.

1576
Martin Frobisher seeks 'Northwest Passage' round
Canada to Asia.

New Worlds

European seafarers had begun to discover the world
beyond their own shores in the 1400s, as they
searched for new trading routes. Portugal and Spain led
the way, exploring the coasts of Africa, Asia and the 'New
World' of the Americas. English exploration began in the reign
of Henry VII, who sent Italian-born navigator John Cabot to
find a northwestern route to Asia. In 1497 Cabot sailed as far
as Nova Scotia, Canada, and discovered rich fishing grounds
off Newfoundland.

**THE AGE OF
EXPLORATION**

In the medieval world,
little was known of the
world beyond Europe,
North Africa and
Western Asia. After
the 1500s, horizons
suddenly expanded.

Drake's ship, the Golden Hind, became the first English vessel to sail round the world. In 1581 he was knighted on board the Golden Hind by Elizabeth I.

EXPLORERS AND COMPANIES

Many more English seafarers sailed off into the unknown. Martin Frobisher reached Labrador, Canada, in 1577. Francis Drake completed his voyage around the world in 1580. In 1595 Walter Raleigh explored the coasts of Trinidad and sailed up the River Orinoco, in South America. Following the explorers, came the merchants. Companies were set up to control foreign trade. The British East India Company opened its first trading post in India at Surat in 1612.

ALL-AMERICAN CROPS

It is easy for us to forget that many of the foods we take for granted today were unknown in Europe before the 1500s and 1600s. New food plants from the Americas included maize, tomatoes, pineapples and potatoes. Spain was probably the first European country to grow potatoes. Legend has it that it was Sir Walter Raleigh who first introduced them into the British Isles, in 1585.

Potato   Pineapple   Tomato

COLONIES IN THE AMERICAS

The Spanish controlled most of Central and South America, but Britain did gain Caribbean islands such as St Kitts (1623), Barbados (1625) and Jamaica (1665), as well as the mainland territory now called Belize (1638). Scottish merchants tried to found a colony in Darién, Panama, in the 1690s, but it failed. Britain's most successful settlements were on the Atlantic coast of North America. The first of these was Jamestown, Virginia (1607). Plymouth Colony was founded in Massachussetts in 1620, by a group of religious exiles from England, known as the 'Pilgrims'.

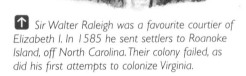

⬆ *Sir Walter Raleigh was a favourite courtier of Elizabeth I. In 1585 he sent settlers to Roanoke Island, off North Carolina. Their colony failed, as did his first attempts to colonize Virginia.*

THE STORY OF POCAHONTAS

Matoaka, or Pocahontas, was born in 1595, the daughter of a native American chief called Powhatan. She became a Christian and married a Virginian settler called John Rolfe. In 1616 she went with him to England and was received at the royal court. Sadly, she died of smallpox in 1617, at Gravesend. Her ship had been preparing to sail down the River Thames for the return voyage to America.

▶ *Pocahontas kept the peace between her people and the settlers.*

THE SLAVE TRADE

The first Europeans came to Africa's Guinea Coast in search of ivory and gold dust, but they soon were dealing in another commodity – human misery. The first Englishman to trade in slaves was John Hawkyns, in 1562. Slave-traders took on board West African men, women and children, who had been captured and put in chains. The slaves were then shipped to the Caribbean and North American colonies and sold into a wretched life of toil on the plantations.

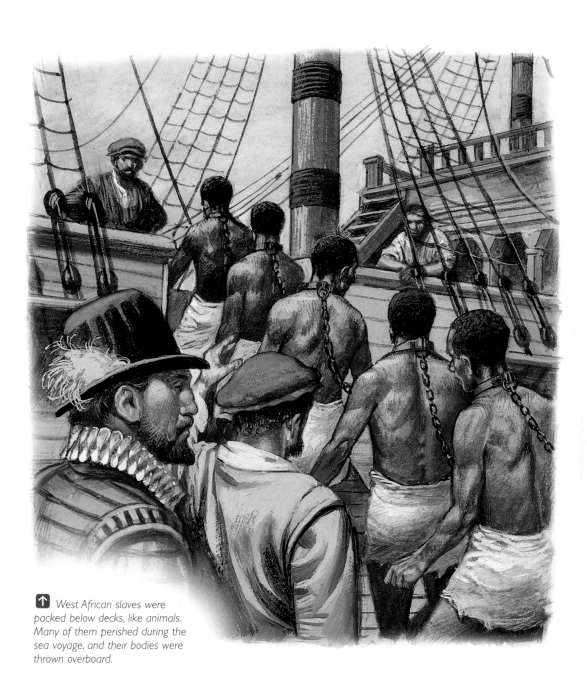

⬆ West African slaves were
packed below decks, like animals.
Many of them perished during the
sea voyage, and their bodies were
thrown overboard.

Treason and Gunpowder

In her old age Elizabeth I was still riding, dancing and hunting, but her face was drawn and haggard. She died of pneumonia, at Richmond palace, in 1603. The throne now passed to James VI of Scotland, the protestant son of Mary, Queen of Scots, and descendant of Margaret Tudor. He was crowned James I of England.

⬆ *This silver coin, minted in 1603–1604, was called a 'crown'. It shows James I on horseback and gives his name in Latin – Jacobus.*

AT THE COURT OF KING JAMES
The thrones of Scotland and England were now united, but in 1607 the English parliament rejected a full union of the two countries. James remained absent from Scotland for 14 years. He brought in harsh anti-Catholic laws, but they were never enough to satisfy the growing number of extreme protestants, or Puritans. People also resented the favours he gave his personal friends at court, such as Robert Carr, Earl of Somerset, and George Villiers, Duke of Buckingham.

⬅ *The first version of the Union Flag was flown from 1606 until 1801. It combined the English flag (a St George's cross, red on a white field) with the Scottish flag of St Andrew (a saltire or diagonal cross, white on a blue field).*

RULERS OF GREAT BRITAIN AND IRELAND

House of Stuart

♣ James I of England
  (VI of Scotland)   1603–1625
♣ Charles I   1625–1649

Commonwealth and Protectorate

♣ Council of State   1649–1653
♣ Oliver Cromwell   1653–1658
♣ Richard Cromwell   1658–1659

House of Stuart

♣ Charles II   1660–1685
♣ James II of England
  (VII of Scotland)   1685–1688
♣ William III of Orange   1689–1702
♣ Mary II   1689–1694
♣ Anne   1702–1714

THE GUNPOWDER PLOT

On the night of 4 November 1605, a search party was sent to Parliament buildings in London. A suspicious letter had been discovered. Was there a Catholic plot to blow up King James there, the following day? In the cellars, lantern light revealed barrels of gunpowder and one of the conspirators, Guy Fawkes. He was arrested, tortured and executed for treason along with seven others. His death is still celebrated each year on 5 November, with dummy 'guys' being burnt on bonfires. However some historians argue that the conspirators were set up – in order to discredit the Catholics.

⬇ *Guy (or Guido) Fawkes (centre) was just one of the people accused of the murder plot. The leader was said to be Robert Catesby.*

Cavaliers and Roundheads

On 22 August 1642, King Charles I raised his standard at Nottingham. His enemy was not a foreign power, but forces loyal to the parliament of his own country. This was a Civil War, which would rage across England, Wales, Scotland and Ireland, dividing communities and even families.

⬆ *Charles I reigned for 24 years. He married Princess Henrietta Maria of France and had six children. However his failure to come to terms with Parliament put the future of the monarchy at risk and cost him his life.*

Royalist musketeer

Soldier of Parliament's New Model Army

⬅ *Both sides in the Civil War fought with swords, muskets, pikes, and pistols. Soldiers wore long hair and broad-brimmed hats. Royalist commanders (often referred to as Cavaliers meaning 'knights') sometimes wore costly, elaborate clothes, whilst the Puritans amongst the Parliamentary troops preferred to dress plainly. A new highly disciplined force was founded by Parliament in 1644. It was called the New Model Army. With their cropped hair and helmets, these soldiers became known as Roundheads.*

1634
Charles I brings in a tax called ship money to fund the navy.

1637
Attempt to force Scots to use English form of worship.

COVENANTERS IN SCOTLAND

Charles I had little understanding of Scotland. The Scottish Church was Presbyterian – it was against having bishops. Charles I tried to force the Scots to follow English forms of worship. In 1638 the Scots drew up a petition, the National Covenant, rejecting his demands. Charles I went to war with the Covenanters in 1639 and 1640, but was forced to make peace. He had made enemies which, in the end, would cost him dearly.

CHANGING TIMES

King James I of England (VI of Scotland) died in 1625. His son, Charles I, came to the throne of a country that was going through many changes. The power of the extreme Protestants, or Puritans, was growing and they were suspicious of his marriage with a Roman Catholic. The middle and lower classes of society were beginning to have more economic power. The country squires and landowners who were members of the House of Commons were demanding more say in running the country. Charles I treated them with disdain.

ROADS AND COACHES

The roads tramped by Civil War armies were still muddy and potholed, but attempts were now being made to map them, improve them and carry out repairs. Road works were the responsibility of each parish. Major roads became the route for postal services, with riders called post boys blowing their horns as they galloped between towns and cities with their satchels of mail.

◀ The first stage coach service began in 1640.

1638
The Covenant is signed in Scotland.

1642
Charles I fails in bid to arrest 5 Members of Parliament.

A GROWING CRISIS

From 1629 to 1640, Charles I summoned no parliaments at all. He brought in unpopular taxes, which caused protests and unrest. In 1641 Parliament demanded that the king replace his ministers and bring in religious reforms. In 1642, Charles I forced his way into the House of Commons and attempted to arrest five Members of Parliament. He failed, and so went to war.

THE FIRST CIVIL WAR

The first battle took place at Edgehill in 1642. Both sides claimed to have won. In 1643 Parliament allied with the Scottish Covenanters and defeated the Royalists at Marston Moor in the following year. They were crushed again at Naseby, near Leicester, in 1645. In 1646, Charles I surrendered to the Scots.

1642
Start of the first phase of the Civil War.

1648
A second phase of Civil War. Charles I is seized by the army.

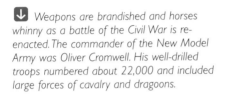
⬇ *Weapons are brandished and horses whinny as a battle of the Civil War is re-enacted. The commander of the New Model Army was Oliver Cromwell. His well-drilled troops numbered about 22,000 and included large forces of cavalry and dragoons.*

THE SECOND CIVIL WAR

Charles I now tried to come to an agreement with the English Parliament, but failed. In 1647 he fled to the Isle of Wight. He made a secret deal with his former enemies in Scotland, promising them the reforms they desired. The Scots marched on England and there were Royalist risings in Wales, too. However all were defeated and by 1649 Charles was imprisoned.

Commonwealth

On 30 January 1649, Charles I was marched from St James's Palace to Whitehall. It was a bitterly cold day in London, with flurries of snow. At one o'clock the king stepped to the scaffold, or execution platform. When the axe had fallen, his head was shown to the ranks of soldiers and the crowd.

THE KING IS DEAD

It was reported that although Charles I had been an unpopular king, a groan passed through the London crowd when he died. Ever since the Middle Ages, people had believed that kings ruled by the will of God. Charles I himself believed in this 'divine right' of kings. He kept silent throughout his trial. News of the king's death spread like wildfire through the British Isles and mainland Europe. To many people, it was simply unbelievable.

➡ *Charles I died bravely, within sight of the Parliament he despised.*

A LORD PROTECTOR

The nation was now a republic, or 'Commonwealth'. Parliament ruled the land instead of a king or queen. It governed through a Council of State, made up of 40 members. However as far as the army was concerned, Parliament was much too cautious in its reforms. In 1653 power was handed over to one man, Oliver Cromwell, who was appointed Lord Protector. His rule was harsh but effective. He attempted to bring in military rule, and in 1556 he was even offered the crown.

⬆ Oliver Cromwell was a squire from the Huntingdon countryside. He made sure that no ruler could ever again afford to ignore the wishes of Parliament.

NO MORE FUN

▲ Playing cards were believed to be the work of the Devil.

Many of Cromwell's supporters were Puritans. The only joy that they could accept was through religious worship. Dancing and theatre were banned. Meat or ale could not be consumed on a Sunday, and even Christmas Day was no longer to be celebrated with plum puddings and merry-making.

THE QUAKERS

In 1646 a Puritan called George Fox preached a new kind of faith. He called upon his followers to 'quake at the word of the Lord'. They became known as 'Quakers', or the Society of Friends. The Friends worshipped God in silence, with no priests or prayers or churches. Many of them were imprisoned for their beliefs or forced to flee the country.

1651
Scots crown Charles II king, but are defeated at Worcester.

1653
Oliver Cromwell becomes Lord Protector.

WHAT KIND OF REVOLUTION?

The English revolution was controlled by landowners and wealthy merchants, but its footsoldiers were poor people, craftworkers, small farmers and tradesmen. Some of these formed a political movement called the Levellers. They demanded true democracy (rule by the people), but were quickly crushed by Cromwell in 1649. In 1650 an even more radical group was broken up. These True Levellers or 'Diggers' demanded equality for all and the common ownership of land.

TUMBLEDOWN DICK

Warfare did not come to an end with the
Commonwealth. In 1651 Charles I's son was
crowned Charles II in Scotland. The Scots marched
south, but were defeated and Charles II fled abroad.
From 1652–1654, Britain fought the Netherlands
(now a free and increasingly wealthy nation) over
trade. Oliver Cromwell died on a stormy night in
1658. His son Richard (known as 'Tumbledown
Dick') was made Lord Protector, but had little taste
for power. The revolution was over.

Oliver Cromwell, who
became Lord Protector in
1653, raises a Bible as he
makes a rousing speech
to Parliament troops.
Religion played a major
role in the Civil War, with
both sides believing that
God would deliver victory
to them.

The Road to Drogheda

More and more lands belonging to Irish Catholics were seized and given over to Protestant English and Scottish settlers. This continuing policy of 'plantation' was supported by the Dublin parliament. In 1628 Charles I decided to allow Roman Catholic worship to continue alongside the Protestant Church, but this infuriated Ireland's Protestants.

↑ *Thomas Wentworth, Earl of Strafford, was recalled from Ireland by Charles I to organise the wars against the Scottish Presbyterians. Following an English defeat, he was executed in London in 1641.*

THE IRISH ECONOMY

Thomas Wentworth was an arrogant man, who had little respect for the Irish people. However he was a capable administrator and built up the Irish economy. He set up new trading links with Spain, stamped out piracy around the Irish coast and developed the linen industry.

▶ *Linen is made from the flax plant.*

WENTWORTH AND ULSTER

In 1633 Charles I appointed a new man to govern Ireland. He was Thomas Wentworth, who later became Earl of Strafford. Wentworth's only aim was to increase royal power in Ireland. He managed to earn the hatred of Catholics and Protestants alike. He drew up plans for further plantation. As a result, violence broke out in Ulster in 1641 and soon spread far and wide. Perhaps 2000 Protestants were killed and many more were stripped and chased naked from their homes.

FROM WAR TO WAR

The tragic fate of the Protestant settlers in Ulster was used to whip up extreme anti-Catholic feelings in Britain. In 1642 an army of Scottish Covenanters arrived in Ulster to defend the Scottish Protestants who had settled there. A Catholic army was formed too by Owen Roe (Eoghan Ruagh) O'Neill. An alliance was made between Old English royalists and Irish Catholics, but there were bitter divisions.

⬆ *The royalist alliance was called the Catholic Confederation. Its general assembly met in Kilkenny Castle (above).*

A ROMAN LIFELINE

Irish Catholics were supported by the Church in Rome, which trained priests for work in Ireland. Political support also came from Roman Catholic countries in Europe. When Oliver Cromwell came to Ireland, he blamed Catholic priests for all the country's problems. Many of them were murdered by his troops.

▶ *Luke Wadding was a monk who founded St Isidore's College in Rome in 1625. He worked tirelessly to keep the Roman Catholic faith alive in Ireland.*

CROMWELL INVADES

Events were overtaken by the Civil War in Britain. Oliver Cromwell invaded Ireland in August 1649, with a battle-hardened army of Puritan troops. They hated all Roman Catholics and wanted revenge for the events of 1641. Cromwell besieged and sacked Drogheda, ordering the defenders to be slain with no mercy. Another massacre at Wexford also claimed many lives. Some have claimed that as many as a quarter of all Irish Catholics were killed during this savage campaign. Cromwell followed it up in 1652 by seizing Catholic lands and granting them to his soldiers and followers. Cromwell's campaign would be remembered with bitterness into modern times.

⬆ The River Shannon became a new frontier after Oliver Cromwell's invasion. Irish Catholic landowners were told that they had until 1 May 1654 to resettle west of the Shannon.

⬅ Oliver Cromwell sacked Drogheda in September 1649. Some of the defenders were burnt alive in a church he set on fire. Cromwell's official report called the massacre 'a righteous judgement of God upon these barbarous wretches'.

1660
The monarchy is restored. Charles II returns.

1661
The Church of England is established.

The Restoration

Great Britain and Ireland had a king again, Charles II. In 1660 Parliament had finally asked him to return from exile and be crowned. In return, Charles had to agree to recognise Parliament and the limits of his power. There was great rejoicing as he entered London on his 30th birthday. Oliver Cromwell's remains were seized from his tomb in Westminster Abbey and publicly hanged from the gallows at Tyburn.

THE WORLD OF POLITICS

During the reign of Charles II, the way in which the British political system was organised became rather more like the one in use today. From 1667–1673, Charles II began to consult with a group of ministers instead of just one. These were rather like the Cabinet in modern times. They were known as the 'Cabal', because of their initials (Clifford, Ashley, Buckingham, Arlington, Lauderdale). The world 'cabal' is still used to describe a small, powerful group of people. The first political parties were formed in the 1680s. They were known as Tories and Whigs.

← Charles II is chiefly remembered as a pleasure-loving king, the 'merry monarch'. He married a Portuguese Catholic, Catherine of Braganza, but was never faithful to her.

THE DIARY OF SAMUEL PEPYS

In January 1660, a Londoner called Samuel Pepys began to write a diary. It was written in a secret code. Pepys offers us a lively look at how people lived in the 1660s. He knew many famous people and was mixed up in all sorts intrigues at the court. He describes the news stories of his day, as when Dutch warships sailed up the River Thames.

◀ Nell Gwyn began her career as an orange-seller. She became a famous actress, much admired by Samuel Pepys, and was a lover of the king himself.

▼ Samuel Pepys wrote freely about his private life and everyday pastimes.

RELIGIOUS FREEDOM?

In 1662 the Church of England was recognised as the official Church. In the following year Charles II declared that both Catholics and Puritans would be free to worship in their own way. However, he was forced to end this offer in 1673, when Parliament ruled that Catholics could not hold public office.

⬇ During Stuart times, the climate was colder than today. Often, the River Thames froze solid. 'Frost Fairs' were held on the ice and people practised ice-skating – a sport recently brought in from the Netherlands.

1672
The Third Anglo-Dutch War (until 1674).

1678
John Bunyan writes first part of *Pilgrim's Progress*.

1678
A ' Popish Plot' is faked by Titus Oates.
Catholics executed.

1685
Charles II has a fit and dies, aged 55.

A MERRY DANCE

After the Restoration, the English began to enjoy life again. Theatres re-opened in 1660. Female parts in plays were now taken by actresses, who became as popular as film stars would be 300 years later. Dancing was never more popular, from the royal court to the village maypole. Women wore make-up and fancy dresses. Fashionable men wore long, curled wigs. There were river trips, fireworks, processions and fairs. In the 1660s and 1670s it became fashionable to drink new beverages – coffee and tea.

THE PLOT THAT NEVER WAS

There was growing anti-Catholic hysteria in England. In 1678 an English spy called Titus Oates claimed that Catholics were plotting to kill the king. He had actually made the whole story up, but 35 Catholics were executed because of this 'Popish Plot'.

← *After the strict rules of the Puritans, people welcomed the more relaxed rule of Charles II.*

THE RESTORATION   223

Great Minds

The 1600s was an age of exploration and discovery. The old ways were challenged and knocked down. This exciting new world was reflected in literature, the arts, in philosophy and especially in science. In 1660 the Royal Society of London was founded to encourage learning. Leading members included Robert Boyle, Samuel Pepys and Isaac Newton.

METAPHYSICAL POETS

In the 1600s many English poets broke away from the forms of poetry that had been popular in Elizabethan times. These 'metaphysical' poets included John Donne, George Herbert, Richard Crashaw and Andrew Marvell. They used unusual and sometimes complicated images, some of them taken from new discoveries in science and geography.

→ *The English scientist Robert Hooke used the newly invented microscope to study the structure of plants and chemicals. His Micrographia was published in 1665.*

← Paradise Lost, *one of the greatest works of English literature, was published by the English poet John Milton in 1667. During the Civil War, Milton was a keen supporter of Parliament. He became blind in middle age.*

GRAVITY AND LIGHT

Isaac Newton was born in Lincolnshire in 1642 and studied at Cambridge University. He was a brilliant mathematician and became one of the world's greatest scientists. Newton studied the nature of light and gravity. He improved the design of the reflecting telescope. He worked out the Laws of Motion and was elected president of the Royal Society in 1703.

➡ *In September 1665, an apple falling from a tree in a garden is said to have inspired Isaac Newton to think about gravity. Could the same process that pulled the apple downwards be applied to moons and planets? Newton worked out that gravity kept the Moon in orbit around the Earth.*

COURT MUSICIANS AND PAINTERS

In the 1630s the great Flemish painters Peter Paul Rubens and Anthony van Dyck came to the court of Charles I, as did the Dutch painter Peter Lely in the 1640s. The English musical composer Henry Purcell wrote the first English opera in 1689 and music for the coronations of James II of England (VII of Scotland).

THE PHILOSOPHERS

Thomas Hobbes (1588–1679) was a keen royalist. He wrote about politics and the human mind. John Locke (1632–1704) argued that governments ruled only with the agreement of the people. If they broke faith, they deserved to be overthrown.

Out of the Ashes

London, by now a city of about half a million people, was hot and stifling on 6 June 1665. That was the day on which an outbreak of plague was reported in the city. It caused little fuss at the time. Since the Black Death of the Middle Ages, the plague had returned time after time.

THE GREAT PLAGUE

This time, though, it was different. The bubonic plague, marked by foul swellings on the body, claimed 70,000 lives in just the first few months. As Londoners fled to the country, they brought the dreaded disease to villages and market towns. Survivors clutched bunches of sweet-smelling flowers to ward off the stench. The air itself seemed poisoned.

↑ Many people took to the river to escape the heat and flames. After the fire, the old city with all its familiar landmarks was gone forever.

← The cobbled streets and alleys of London had changed little since medieval times. They still swarmed with rats and their deadly fleas. The plague was first brought to England by black rats that infested almost every ship.

1677
The Monument is completed in memory of the
Great Fire.

1710
The new St Paul's Cathedral is completed.

LONDON BURNS

After more than a year of plague, another disaster struck London. In the early hours of 2 September 1666, a fire started at a baker's in Pudding Lane. The flames were soon blazing over a wide area and continued to do so for five whole days, driven by the wind. Timber houses had to be blown up to stop the fire spreading. By the time it was over, the Great Fire had burnt down 13,200 houses, the old city gates, the Guildhall, 89 churches and the great cathedral of the City of London, St Paul's.

ASYLUM SEEKERS

The British Isles were not the only part of Europe to experience religious conflict in the 1500s and 1600s. In France there were wars between Roman Catholics and the Protestant followers of John Calvin, known as Huguenots. After 1598, Protestant rights were protected by the Edict of Nantes, but during the reign of Louis XIV many Huguenots were persecuted or forced to become Catholics. In 1685 the Edict of Nantes was cancelled, and 400,000 Huguenots fled the country. Many sought refuge in London. France's loss was England's gain, for many were skilled workers.

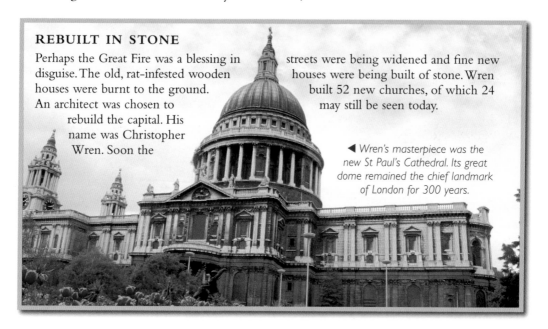

REBUILT IN STONE

Perhaps the Great Fire was a blessing in disguise. The old, rat-infested wooden houses were burnt to the ground. An architect was chosen to rebuild the capital. His name was Christopher Wren. Soon the streets were being widened and fine new houses were being built of stone. Wren built 52 new churches, of which 24 may still be seen today.

◀ Wren's masterpiece was the new St Paul's Cathedral. Its great dome remained the chief landmark of London for 300 years.

James, William and Mary

Charles II died in February 1685. He was followed as king by his brother, who became James VII of Scotland and II of England. James was a Roman Catholic and this dismayed the Protestants. Many belonged to the more radical political party, the Whigs. They had had enough of Stuart kings who showed little regard for the people's wishes.

← *Rebel fighters gathered at Sedgemore, Somerset, in support of Monmouth's rebellion. They were defeated by forces loyal to King James.*

LILLIBOLERO

The dramatic events of the Glorious Revolution of 1688 were played out to a popular political song of the day. It was called *Lillibolero*. The music was a march by Henry Purcell while the words, written by Thomas Wharton in 1686, mocked King James and the Catholics of Ireland. The song was sung as violent anti-Catholic mobs celebrated James's downfall in London.

BLOODY ASSIZES

In June 1685 the Protestant James, Duke of Monmouth, a son of Charles II born outside marriage, landed in Lyme Regis, in southern England. He claimed the throne, but was defeated in July at Sedgemoor and executed. His followers were dealt with savagely by a judge called George Jeffreys, in a series of trials called the Bloody Assizes. A death sentence was passed on 320 people and 840 more were sold into slavery. It was a bitter start to the reign.

THE GLORIOUS REVOLUTION

By 1688 leading politicans had decided on a drastic plan. They invited the Dutch ruler, William of Orange, to become king. He was a Protestant and married to Mary, the king's daughter. William landed at Torbay in Devon and gained rapid support. James fled to France and it was agreed that William III and Mary II would rule jointly. This change of power became known as the Glorious Revolution.

→ In 1688, Mary II and her husband William were called back to Britain from the Netherlands to become king and queen.

REIGNING TOGETHER

Both Mary II and William III ruled together, as joint monarchs with equal rights. It was the only time this had happened in English or Scottish history. This reign confirmed that the state would be Protestant rather than Roman Catholic, and brought to an end the long years of strife between the kings and parliament. After the death of Mary, from smallpox in 1694, William ruled the country on his own.

⬇ *At the battle of Boyne in 1690, the Protestant William III finally defeated the Catholic James II, an event still celebrated by the Protestants of Northern Ireland.*

ENGINEERS AND BUILDERS

Engineering works began to change the face of many parts of Britain in the 1600s and early 1700s. The wetlands of East Anglia were drained and channelled by experts from the Netherlands. Harbours were rebuilt and new lighthouses guarded rocky shores. Gates called turnpikes were set up along the highways to collect money from travellers for repairs and road-building.

▶ *The first Eddystone lighthouse was built off Cornwall between 1695 and 1699, but was destroyed by severe autumn gales in 1703.*

1689 May
Highland Scots rebel in support of James.

1690
Battle of the Boyne in Ireland. James is defeated.

SCOTLAND AND IRELAND

William and Mary did not enjoy an easy reign. The Highland Scots rose up in support of James. Their leader was John Graham of Claverhouse, Viscount Dundee, a persecutor of the Covenanters. They won the battle of Killiecrankie in May 1689, but Dundee was killed and the rising failed. James now landed with French troops in Ireland, trying to regain the throne. William too led an army into Ireland, reinforced with Ulster Protestants. They met at the battle of the Boyne in 1690 and James was defeated.

A BILL OF RIGHTS

The most important outcome of the Glorious Revolution was a Bill of Rights, passed in December 1689. This made it very clear that Parliament was now the chief governing body in the land, and that the power of kings and queens was strictly limited.

MASSACRE AT GLENCOE

At this bleak spot, Glencoe in Stratchclyde, 37 members of the MacDonald clan were massacred in 1692. William III demanded that all the clans in the Scottish Highlands swear an oath of loyalty. They obeyed, but MacIain MacDonoald of Glencoe signed late, due to a misunderstanding. Troops sealed off the ends of the glen, while others, billeted in MacDonald homes, carried out a brutal attack. They were commanded by Campbells, old enemies of the Macdonalds.

▼ *Glencoe in Stratchclyde*

1701
Act of Settlement decides the royal succession.

1702
William III falls from horse and dies. Anne becomes queen.

Queen Anne

Queen Anne came to the throne in 1702, after William III died in a fall from his horse. She was a Protestant, the daughter of James VII of Scotland (II of England) and the sister of Mary II. It was during her reign, in 1707, that the Scottish and English parliaments united. Great Britain, for the first time, was a single political unit rather than a union of kingdoms.

Queen Anne married Prince George of Denmark in 1683, but all their 17 children died, mostly in infancy.

LAST OF THE STUARTS

Anne was the last Stuart monarch. In 1701 she had agreed that on her death, the throne would pass to the royal house of Hanover, in Germany. Anne was easily influenced by her circle of friends. Her closest companion was Sarah, wife of a brilliant soldier called John Churchill. Anne made him Duke of Marlborough in 1702. After 1710 Anne quarrelled with the Churchills and fell under the spell of Sarah's cousin, Abigail Masham.

WAR OF SPANISH SUCCESSION

In 1701 a wrangle broke out between the great powers of Europe. Who would inherit the throne of Spain? On one side was Louis XIV's France, the south German kingdom of Bavaria and Spain. On the other was the Grand Alliance – Britain, Austria, the Netherlands, Denmark and Portugal. John Churchill, the first Duke of Marlborough, commanded the Dutch and English armies and won spectacular victories at Blenheim in Bavaria, and Ramillies and Oudenaarde in what is now Belgium. Casualties were very high on all sides. Peace was made at the treaties of Utrecht (1713) and Rastatt (1714). The war was a success for Britain and its allies and signalled the decline of Spain as a great power. Britain gained from Spain the territory of Gibraltar, the great rock that guards the entrance to the Mediterranean Sea.

⬇ *Gibraltar is a small patch of land, but it was of great strategic importance as a naval base for the British.*

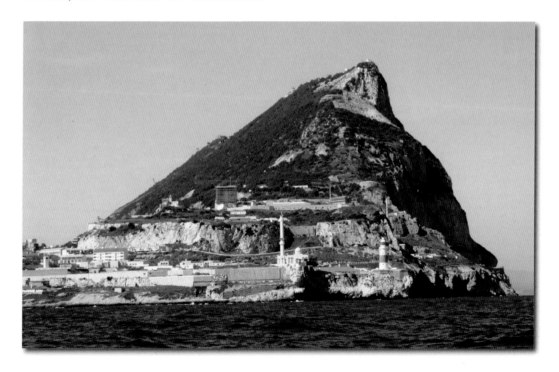

⬇ *Blenheim Palace was named after the Duke of Marlborough's most famous victory. It was largely paid for by public funds, as a reward for the Duke's military successes in Europe. It was decorated by the finest craftsmen of the day, such as the woodcarver Grinling Gibbons, and it was surrounded by lakes and gardens. It was here that Winston Churchill, a descendant of the first duke, was born in 1874.*

WHIGS AND TORIES

In the days of Queen Anne, society was rigidly divided between the two political parties of the day. The Whigs were supporters of the Bill of Rights and of the Hanoverian succession. Many of them were merchants and business men with radical Protestant views. The Tories were conservative and royalist, and included many churchmen. Queen Anne disliked the Whigs and was determined to use all her personal powers to control British politics.

'QUEEN ANNE' FURNITURE

Furniture made by craftsmen in the reign of Queen Anne is still much admired today. It is simpler than the furniture of the Restoration period, and is much more practical. It includes bureaus, card-tables, chests of drawers, mirrors and dressing tables. The most popular wood was English walnut.

◀ The finest pieces of the period are chairs that are comfortable and solid. By the end of Anne's reign, more ornamental styles were coming back into fashion.

BAROQUE PALACES

A new European style of architecture became fashionable in Britain during the reign of Queen Anne. The 'baroque' style was exuberant and ornamental, packed with artistic detail and designed to impress. There were grand staircases and ornate mirrors. Two of the finest examples are palaces. Castle Howard, to the north of York, was built from 1699 to 1712 for the Earl of Carlisle. Blenheim Palace, in Oxfordshire, was built between 1705 and 1722 for the Duke of Marlborough. Both were designed by the architect Sir John Vanburgh, who was also a playwright, a theatre manager, a soldier, and a political activist who supported the Whigs.

A World Power
1714–1901

THE WORLD AT A GLANCE

ELSEWHERE IN EUROPE

1720
Russia defeats Sweden in the Great Northern War, gains Estonia.

1740
Frederick II becomes King of Prussia, Maria Theresa becomes Empress of Austria.

1789
Outbreak of the French Revolution in Paris. King Louis XVI is executed in 1793.

1804
Napoleon Bonaparte is crowned Emperor of France. Draws up new code of laws.

1815
The Congress of Vienna redraws the map of Europe. Poland is united with Russia.

1821
Greeks rise against Turkish rule. Greece is recognised as independent in 1832.

1871
Germany unites as a single empire under the rule of Wilhelm I, King of Prussia.

1871
Rome becomes capital of a united Italy for the first time since the Roman empire.

ASIA

1739
Persia (Iran) invades India and captures the city of Delhi.

1750
The French gain control of southern India.

1819
British empire-builder Stamford Raffles founds modern port at Singapore.

1858
Rule of India passes from the East India Company to the British government.

1867
The Meiji Restoration: Japan modernises under the rule of Emperor Mutsuhito.

1883
One of the world's worst ever volcanic eruptions destroys island of Krakatoa.

1891
Work begins on the Trans-Siberian Railway (from Moscow to the Pacific).

1900
Defeat of nationalists ('Boxers') rebelling against foreign influence in China.

AFRICA

1720
Sultan of Zanzibar takes control of the East African coast.

1730
Revival of the Bornu empire, south of the Sahara Desert.

1806
Britain gains control of Cape Colony, South Africa, from the Dutch.

1818
Shaka founds the Zulu kingdom in South Africa.

1822
Liberia is founded in West Africa, as a colony for liberated slaves.

1869
Suez Canal opens, European powers have growing influence in Egypt.

1896
Emperor Menelik II of Ethiopia defeats an Italian army at Adowa.

1899
Boer War begins between British and Afrikaners in South Africa.

"A British empire is founded on cotton, coal and toil..."

NORTH AMERICA

1718
French found the port of New Orleans, Louisiana.

1759
Britain defeats France to capture the Canadian city of Quebec.

1776
American colonists declare their independence from Britain.

1823
Mexico becomes an independent republic.

1838
Slavery ended in Jamaica and other British Caribbean colonies.

1861
Civil war in the United States (until 1865, abolition of slavery).

1867
Canada becomes a self-governing Dominion within the British empire.

1876
Native Americans defeat US Cavalry at the Battle of Little Bighorn.

SOUTH AMERICA

1763
Rio de Janeiro becomes capital of Spanish Brazil.

1780
Uprising of indigenous peoples in Peru under Tupac Amaru II.

1816
Argentina declares its independence from Spain.

1818
Chile becomes independent from Spain, under Bernardo O'Higgins.

1819
New Granada (Colombia, Venezuela, Ecuador) independent under Simon Bolívar.

1822
Brazil proclaims its independence from Portugal under Pedro I.

1826
Peru gains its independence from Portugal.

1888
Slavery is finally abolished in Brazil.

OCEANIA

1768
British navigator James Cook visits Tahiti, New Zealand and Australia (to 1771).

1788
British convicts and settlers arrive at Botany Bay, southeast Australia.

1840
Treaty of Waitangi: Maori chiefs cede New Zealand to British.

1843
First Maori War, start of many conflicts with the British colonists (into the 1860s).

1850
Self-government granted to Britain's Australian colonies (New Zealand 1856).

1851
A Gold Rush begins in Australia.

1884
Northeastern New Guinea taken over by Germany. Britain claims the southeast.

1901
Australian colonies unite within a federal Commonwealth.

1714
Start of rule by the House of Hanover.

1739
Trade dispute with Spain, the War of Jenkins's Ear.

The House of Hanover

George I, ruler of Hanover in Germany, came to the throne as a distant descendant of James VI of Scotland (I of England). He was 54 years old, a dull and uninspiring man. His kept his divorced wife, Sophia Dorothea, imprisoned in a German castle from 1694 until her death in 1726. George I cared little for life in Britain and never learned to speak English.

⬆ *This medal was made in memory of the coronation of George I, the first Hanoverian ruler of Britain, in October 1714.*

THE NEW DYNASTY

George I was unpopular, but he was supported by the Whigs simply because he offered the best chance of stopping a return to Stuart rule. In return, he supported the Whigs against the Tories. His son came to the throne in 1727. In 1743 George II became the last British king ever to lead his troops onto the field of battle – at Dettingen, in Bavaria, against a French army. Under his rule, the British began to build up a large overseas empire.

➡ *George II's reign saw war and rebellion, bitter quarrels within the royal family, and the growing power of politicians.*

RULERS OF GREAT BRITAIN AND IRELAND
House of Hanover

♣ George I Elector of Hanover	1714–1727
♣ George II	1727–1760
♣ George III	1760–1820
♣ George IV	1820–1830
♣ William IV	1830–1837
♣ Victoria	1837–1901

A MAN OF MUSIC

George Friedrich Händel was from Saxony, in Germany. In 1710 he was appointed court musician to the Elector of Hanover, but irritated his employer by spending more and more time in London. When that ruler was crowned King George I in England, Händel made his peace by composing his *Water Music*, for a royal procession on the River Thames. Händel wrote 46 operas, but his best-loved piece of music was *The Messiah*, first performed in Dublin in 1742. He died and was buried in Westminster Abbey in 1759.

▲ Händel liked to write music for public festivities. His Music for the Royal Fireworks *was first performed in Green Park, London, on 27 April 1749.*

THE HOUSE OF HANOVER **239**

1752
Public protests when the calendar is revised by removing 11 days.

1756
Seven Years War: European powers fight over their empires.

THE MADNESS OF GEORGE III

George III, grandson of George II, came to the throne in 1760 and ruled for 60 years. He was an energetic but obstinate ruler, often clashing with the politicians of his day. His reign saw Britain lose its colonies in North America. In 1810 George became mentally ill, probably as a result of a body disorder called porphyria.

← *George III, whose long reign saw rebellions in America and Ireland, and a war in France.*

THE EAR THAT STARTED A WAR

The great powers of Europe were almost continuously at war in a pattern of shifting alliances. Wars were caused by disputes over trade and territory and rival claims to thrones. In 1739, a British sea captain claimed that his ear had been cut off by Spanish customs officials, so Britain went to war with Spain in the 'War of Jenkins's Ear'. This was followed by the War of the Austrian Succession (1740–48) in which Britain supported Austria against France. That was followed in turn by the Seven Years' War (1756–63), in which Britain was allied with the growing military power of Prussia against France. This war spread far beyond Europe to North America and India. As European colonies were established around the globe, warfare increasingly took on a global dimension.

FROM ORCHARD TO PALACE

In 1762, George III bought a large residence near St James's Park, in London. It was called Buckingham House, because it had originally been built for the Duke of Buckingham, a friend of Queen Anne's, in 1703. A century before that, the land had been used as a mulberry garden by King James I. George III gave the house to his wife, Charlotte, and it became known as Queen's House. It played an important part in the life of the royal family, and was much enlarged over the years. The building took on its modern appearance in the 1820s and in 1837 it became the official chief residence of the British monarch. Since then it has been known to the public as Buckingham Palace.

How people dressed

The fashions of the 1700s were similar to those of the 1600s, only rather more practical. The long, full wigs worn by important men (giving them the nickname 'bigwigs') were replaced by smaller wigs. Women wore gowns based upon the latest Paris fashions. The first fashion plates appeared in *The Lady's Magazine* in the 1770s. Children's clothes were scaled-down versions of adult clothes, with the boys in knee breeches and the girls in full-skirted dresses.

↑ *Men wore a coat and waistcoat, breeches, stockings and buckled shoes. Wigs were still worn, but it became the fashion to tie them at the neck. Hats were three-cornered and made of felt.*

→ *Women wore dresses with full skirts, often made of cotton or silk. Court dresses were stretched out over wooden hoops and decorated with frills. Women too now wore high, powdered white wigs.*

1708
The Old Pretender lands in Scotland, but rising fails.

1715
The Old Pretender joins Jacobite rising, which again fails.

Bonnie Prince Charlie

Support for the exiled Stuarts did not suddenly disappear. People who wished them to return to rule Britain and Ireland were called Jacobites (from Jacobus, the Latin for 'James'). They presented a serious threat to the House of Hanover, for they had supporters all over the British Isles. However their most loyal supporters were to be found in the Highlands of Scotland.

↑ James Francis Edward Stuart (1688–1766) was raised in exile in France. His refusal to give up the Roman Catholic faith barred him from the throne, and he failed to raise enough popular support to win it back by force during campaigns in 1708 and 1715. He died in Rome.

THE OLD PRETENDER

Someone who claims to be king or queen is called a 'pretender' to the throne. James Francis Edward Stuart became known as the Old Pretender. A Roman Catholic, he was the son of James VII/II and had been taken away to France as a baby. He landed in Scotland in 1708, but the French fleet sent in his support was defeated. In 1715 the Earl of Mar launched a Jacobite rising and James landed once more at Peterhead.

THE '15 RISING FAILS

The rising, known as the '15, came to grief at Preston and Sherrifmuir. James fled to exile in Rome and his followers were executed. The Jacobite cause had many supporters in Catholic Europe, and in 1719 Spanish troops invaded Scotland, but were defeated at Glenshiel. The Old Pretender married a Polish princess, Clementina Sobieski, and died in 1766.

THE OUTLAW ROB ROY

Robert MacGregor, known as Rob 'Roy' (meaning the 'red-headed') was born at Buchanan in Stirlingshire in 1671. He raised a private army that supported the Jacobites. In 1712 his lands were seized by the Duke of Montrose and he became an outlaw. A raider and rustler, he became famous for his daring exploits and his help for the poor and needy. He died in 1734.

BONNIE PRINCE CHARLIE

The Young Pretender was James's son, Charles Edward Stuart. He landed at Eriskay in the Hebrides in 1745 and raised his father's standard at Glenfinnan. The '45 rising very nearly succeeded. 'Bonnie Prince Charlie' won a victory at Prestonpans, captured Carlisle and reached Derby. London was in a state of panic, and Jacobites were planning to rise in Wales. Then, Charles's support began to falter and he turned back to Scotland.

← *The rebellion of Bonnie Prince Charlie (1720–1788) was more successful than that of his father, but it was doomed once the Jacobite sympathisers in England and Wales failed to rally to his cause.*

1744
Charles Edward Stuart plans invasion.
French fleet is scattered.

1745 July
Charles raises battle standard in Glenfinnan.

LIFE OF EXILE

Flora Macdonald disguised Bonnie Prince Charlie as her maid and spirited him out out of Scotland. A ship carried him from the island of Benbecula into a life of exile.

1745
Battle of Prestonpans: Jacobite victory.

1746
Battle of Culloden. Jacobites defeated by Duke of Cumberland.

CULLODEN AND AFTER

In 1746 Charles won another battle at Falkirk, but his Jacobites soon received a crushing defeat on Culloden moor, Inverness, at the hands of William, Duke of Cumberland – 'the Butcher'. In England a flower was named 'sweet william' in honour of Cumberland, but Scottish Jacobites called it 'stinking billy'. Highland clansmen were ruthlessly hunted down. The carrying of weapons, even the wearing of the kilt and the playing of bagpipes were banned. Scotland's future now lay in the growing towns of Lowlands, where manufacturers and merchants were becoming wealthy.

◀ Burns died in 1796, but his birthday is still honoured around the world each 25 January.

AULD LANG SYNE

Scotland's greatest poet was born in 1759 in Alloway, near Ayr. Robert Burns created simple, bold verse in the language of the Lowlands Scots. He wrote about country life, nature and love. His most popular poems include *A Red, Red Rose*; *Scots, Wha Hae*; *John Anderson, my Jo*; *Tam O'Shanter* and *Auld Lang Syne*.

↩ *Jacobite forces at Culloden included massed ranks of clansmen from the Scottish Highlands. They were gunned down and bayoneted without mercy. Charles became a fugitive with a price in his head.*

Money and Politics

The gap between rich and poor people in the British Isles was growing ever wider. London society in the 1730s and 40s is shown up in the paintings and engravings of William Hogarth. Poor families brawl, desperate young mothers drink cheap gin on the street until they fall into a stupor. Adventurers are on the make, climbing their way up the all too corrupt social scale, only to fall back down and end their days in a debtors' prison.

Dealers in shares, or stockjobbers, drove up the trading price far beyond the real value.

THE SOUTH SEA BUBBLE

Trading shares in the hope of making a profit is called speculation. It is a form of gambling, and can lead to reward or ruin. Britain's first great financial crash happened in 1720. Shares in the South Sea Company, founded in 1711 to trade with South America, rose to a ridiculous value, driven up by feverish speculation and crooked government dealings. When this South Sea 'bubble' burst, thousands of people were ruined. Many committed suicide.

BANKS AND MONEY

Paper bank notes were first issued in Britain in 1695. There was a growing view of wealth as an abstract idea, of deals made on paper rather than as chests full of gold coins. New companies, many of them founded in order to make money in distant colonies overseas, issued shares. At first these were bought and sold in coffee shops. A Stock Exchange was founded in the City of London in 1773.

1773
Founding of the London Stock Exchange.

1776
Adam Smith argues that government should not interfere in trade.

PRIME MINISTERS AT NO 10

Because George I spoke no English and was often away in Hanover, government affairs began to be dealt with by his chief ('prime') minister, who chose a working committee of ministers (the 'cabinet'). From 1721 the first – unofficial – Prime Minister was a formidable Whig politician, Sir Robert Walpole. The use of Number 10 Downing Street as the London residence of British Prime Ministers dates back to 1731.

→ *Robert Walpole entered politics in the reign of Queen Anne and was made Chancellor of the Exchequer by George I, in 1715. He died in 1745.*

↑ *The few men who were allowed to vote did so in public. There was opportunity for bullying and corruption. Drunken crowds, in the pay of one party or another, often rioted at election time.*

PRIME MINISTERS OF GREAT BRITAIN

✤ Sir Robert Walpole (Whig)	1721–1742
✤ Earl of Wilmington (Whig)	1742–1743
✤ Henry Pelham (Whig)	1743–1754
✤ Duke of Newcastle (Whig)	1754–1756
✤ Duke of Devonshire (Whig)	1756–1757
✤ Duke of Newcastle (Whig)	1757–1762
✤ Earl of Bute (Tory)	1762–1763
✤ George Grenville (Whig)	1763–1765
✤ Marquess of Rockingham (Whig)	1782
✤ Earl of Shelburne (Whig)	1782–1783
✤ Duke of Portland (coalition)	1783
✤ William Pitt the Younger (Tory)	1783–1801

THE GREAT DEBATERS

Powerful debaters could be heard in the House of Commons. William Pitt the Elder entered politics in 1735, part of a group within the Whigs who were opposed to Walpole. He was a great supporter of Britain's overseas wars. His popular son, William Pitt the Younger, served over 17 years as Prime Minister. His great opponent was Charles Fox, who became a Member of Parliament at the age of just 19.

MONEY AND POLITICS 247

Faraway Lands

Ramrod
Each new charge had to be rammed down the muzzle. The iron ramrod could be fitted under the barrel.

Long barrel
The great length of the musket's barrel was meant to help it fire straight, but it was not very efficient. Later gun barrels were 'rifled', having spiral grooves that made the bullet spin.

By the 1740s, Europe's most powerful countries were warring with each other around the world. The stakes were extremely high – rich trade and new lands. The first overseas colonies were often founded by commercial companies, which had their own armies and fleets of ships. Local people were powerless in the face of heavily armed European troops.

Bayonet
A long dagger could be fitted to the barrel for hand-to-hand fighting.

'BROWN BESS'

To fire a musket, the cock first had to be set at the safety position. The metal pan was opened, filled with a small amount of gunpowder and closed. The main charge of gunpowder and a ball were then rammed down the muzzle. When the trigger was pressed, it released a hammer containing a flint. This struck against the raised pan cover, dropping sparks into the gunpowder. When this ignited, the shot was fired.

The flintlock
The flintlock mechanism was slow to use and unreliable. Gunpowder had to be kept dry.

◀ British troops carried a type of flintlock musket known as 'Brown Bess'.

THE EAST INDIA COMPANY

As India's mighty Moghul empire fell into decline in the 1740s and 50s, the British East India Company seized land from local rulers. It ended up controlling much of the country, fighting its French rivals every step of the way. British success was largely due to a brilliant general called Robert Clive. By fair means or foul, Company officials became hugely rich. When they returned to Britain, they found themselves not only envied but mocked for their new-found wealth. They were nicknamed 'nabobs' (from the Hindi word *nawab*, 'governor').

In 1757 the British defeated the 43,000-strong army of Siraj-ud-Dawlah at Plassey, to the north of Calcutta. Clive's victory brought the whole of Bengal under British control.

1763
Treaty of Paris. Britain gains Canada and
Caribbean islands.

1768
James Cook explores the Pacific Ocean (to 1771).

ACROSS THE ATLANTIC

In Canada, the story was similar. The French had a colony
on the St Lawrence River, while the British Hudson's
Bay Company controlled land to the north. In 1759
British troops captured Quebec. By the Treaty of
Paris, which ended the Seven Years' War in 1763,
Britain gained Canada and also some of France's
Caribbean islands – Tobago, St Vincent, Grenada
and Dominica.

AUSTRALIA AND THE PACIFIC

In 1761, a naval captain called James
Cook sailed to explore the Pacific
Ocean. He mapped the coast of
New Zealand and landed in
Australia, claiming New South
Wales for Britain. On later
voyages, Cook explored the coasts
of Antarctica and discovered many
Pacific islands. He also sailed along
the North America's west coast as
far as the Bering Strait. He was
killed in Hawaii in 1779.

FROM AFRICA TO ENGLAND

In about 1760, a 10 year-old Nigerian boy
called Olaudah Equiano was kidnapped from
his West African home and sold to slave
traders. He was transported to the Caribbean,
but ended up buying his freedom from his
master. He became a sailor and took ship to
London, where he campaigned against slavery
until his death in 1797. He wrote about his
experiences in a book published in 1789.

1770
James Cook claims New South Wales, Australia
for Britain.

1789
Crew of *HMS Bounty* mutiny on Pacific voyage.

⬇ *James Cook was a Yorkshireman, the son of a farm worker. He captained British ships to the far ends of the Earth. A brilliant navigator, he was well-liked by his crews.*

Dividers   Sector   Pen holder

Parallel ruler

⬆ *Precise measuring instruments and advances in the making of chronometers (accurate time-keepers) improved seafarers' ability to navigate and draw up charts.*

DISTANT DISCOVERIES

Explorers such as Captain James Cook (1728–1779) opened up the world to the Europeans. Navigators charted unknown coasts and discovered new lands. They made geographical, botanical and other scientific discoveries that brought about a new understanding of the world. However the explorers were followed by settlers and colonisers and soldiers. The peoples who already lived in these lands now often suffered from war, exploitation and the destruction of their traditional ways of life. This happened across North and South America, Africa, Asia, Australia, New Zealand and the Pacific.

1732
Colony of Georgia is founded, named after George II.

1763
Treaty of Paris gives Britain territory west to the Mississippi.

The Loss of America

By 1763, Britain had gained control of North America from the Atlantic shore to the Mississippi River. Their lands were divided into 13 colonies. The colonists were independently minded. Many of them were descended from people who had come to America to escape injustice – Puritans, Quakers, political rebels. They resented the British government's strict controls on shipping and trade across the Atlantic Ocean. They were furious when the British demanded that they pay for the wars against the French – through taxation.

➡ *This statue commemorates Paul Revere, a famous American rebel against British rule. He kept a secret watch on British troop movements and on the night of 18 April 1775 he made a ride from Boston to Lexington and Lincoln, to warn the people that the regular troops were on their way. The colonies were now at war with their masters.*

⬅ *Native American warriors were used by the British in their colonial wars with the French.*

➡ *A colonist militia, the Green Mountain Boys were formed in Vermont as early as 1770.*

⬅ *In 1776 Britain recruited about 29,000 Hessian troops (German mercenaries) to fight for them in North America.*

In 1773, colonists disguised themselves as Native Americans and boarded British ships anchored in Boston harbour. They threw the cargoes of tea into the sea. This protest against taxation was jokingly called the 'Boston Tea Party'.

THE RIGHTS OF MAN

Thomas Paine was an English political thinker. He went to live in Philadelphia in 1774 and became a keen supporter of American independence. In England in 1791, he started to write *The Rights of Man*, supporting the French Revolution and calling for an end to monarchy in Britain. Accused of treason, Paine fled to France. His last years were spent in America, but his refusal to believe in God made him few friends in his old age.

TAXES – BUT NO VOTES

Britain first attempted to tax its American colonies in 1765. A costly tax was placed on all legal documents. This was soon withdrawn, but it was replaced by other taxes. Customs duties had to be paid on European goods. The colonists declared that it was unfair for them to pay taxes to a government in which they were not represented. Britain responded by sending in troops and in 1770 they massacred protestors in Boston.

AN AMERICAN REVOLUTION

The American War of Independence broke out in April 1775 when George Washington defeated the British at Lexington. In 1776 the American colonists declared their independence from Britain. One of them, a Scot called John Paul Jones, sailed across the Atlantic to attack British shipping. In 1778 both France and the Netherlands joined the American side against Britain. The fighting continued until 1781, when the British surrendered at Yorktown, in Virginia. Britain had lost its richest prize.

BATTLES IN THE AMERICAN WAR OF INDEPENDENCE

* ✤ Bunker Hill *British victory* 1775
* ✤ Lexington *American victory* 1775
* ✤ Saratoga Springs *American victory* 1777
* ✤ Brandywine Creek *British victory* 1777
* ✤ Yorktown *American victory* 1781

⬇ The 'Redcoats' fought the rebel colonists for six long years. Britain's defeat led to the creation of a new federal republic, the United States of America.

1709
Abraham Darby uses coke instead of charcoal to smelt iron.

1712
Thomas Newcomen's piston-operated steam engine.

New Technologies

Britain was rich in coal and its overseas empire could provide valuable raw materials such as cotton or jute. These new lands also offered a huge market for manufactured goods such as textiles. Clever inventions made it possible to produce goods more quickly and cheaply than ever before. A new system of canals made it much easier to move goods from cities to ports. An 'industrial revolution' had begun.

← Tin and copper had been mined in Cornwall since ancient times. By 1800 this industry was being transformed, with steam engines pumping out the mines, and with new roads and foundries being constructed. Soon the Cornish mines were employing 50,000 workers.

1730
Charles Townshend's theories on the rotation of crops.

1733
John Kay's flying shuttle for the weaving industry.

STEAM AND COAL

Steam power was developed in 1712 by two Devonshire engineers, Thomas Savery and Thomas Newcomen, to pump out water from mines. In the 1770s the steam engine was perfected by a Scottish engineering genius called James Watt. His successful steam pumps allowed deep mine shafts to be bored into the Northumberland and Durham coalfields.

↑ *Massive, hissing steam engines provided the power for Britain's industrial revolution.*

MILLS AND MINES

Britain became the world's first industrial country. By 1757 glowing furnaces rose from the heads of the South Wales valleys. The great ironworks at Carron brought industry to the Scottish Lowlands in 1759. The world's first iron bridge spanned the River Severn in Shropshire, England, by 1779. Factories and mills spread through Yorkshire, Lancashire and the English Midlands. Tin was mined in Cornwall, lead in Derbyshire, copper in Wales. The poet William Blake wrote of 'dark, satanic mills' appearing in a 'green and pleasant land'.

THE POTTERIES

Staffordshire, in the northwest of England, became the centre of pottery manufacture. The leading producer was Josiah Wedgwood, who set up the famous Etruria works in 1769. He produced black-and-cream-coloured wares, but his most famous design was of an unglazed blue decorated with a raised white pattern.

▲ *Wedgwood was inspired by classical designs. He made a copy of the Portland Vase, a fine piece of Roman glassware.*

SCIENCE AND TURNIPS

Science and technology were beginning to change farming as well as manufacture. In 1701 Jethro Tull invented a drill that dropped seeds in rows instead of scattering them across the field. In 1730 a retired politician called Charles Townshend (nicknamed 'Turnip') developed a new system of improving the soil by switching ('rotating') crops, using wheat, grass and turnips.

⬇ *From the 1760s, a network of canals was dug by gangs of labourers called navigators, or 'navvies'. Pottery and other manufactured goods were transported in horse-drawn boats. Seed drills allowed crops to be planted in straight rows, which made hoeing easier during the growing season.*

➡ *The spinning-jenny of 1768 was a machine that operated several spindles at once. It was developed in Lancashire, England, by James Hargreaves and mechanic Thomas Higgs, who named it after his daughter.*

A TEXTILE REVOLUTION

Few industries changed so much in the 1750s and 60s as spinning and weaving. Output soared as new spinning frames and shuttles were invented by pioneers such as Richard Arkwright, James Hargreaves and Samuel Crompton. Work once carried out in the home was transferred to big textile mills powered by water or, later, by steam. By the 1800s, the industrial revolution was gaining speed. It would change the world forever.

Irish Rebellion and Union

In the 50 years after the Battle of the Boyne, the Irish economy improved. Trade passed along rivers, canals and much improved roads to the the seaports of the east and south. Farms prospered on the more fertile lands, although the Irish-speaking peasant farmers of the west struggled along on the verge of famine. The Protestant ruling class built splendid country homes. From the 1750s onwards, Dublin was laid out with broad streets of fine brick town houses and bridges over the River Liffey. The population of Ireland rose to about five million.

▲ *Swift uses the experiences of Gulliver to point out human follies.*

GULLIVER'S TRAVELS

Jonathan Swift was born in Dublin, of English parents. He became known for his poetry. He was appointed Dean of St Patrick's Cathedral, in Dublin, and campaigned against British restrictions on Irish trade. In 1726 Swift wrote *Gulliver's Travels*, in which the hero describes his visits to various fantastic worlds. The result is a bitter but humorous look at the foolishness of mankind.

DUBLIN AND LONDON

At the beginning of the 1700s, Catholics made up 90 percent of the Irish population, but owned only 14 percent of the land. The British attitude to Ireland was that of a colonial power. When Irish exports in woollen cloth and cattle were so successful that they threatened trade in England, they were simply banned. Catholics were not allowed to worship freely or even to vote. Ireland still had its own parliament in Dublin, but real power lay in London.

⬇ The tidal reaches of the River Liffey pass through the heart of Dublin, the Irish capital. The domed Four Courts building was the centre of Ireland's judicial system under British rule. It was constructed between 1796 and 1802.

1795
Foundation of the Orange Order by Irish Protestants.

1798
Uprising in Wexford. French land in Killala.

→ *Politician Henry Grattan speaks to the Irish Parliament in 1780. He campaigned tirelessly for Ireland to be allowed to make its own laws.*

WHO HOLDS POWER?

More and more people in Ireland, Protestant as well as Catholic, wanted to see political reform. One leader of opinion was a member of the Irish Parliament called Henry Grattan. Many of his supporters were inspired by the American War of Independence and the calls for freedom grew louder. When the French Revolution took place in 1789, the British decided it might be best if they went along with Grattan's demands.

↑ *The production of linen cloth from flax was a major industry among the Protestants of Ulster. Much of the work was home-based.*

UNITED IRISHMEN

After 1791 a Protestant from Kildare called Theobald Wolfe Tone recruited many Irish people to a society called the United Irishmen. It called for equal religious rights and Irish independence. At first it had support both from Protestant militias called the Volunteers and from Irish Catholics. It soon became linked with more radical groups and sought help from the revolutionary government in France. In 1796 a French revolutionary fleet appeared off Bantry Bay in the south, but was scattered by storms.

1801
Act of Union between Great Britain and Ireland.

1803
Robert Emmet's rising Union Flag includes red saltire (cross) of St Patrick.

DEFEAT OF THE REBELS

In May 1798 the Irish rebellion began in Wexford, and in August the French landed troops in support. It was too late. Both were defeated and many Irish rebels were hanged. Grattan's reforms were thrown out. A new Act of Union, in force from 1 January 1801, abolished the Irish parliament. Ireland was now a part of the United Kingdom, and the red saltire (diagonal cross) of St Patrick was added to the Union flag. The United Kingdom had reached its greatest extent, an arrangement that lasted over 100 years.

A TROUBLED UNION

The new political order was in trouble from the start. A United Irishman called Robert Emmet organised another uprising. He manufactured guns and explosives, and attempted to seize Dublin Castle in 1803. The Lord Chief Justice was killed in the street. However the rebellion was suppressed and Emmet was executed. Although he had failed, Emmet's fame spread far and wide and he became widely seen as a martyr, as a symbol of the Irish nationalism that would grow throughout the coming century.

← The 1798 rebellion came to an end at Vinegar Hill, near Wexford, on 21 June. That September, Wolfe Tone was captured. He committed suicide in prison.

The Napoleonic Wars

Georege III's Britain and the revolutionary government in France were bitter enemies. They hated each other's politics and they were rivals for power. They went to war in 1791. Two remarkable characters made their name in the 11 years that followed. One was a popular British naval commander called Horatio Nelson. He defeated the French fleet at Aboukir Bay, Egypt, in 1798. The other was a brilliant French soldier called Napoleon Bonaparte. Napoleon had political ambitions.

⬆ *Admiral Horatio Nelson was killed in battle at Trafalgar, on the deck of HMS Victory.*

⬅ *Napoleon was a military genius, great law-maker and a ruthless politician.*

A NEW EMPEROR IN EUROPE

A peace made between Britain and France in 1802 did not last. By 1804 the two countries were at war again – only by now Napoleon Bonaparte had crowned himself emperor of France and was planning to invade Britain. Round forts called 'Martello towers' were built to defend the Channel coast. The English anxiously peered through telescopes across the Straits of Dover. Mothers threatened naughty children that 'Boney' would come for them in the night if they did not behave – but the bogeyman did not invade.

1803
Start of Napoleonic Wars with France.

1805
British defeat French and Spanish at Trafalgar. Nelson is killed.

Nelson's defeat of the French and Spanish fleet at Trafalgar was a major blow to Napoleon's plans to control Europe.

LAND AND SEA

In 1805 a French-Spanish fleet was defeated by Nelson off Cape Trafalgar, in Spain. Britain's navy ruled the seas. On land, however, Napoleon won stunning victories against the great powers of the day – Austria, Prussia, Russia. His empire soon stretched across Europe. In 1812 Napoleon invaded Russia, but his troops were caught in the winter snows and many perished. By 1814 France's enemies were in Paris. Napoleon was forced from power and exiled to the Mediterranean island of Elba.

BELOW DECKS

A sailor's life was tough during the 1700s and 1800s. Naval discipline was severe and punishment included floggings. Voyages were long, with hammocks slung between the decks for sleeping. Hard biscuits and salted-down meat were eaten, and a ration of rum was allowed. Battle conditions were terrifying, as cannon balls splintered masts and brought down rigging. In 1797 there were major mutinies by British sailors at Spithead and the Nore. Admiral Horatio Nelson, however, was popular with all ranks under his command and inspired loyalty.

↑ Sailors rest in their hammocks, exhausted afer a long session of hard work. Conditions below deck were cramped and dark.

THE PENINSULAR WAR

In 1808 Napoleon invaded the Iberian peninsula (Portugal and Spain). He made his brother Joseph King of Spain. The British sent a force under Sir Arthur Wellesley (the later Duke of Wellington) to help Spanish and Portuguese resistance fighters. The British suffered setbacks during the campaign, with a desperate retreat to La Coruña in 1809. They won a great victory at Salamanca (1812) and also at Vittoria (1814).

▶ Arthur Wellesley, 1st Duke of Wellngton, was born in Dublin in 1769. He was a brilliant soldier, cautious but thorough in his organisation.

1814
End of war in Spain. Napoleon exiled to island of Elba.

1815
Napoleon escapes. Defeated by British and Prussians at Waterloo.

WATERLOO

Napoleon slipped away from Elba and on 1 March 1815 he landed in France. Loyal troops rallied to him as he marched through the land. On 18 June they reached Waterloo, near Brussels, for a final and terrible battle. They were defeated by Prussian, Dutch and British troops under the command of the Duke of Wellington. The victors met in Vienna in 1815 to re-draw the map of Europe. Napoleon was sent to the remote Atlantic island of St Helena, where he died in 1821.

THE 'IRON DUKE'

After Waterloo, the Duke of Wellington took up a career in politics. He became Prime Minister for the Tories in 1828. Wellington supported Catholic rights in Ireland, but his past fear of French revolutionary ideas and his rigid military discipline made him extremely conservative and he was against more people getting the vote. He became very unpopular and rioters attacked his house in London. Wellington fell from power in 1830 and retired from politics in 1846. He died in 1852 and was buried in St Paul's Cathedral – next to Lord Nelson.

⬇ *Waterloo was one of the most famous battles in British history. The British infantry formed squares, with the men facing outwards and firing in turn. The French cavalry could not break their ranks. The French suffered 25,000 dead and wounded, the British 15,000 and the Prussians about 7000.*

1805
The artist JMW Turner paints *The Shipwreck*.

1812
The waltz becomes the most popular dance in Britain.

The Regency

George III was getting old and increasingly insane. His son George was eager for power and in 1811 he was made Prince Regent, to rule in his father's place. The years until his father's death in 1820 are known as the Regency period. For noble ladies and gentlemen, this was a time of high fashion and society scandals. Horse-drawn carriages bowled through newly laid out green parks. Elegant, candle-lit balls were held at Bath or at the Prince's new palace beside the sea at Brighton, Sussex.

↑ *The Royal Crescent, Bath. This city in Somerset became a centre of fashion, theatre — and gossip.*

THE DANDIES

Some Regency fashions for men were extreme. 'Dandies' squeezed into corsets and wore wide trousers and frock coats that flared from the hips. Extraordinary hair styles peeked out from top hats. They were a source of amusement to many. Leader of the dandies and self-appointed judge of all that was fashionable was George 'Beau' Brummell. He fell out with 'Prinny' (the Prince Regent) in 1813. Ruined by his gambling debts, he fled to France, where he died in the madhouse in 1840.

◄ *Standard dress for a Regency gentleman included trousers rather than breeches, a frock coat and a waistcoat.*

1820
Prince Regent becomes George IV on the death of his father.

1820
The artist John Constable paints *Flatford Mill*.

CARTOONS – AND CAROLINE

The Prince Regent was a well-meaning, intelligent and witty man, a lover of art, literature and fine architecture. However, he was savagely mocked by the cartoonists of his day. He was despised for his lavish, extravagant way of life. Dinner guests at his Brighton Pavilion could be offered a choice of 116 dishes, at a time when large sections of society were desperately poor and hungry. When George tried to divorce his second wife, Caroline of Brunswick, his treatment of her outraged the public.

← *Public opinion supported Queen Caroline over King George, as shown in this cartoon of the day.*

PEN TO PAPER

The 1800s was an exciting time for writers. Jane Austen's novels tell us just what it was like to live in Regency England, describing courtship, marriage and money. The Romantic poets were fired by imagination and emotion. William Wordsworth and John Keats praised the power of nature. The poets George Byron and Percy Bysshe Shelley led wild lives. Lord Byron went to fight in the Greek war of independence, but died of fever in 1824.

▼ *Shelley was drowned in a storm off Italy in 1822.*

▼ *Byron's most popular work was Childe Harold, which he completed in 1817.*

1826
Royal Zoological Society founded in London.

1830
George IV dies. His brother becomes William IV.

A TIME OF CHANGE

The Prince Regent escaped an assassination attempt in 1817 and was crowned George IV in 1821. He had always been pro-Whig, but as ruler he gave his support to the Tories, who opposed political reform. When his brother William came to the throne nine years later, he opposed the Reform Act of 1832. However democratic reform could not be held back for long. All over Europe old empires were breaking up. New nations were being created and their citizens were calling for freedom.

→ By 1822 the Prince's Pavilion beside the sea at Brighton, in Sussex, had been transformed by the architect John Nash into a splendid palace in the Asian style. Here was a lavish banqueting room, a magnificent music room, galleries and saloons. The rooms were filled with mirrors and chandeliers, and all sorts of ornament in the Chinese style that was fashionable at the time.

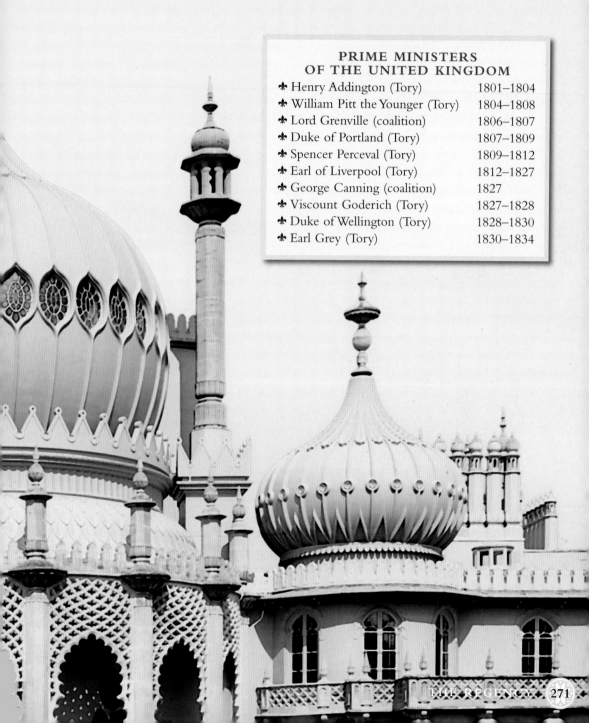

PRIME MINISTERS OF THE UNITED KINGDOM

✤ Henry Addington (Tory)   1801–1804
✤ William Pitt the Younger (Tory)   1804–1808
✤ Lord Grenville (coalition)   1806–1807
✤ Duke of Portland (Tory)   1807–1809
✤ Spencer Perceval (Tory)   1809–1812
✤ Earl of Liverpool (Tory)   1812–1827
✤ George Canning (coalition)   1827
✤ Viscount Goderich (Tory)   1827–1828
✤ Duke of Wellington (Tory)   1828–1830
✤ Earl Grey (Tory)   1830–1834

Puffing Billies

The countryside of Britain and Ireland had been quiet and unspoiled throughout its history. In the 1800s, that peace was shattered. First came railway engineers, laying track, digging cuttings and building bridges. Then came clanking, steam-powered locomotives, huffing and puffing through the fields. Horses bolted in fright.

Chimney

Piston

Boiler

Coal tender

➡ Puffing Billy,
*now in London's Science
Museum, is the oldest steam
locomotive still in existence.*

THE RAINHILL TRIALS

In October 1829 the Manchester to Liverpool railway company offered a prize for the most reliable steam locomotive. Huge crowds gathered to see the locomotives battle it out on a length of track near Liverpool. *Perseverance* was much too slow. *Novelty* could travel at 48 kilometres an hour, but kept breaking down. *Sans Pareil* burned too much coal. The winner was the *Rocket*, built by George and Robert Stephenson.

▼ The Stephensons' *Rocket* could average a speed of 24 kilometres an hour and it did not break down once.

⬇ Trevithick's second locomotive was called Catch Me Who Can. He demonstrated it in 1808 on a circular track in London. It travelled at 16 kilometres an hour.

BIRTH OF THE RAILWAYS

The railway age began in 1804. A Cornish engineer called Richard Trevithick was working at Penydarren, near Merthyr Tydfil in South Wales. He mounted a steam engine on a wagon and created the world's first locomotive. He proved it could haul a heavy industrial load – and passengers too. By 1813 William Hedley's famous *Puffing Billy* was steaming away at Wylam Colliery, near Newcastle. Wylam was the birthplace of engineering genius George Stephenson. He greatly improved the design of locomotives and rails and between 1821 and 1825 he built the Stockton and Darlington Railway. His son Robert was also an engineer, and in the 1840s and 50s he constructed magnificent railway bridges across the Menai Strait and the Conwy, Tyne and Tweed rivers.

1830
Passenger service opens, Liverpool to
Manchester railway.

1833
IK Brunel appointed chief engineer of the
Great Western Railway.

 Brunel's magnificent railway bridge across the River
Tamar, between Plymouth and Saltash, opened in 1859.

ISAMBARD KINGDOM BRUNEL

The son of an engineer, IK Brunel (right)
was born in Portsmouth, England in 1806.
He was a great builder of bridges, tunnels
and docks and in 1833 became chief engineer
of the Great Western Railway.
He also designed great
steamships for the Atlantic
crossing. *Great Britain*
(1845) was driven by
propeller screws, and
Great Eastern (1858)
held the record of
the world's biggest
ever vessel for
over 40 years.

SS *Great Eastern*

ACROSS THE OCEAN

In 1819 an American paddle steamer docked in Liverpool, and in 1821 the British steamer *Rising Star* left Gravesend for South America. These early ships used sail as well as steam, but by the 1830s steam-only crossings of the Atlantic Ocean were also being made.

The master of building the new iron ships was the engineer IK Brunel. Tall sailing ships were at this time reaching perfection in their design, and it would be another 100 years before they disappeared from the seas.

→ The SS Great Britain *in her original dock at Bristol. The British empire relied on the profitable shipping of goods and passengers around the world. After the 1820s, steam power was an added bonus.*

Long May She Reign

In June 1837 Princess Victoria, niece of William IV, was woken to be told she was queen. She was only 18 years old. Victoria ruled the United Kingdom at a time when it was the world's most powerful nation, with a vast overseas empire. In 1840, Victoria married a German prince, Albert of Saxe-Coburg and Gotha. They had four sons and five daughters, who married into many of Europe's royal families.

→ *Prince Albert and Queen Victoria. The Queen ruled for 63 years, becoming the United Kingdom's longest-reigning monarch.*

VICTORIAN MORALITY

In 1861 Albert died of typhoid fever. Victoria was grief-stricken and disappeared from public view for many years. People began to grumble about this, but towards the end of her reign she did regain her popularity. Victoria was not known for her sense of humour or fun. She believed in strict religious morality and in duty to one's country. These values were shared by many of her subjects. The Victorian upper and middle classes preached of progress, of doing good and improving society. Improvements were certainly needed. Living conditions for the poor in both cities and countryside were very harsh.

THE PEELERS

The first uniformed police went on parade in London in 1829. The force was founded by Sir Robert Peel and so the constables became known as 'Peelers' or 'Bobbies'. They wore blue-frock coats and top hats reinforced with metal. Helmets and tunics were worn as from 1864.

▶ The Peelers worked 12 hours a day, seven days a week. At first they were treated with little respect by the public.

◀ From about 1855, women wore a dress called a crinoline, whose bell-shaped skirt stretched out over hoops of whalebone and steel. Hair was worn in ringlets. By 1875 dresses were narrower, with a bottom pad called a bustle. Underwear included tightly-laced corsets.

1852
Balmoral Castle becomes Victoria's
Scottish residence.

1861
Prince Albert dies of typhoid. Victoria retires
to Windsor.

THE QUEEN AND POLITICS

In the 1830s the old political parties
changed their names. The Tories became
known as the Conservatives and the Whigs
as the Liberals. Queen Victoria took a great
interest in politics. Viscount Melbourne, the
first Prime Minister of her reign, was her
personal friend and advisor. She did not
take so well to Sir Robert Peel or
Viscount Palmerston. Later in
her reign, Victoria clearly
preferred the charming,
conservative Benjamin
Disraeli to William
Gladstone, his more
radical rival.

⬇ *The Great Exhibition of 1851 was planned
by Prince Albert. It was staged in Hyde Park,
London, in a huge building made of iron and
glass, designed by Joseph Paxton. This was
nicknamed the 'Crystal Palace'. The exhibitions
showed off produce and craft work from all over
the world. They attracted over 6 million visitors. In
1854 the Crystal Palace was moved to South
London, where it was destroyed in a fire in 1936.*

THE PENNY POST

A modern postal service using
stamps paid for by the sender was
introduced by Rowland Hill, the
Postmaster General, in 1840. The
first stamps were called 'Penny
Blacks' and 'Twopence Blues'.

Ribs and pillars
The glass panels were supported by 4064 tonnes of prefabricated iron ribs and pillars.

PRIME MINISTERS OF THE UNITED KINGDOM

✤ Viscount Melbourne (Whig)   1834
✤ Sir Robert Peel (Conservative)   1834–1835
✤ Viscount Melbourne (Whig)   1835–1841
✤ Sir Robert Peel (Conservative)   1841–1846
✤ Lord Russell (Liberal)   1846–1852
✤ Earl of Derby (Conservative)   1852
✤ Lord Aberdeen (Peelite)   1852–1855
✤ Viscount Palmerston (Liberal)   1855–1858
✤ Earl of Derby (Conservative)   1858–1859
✤ Viscount Palmerston (Liberal)   1859–1865
✤ Lord Russell (Liberal)   1865–1866
✤ Earl of Derby (Conservative)   1866–1868

Enclosure
The exhibition building covered 8 hectares of parkland, enclosing fully grown elm trees.

LONG MAY SHE REIGN   279

The Factory Age

Families were leaving the countryside to seek
work in the new factories and mines. They left
a hard life for an even harder one. They toiled in the
cotton mills of Manchester, in the steel mills of Sheffield,
on the docksides of Liverpool, Glasgow and Newcastle-
upon-Tyne. Industry depended on steam and steam
depended on coal. The number of miners in Britain's
coalfields doubled between 1851 and 1881.

⬇ *Children worked underground in the mines, hauling coal
waggons with chains or opening trap doors in the tunnels.*

▶ *The Davy
lamp was first
tested in 1816,
at Hebburn
Colliery.*

THE DAVY LAMP

Mining disasters killed
hundreds of people in
Victorian times. Deep
underground, just one
spark amongst the coal
dust could set off an
explosion, causing fires to
rage or shafts to collapse.
One invention that saved
the lives of many miners
was a safety lamp,
developed by Cornish
scientist Humphry Davy
in 1815.

1842
It becomes illegal for women and children to work down mines.

1848
Health of Towns Act, to improve water supply and drainage.

WORKING CONDITIONS

Many factory owners put profit above the health and safety of their workers. Children and young women were employed in wretched conditions in textile mills and mines. Small boys worked as sweeps, being made to crawl up tall, narrow chimneys in houses and factories until they bled. Furnaces were operated without proper safety checks. Workers in factories and mills were deafened by steam hammers and machinery. Hours were long and there were no holidays.

↑ *A cotton mill in about 1830 uses a new type of 'spinning mule' invented by Richard Roberts. It produced good quality yarn and kept its place in the textile industry until the 1950s. In the 19th century a young boy (top right) would be employed to crawl underneath and sweep up.*

1799
Socialist pioneer Robert Owen purchases New
Lanark Mills, Scotland.

1811
'Luddites' destroy industrial machinery in north
of England.

Changing Society

The industrial age, which was now spreading rapidly through Europe and North America, completely changed society. However old methods of government stayed in place. Some people campaigned against injustice and tried to reform society. Many called for greater democracy. Some revolutionaries wanted the workers to seize power for themselves.

FIGHTERS AGAINST INJUSTICE

William Wilberforce, Member of Parliament for Hull, led a long campaign against the slave trade in the colonies. In 1807 British ships were banned from carrying slaves and in 1833, one month after Wilberforce died, slavery was finally abolished throughout the British empire. Another great reformer was a Quaker called Elizabeth Fry, who from 1813 campaigned against terrible conditions in the prisons. Changes were made to the system, but Victorian prisons remained grim.

⬇ *Prisoners are exercised in the yard. Political protest and petty crimes were met with harsh sentences. Many convicts were transported to prison colonies in Australia.*

↑ As new machinery was brought into farming, labourers began to fear for their jobs.

VIOLENT PROTEST

New machines meant fewer jobs. In 1811, laid-off Nottingham workers began to smash machinery. In the five years that followed, protests spread across northern England. The protestors claimed their leader was a 'General Ludd', so they were called 'Luddites'. Many were hanged or transported to Australia. New machines were replacing labourers on farms, too. In 1830, farm workers in south England destroyed threshing machines and set fire to haystacks. Their leader was commonly known as 'Captain Swing'.

THE COMMUNIST MANIFESTO

Karl Marx was a German writer on economics who moved to London. Friedrich Engels, another German, came to Manchester to work for his family's textile business. In 1848 Marx and Engels wrote the *Communist Manifesto*. They described how economic systems had developed through history and the conflict between social classes. They called upon workers all over the world to overthrow capitalism and create a society in which classes would exist no more.

▶ The writings of Marx (right) and Engels had a great influence on world history.

1834
'Tolpuddle Martyrs' – farm workers arrested for joining trade union.

1839
First National Convention of the Chartist Movement.

A PEOPLE'S CHARTER

The Reform Act of 1832 gave the vote to more people and representation to the new cities. Between 1838 and 1848, working people campaigned for further reforms. They were called Chartists, because they presented a 'People's Charter' to Parliament. This demanded that all adult men should have the vote, that ballots should be secret and that anyone could become a Member of Parliament (MP).

Parliament rejected the Charter, in 1840 and 1842. Mass protests and armed risings followed, but were put down by troops. However laws passed in 1867 and 1884 did bring in many democratic reforms.

In 1819, reformists meeting in St Peter's Fields, Manchester, were charged by mounted troops and volunteers. Eleven of the crowd were killed and 500 injured. Just four years after the Battle of Waterloo, the event became known as the Peterloo Massacre.

1844
Cooperative movement set up in Rochdale for mutual help in trade and housing.

1846
Corn Laws, which kept the price of bread high, abolished by Robert Peel.

▼ The poverty, violence, humour and humanity of Victorian London was recorded by Charles Dickens.

DICKENSIAN LONDON

Charles Dickens, born in 1812, had a hard childhood. His father was imprisoned for debt and he had to work in a factory making boot blacking. In 1828 he became a journalist and from the 1830s onwards began to write popular novels, many of them serialised in magazines. They tell us how the Victorians lived. *Oliver Twist* (finished in 1839) shows us life in the workhouse and the beggars and thieves of the London slums. Such tales shocked many people and encouraged social reform. Dickens died in 1870.

TRADE UNIONS AND SOCIALISTS

Many working people organised trade unions, to fight for better conditions. Six Dorsetshire farm workers did this in 1834. Transported to Australia for this 'crime', they became known as the 'Tolpuddle Martyrs'. The richest people in Victorian society did not work. They used their money ('capital') to speculate, buying and selling shares. Socialists believed that the profits made by capitalists belonged rightfully to the workers who actually produced the goods.

➡ The glittering world of the rich and fashionable depended on the hard work of countless poor labourers, servants and maids.

Nature, Science and Technology

The Victorians were fascinated by the natural world and how it worked. There were breakthroughs in the understanding of physics, chemistry, botany, zoology and geology. Science was now studied at universities, and introduced to the public in splendid new museums, botanical gardens and zoos.

↑ *From 1831–1836 the crew of HMS Beagle carried out a scientific survey of South American waters. The chief scientist was a naturalist called Charles Darwin. He collected and studied fossils, animals and plants.*

THE FOSSIL COLLECTOR

Mary Anning was born in Lyme Regis, Dorset in 1799. She was already a first-rate fossil collector as a child, discovering the first fossil skeleton of an ichthyosaur in 1810. In 1821 she found the first fossilized plesiosaur and in 1828 the first *Pteranodon*.

▼ *By studying Mary Anning's fossil ichthyosaur, scientists could work out how such creatures lived in prehistoric times.*

LIFE ON EARTH

Many people were becoming interested in the fossils of animals and plants. The scientists Alfred Russel Wallace and Charles Darwin both travelled the world, studying wildlife. They came to believe that life forms on Earth had evolved, or gradually developed, over many millions of years. Their ideas were opposed by many Christians, who believed that the world was only a few thousand years old and that all existing life had been created by God in its present form.

SCIENCE AND ELECTRICITY

Michael Faraday's discoveries about electricity and magnetism in the 1830s changed the way in which people lived. In 1878 Joseph Swan demonstrated an electric light bulb in Newcastle upon Tyne. The first electric telegraph was developed by WF Cooke and Charles Wheatstone in the 1830s. The telephone was first demonstrated in the USA in 1876, by Scottish-born inventor Alexander Graham Bell. The 'wireless telegraph' or radio was invented by Italian scientist Guglielmo Marconi. He sent the first trans-Atlantic radio signal, from Cornwall to Newfoundland, in 1901.

⬆ Alexander Graham Bell experimented with different machines for transmitting sound, especially speech, while working as a teacher of deaf people.

⬇ The Royal Botanical Gardens at Kew, to the west of London, became a world centre of research into plants and seeds. A fine palm house, built of glass and iron, was completed there in 1848.

1839
The Rebecca Riots in West Wales (until 1844).

1855
The first coal mine is opened in the Rhondda valley, South Wales.

Victorian Wales

Wales had known peace since the Civil War, apart from a brief landing by French revolutionary troops at Fishguard in 1797. However the 1800s were less peaceful. There were no more wars or foreign invasions, but there was a period of violent social unrest brought about by rapid economic change.

↑ The demand for social reform and voting rights led to violent clashes with the authorities in the 1830s.

THE MERTHYR RISING

In 1829 there was widespread unemployment in South Wales and wages were cut. The troubles came to a climax in 1831. Prisoners were broken out of jail and a series of marches and riots turned into a full-scale uprising. In Merthyr Tydfil, troops were brought in to face a crowd of some 10,000 people. The soldiers opened fire, killing about 24 and wounding many more. A young miner called Richard Lewis, nicknamed 'Dic Penderyn' was later hanged for wounding a soldier, despite his innocence. The Merthyr rising was followed by ten years of bitter political protest.

CHANGING TIMES

The economy of 19th century Wales still depended on agriculture, but also on fishing, shipbuilding, and in North Wales copper mining and the quarrying of limestone and slate. In the south, coal was exported through the growing port of Cardiff. For 130 years from 1855, coal would rule the Welsh economy. Religious differences emerged too, as more and more people turned away from the Church of England to follow 'non-conformist' forms of worship in the chapels. The Wesh language, often forbidden in the schools, was kept alive by the chapels' Sunday schools.

OLD AND NEW

The ancient poetry festivals called *eisteddfodau* were reinvented in the 1790s. After the 1850s, these annual meetings became a focus for Welsh cultural – and often political – life. Young Wales (*Cymru Fydd*), a movement for Welsh self-government, was started in 1886. It was soon eclipsed by support for a rising star in the world of politics, a young Liberal called David Lloyd George. He became MP for Caernarfon in 1890. By 1916 he would be Prime Minister.

WALES IN PATAGONIA

In 1865 a group of Welsh settlers sailed to Argentina, in South America. They founded a colony in the Chubut valley, in the remote region of Patagonia. Another colony was later founded at Cwm Hyfryd, at the foot of the Andes mountains. The settlements prospered and the colonists built their own farms, chapels and law-courts. During the 1900s they became outnumbered by new Spanish and Italian settlers, but the Welsh language can still be heard in Patagonia to this day.

⬇ *The Menai Suspension Bridge, an engineering marvel of its age, was built by Thomas Telford and opened in 1826. It lay on a new road built from London to Holyhead, the port for Ireland.*

Victorian Scotland

Queen Victoria liked to visit Scotland. Her family would hunt the moors and fish for salmon. They made popular a romantic view of Scotland that was quite at odds with the harsh reality. In the Highlands, poor people were being forced from their cottages. In the industrial Lowlands, fortunes were being made while children starved in the sprawling slums of Glasgow.

ROMANTIC TALES

Two great writers of adventure tales lived in 19th-century Scotland. Sir Walter Scott wrote thrilling historical novels such as *Ivanhoe* (1819). Robert Louis Stevenson, wrote *Kidnapped* (1886) and that unforgettable story of buccaneers and gold, *Treasure Island* (1883).

▶ Robert Louis Stevenson (1850–1894).

HIGHLAND CLEARANCES

Between the 1750s and the 1860s, landowners in the Scottish Highlands reorganised their estates along more commercial lines. They brought in sheep, which were more profitable than cattle. In the Victorian age, they encouraged deer hunting and fishing. A large workforce was no longer needed and tenants simply stood in the way of the landowners' profits. Families were evicted by force and their cottages were destroyed. By the 1860s, the Highlands had become largely depopulated and the Gaelic language spoken there was under threat. It was the 1880s before the rights of remaining tenants were protected by law.

1848
Scotland linked with England by rail.

1850s
Number of homeless people in Scotland reaches 200,000.

LEAVING THE OLD COUNTRY

Many of the evicted Highlanders sought work in the Lowland cities. Others gave up and sailed off to foreign lands. Many emigrated to the coastal regions and cities of eastern Canada, to the United States and Australia.

The 'clearance' of the Highlands caused great hardship. In the 1830s and 40s things were made even worse by food shortages and starvation.

1884
The Highland Land League is founded.

1886
The Crofters' Act protects the rights of
Highland tenants.

SCOTTISH CLOTH

The tartan cloth of the Scottish
Highlands, which had been banned
after the Jacobite rebellion of 1745,
was made fashionable once more
by the novels of Sir Walter Scott
and by the royal family.

THE DISRUPTION

In 1843 there was a major crisis in the
Church of Scotland. In this 'Disruption',
large numbers of people left the established
Church. They were unhappy with the way
in which it was influenced by the state, so
they set up their own Free Church. In an
age when
Churches were
deeply involved
in education
and social
welfare, this had
a great effect on
everyday life.

RADICAL POLITICS

The economic changes in Scotland encouraged calls
for political change. In the early 1800s a Welsh
socialist called Robert Owen set up the New Lanark
Mills, with the aim of benefiting the workers. In
1819–1820 there was widespread rioting and three
Scottish radicals, James Wilson, Andrew Hardie and
John Baird were hanged. Scotland remained a centre
of Chartist and Liberal politics and in 1893 a former
Scottish miner called Keir Hardie founded the
Independent Labour Party, the forerunner of the
modern Labour Party.

➡ *Keir Hardie became an MP in 1900. His new Labour Party transformed
British politics and led to the decline of the Liberal Party. Hardie also
campaigned for women's rights and self-government for India.*

SCOTLAND AT WORK

The eastern ports of Scotland were home to large fleets of sailing ships, which trawled the North Sea for herring. Women worked on shore gutting and cleaning the fish. Textiles and iron were the major industries around Lanark and Glasgow, and the River Clyde became a great centre for shipbuilding and shipping. Dundee grew wealthy processing jute imported from the lands of the British empire. By the time of Queen Victoria's death in 1901, one in three Scots lived in the cities – in Edinburgh, Glasgow, Dundee or Aberdeen.

A new railway bridge over the Firth of Forth was opened in 1890. It was the world's first big steel bridge, with spans of 521 metres, and it immediately became one of the best-known sights in Scotland. It restored confidence in engineering that had been set back by a disaster on the Tay Bridge, destroyed by a storm in 1879.

Famine in Ireland

In Ireland, industry chiefly developed in the north. Belfast soon grew to be larger than the Irish capital, Dublin. Belfast's economy depended upon linen textiles, engineering and shipbuilding. At the same time, much of rural Ireland was suffering from poverty and hunger. Ireland may now have been part of the United Kingdom, but its citizens did not seem to be treated equally. The Union was challenged time after time.

THE BOYCOTT

A new word entered the English language in 1880: 'to boycott'. It meant 'refusing to deal with someone'. The name came from Charles Boycott, the land agent for Lord Erne, who had an estate in County Mayo. When Boycott would not lower the rents, the tenants protested by refusing to speak or deal with him in any way.

O'CONNELL AND 'YOUNG IRELAND'

The fight for Irish Catholics to be able to vote was taken up by Daniel O'Connell, a popular lawyer known as 'the Liberator'. His campaign succeeded in 1829, but most Catholics did not own enough property to qualify for the vote. O'Connell went on to campaign against the Union with Great Britain. At first he was allied with a nationalist movement called 'Young Ireland', but its members soon disagreed with his policy of non-violence. They organised an armed uprising in 1848, but it was too small to succeed.

← *Daniel O'Connell, lawyer, politician and veteran campaigner for Irish rights, died in 1847, heartbroken by the tragedy of the famine.*

THE IRISH FAMINE

Tenant farmers of rural Ireland lived a wretched life. The rents they had to pay to landlords meant that they had to sell all the grain they could grow. For their own food, they relied on potatoes and little else. In 1845 the potato crop was struck by a blight, or mould. People starved and began to die of fever and dysentery. The landlords never went hungry and crops that could have saved lives were exported to England. The blight continued and the famine lasted three years.

⬇ *In 1841 the population of Ireland was about 8 million. Perhaps 800,000 to a million people died during the years of famine.*

LANDLORDS AND FENIANS

The famine left lasting bitterness. It was felt that the government had done very little to prevent the tragedy and that landlords had neglected their tenants. New campaigns were now launched to protect tenants, in a long 'land war'. The Irish Republican Brotherhood grew up in the late 1850s. Its members, known as Fenians ('warriors') organised unsuccessful risings in 1865 and 1867 and campaigns of violence in England. Their aim was an independent Ireland.

IRISH AMERICANS

Many Fenians did not live in Ireland, but in the large Irish communities that were growing up overseas. The Irish who had settled in the eastern United States kept the campaign for Irish independence alive.

← *The Statue of Liberty was presented to the United States of America by France in 1886. It was erected at the entrance to the harbour in New York City, and so became a symbol of freedom and hope to the many poor people fleeing Europe at that time. These included generation after generation of Irish emigrants.*

EMIGRATION

During the famine and the years that followed, some 1½ million Irish people left their homeland to seek a better life overseas. Many ended up in Glasgow, Liverpool or London. Others sailed to seek a new life in the United States, Canada and Australia. They left behind deserted villages – and large areas where the Irish language was no longer heard.

HOME RULE FOR IRELAND?

In the 1870s the campaign for Irish tenants' rights was taken up by a Protestant politician called Charles Stewart Parnell. He won the support of many Fenians, but was cleared of involvement in acts of terror such as the murder of two English officials in Phoenix Park, Dublin, in 1882. Parnell's constant demands for 'home rule' by an Irish parliament were at last supported in London by the Liberal leader, William Gladstone. New laws were brought in to protect tenant's rights in the 1880s, but when Parnell died in 1891, Parliament still had not agreed to Irish home rule.

➡ *Charles Stewart Parnell (1846–91) was known as the 'uncrowned king of Ireland'. He became a Member of Parliament for Meath in 1875, standing for the Home Rule League. His tireless campaigning on the Irish question made it one of the leading issues of the day.*

SEXTON, M.P.   J.W. SULLIVAN, M.P.   PATRICK EGAN, T
CHARLES STUART PARNELL, M.P.
PRESIDENT OF THE IRISH LAND LEAGUE - ADDRESSING A MEETING.

THE GAELIC ATHLETIC ASSOCIATION

A Gaelic Athletic Association (*Cumann Lúthcleas Gael*) was founded in 1884 at Thurles, in County Tipperary. Its aim was to revive interest in traditional Irish sports and to give them formal rules. Chief amongst them were hurling, a fast stick and ball game, and Gaelic football, a variety of the sport in which the ball is punched as well as kicked. The Association was a success and became a cultural focus of the Irish nationalist movement, promoting the Irish language. With its headquarters at Croke Park in Dublin, the Association still plays an important part in Irish life today.

▲ *Emblem of the Gaelic Athletic Association.*

The Great powers

Russia had grown into a huge empire, stretching from Central Europe into Asia. In 1853 it invaded the region now known as Romania. At that time, this was ruled by the powerful Ottoman empire of the Turks. Turkey went to war with Russia. Because the United Kingdom and France wanted to stop Russia gaining control of the Balkan region, they joined forces with the Turks.

THE CRIMEAN WAR
In 1854 France and Britain sent troops to the Black Sea, even though the Austrians had already forced the Russians out of Romania. The allies landed on the Crimean peninsula, part of the Russian empire, and laid siege to the Russian naval base of Sebastopol. They won victories on the River Alma, at Balaclava and Inkerman, but the war is chiefly remembered for a disastrous charge by the British cavalry. Ordered in error to launch a direct attack on Russian guns at Balaclava, the Light Brigade galloped to certain death. The war was won in 1855, when a French force finally burst through the defences of Sebastopol.

➡ *The charge of the 600-strong Light Brigade at Balaclava in 1854 was commemorated by the great Victorian poet Alfred, Lord Tennyson. He described them riding 'Into the jaws of Death, Into the mouth of Hell'.*

REPORTS FROM THE BATTLEFIELD

Magazines such as the *Illustrated London News*, with its drawings of current events, were very popular with the Victorians. However reports of the Crimean War, published by *The Times* newspaper, shocked the public. They were sent directly from the war zone by an Irish journalist called William Howard Russell. It was during the Crimean War that the first war photographs were taken, too. For the first time in history people could read about distant battles and see the reality of warfare for themselves.

▲ This van was used to process photographs taken during the Crimean War.

THE LADY WITH THE LAMP

The blunder at Balaclava showed that the British army was run by ageing aristocrats who had little understanding of modern warfare. The troops were poorly dressed and equipped and died in their thousands from cholera and frostbite. One person did care for the wounded and dying. In 1854 an English woman called Florence Nightingale arrived at Scutari (Üsküdar) with 38 nurses. With her strict concern for hygiene, she saved countless lives. On return to England, Florence Nightingale started the training of professional nurses.

PRIME MINISTERS OF THE UNITED KINGDOM	
✤ Benjamin Disraeli (Conservative)	1860
✤ William Gladstone (Liberal)	1868–1874
✤ Benjamin Disraeli (Conservative)	1874–1880
✤ William Gladstone (Liberal)	1880–1885
✤ Marquess of Salisbury (Conservative)	1885–1886
✤ William Gladstone (Liberal)	1886
✤ Marquess of Salisbury (Conservative)	1886–1892
✤ William Gladstone (Liberal)	1892–1894
✤ Earl of Rosebery (Liberal)	1894–1895
✤ Marquess of Salisbury (Conservative)	1895–1902

↑ *Florence Nightingale visited the sick and wounded by night, with a lantern. She became known as the 'lady with the lamp'.*

AT THE FRONT LINE

Another British nursing hero was Jamaican-born Mary Seacole. She came to London to volunteer as a nurse, but was turned down. She therefore travelled by herself to the Crimea in 1855, opened a hotel there and treated wounded soldiers on the battlefield, often when under fire. She helped British, French and Russian soldiers alike. Left in poverty after the war, a public fund was raised to help her, in recognition of her work.

1856
Introduction of the Victoria Cross, the highest military award for bravery.

1856
Florence Nightingale starts training nurses in England.

RIVAL NATIONS AND EMPIRES

New nation states were being founded across Europe. Italy united as a single kingdom in 1861. In 1867 the twin nation of Austria-Hungary was created. In 1871 Germany became a single country for the first time. Its *Kaiser* (emperor) was Wilhelm I. He was followed onto the throne in 1888 by Wilhelm II, a grandson of Queen Victoria. This was an age of petty nationalism, or 'jingoism', in which each nation tried to outdo the others.

By 1914, this would lead to the bloodiest war in history. In the meantime, European nations were building up vast empires overseas. The British empire now stretched around the world.

⬇ *Italian nationalist Giuseppe Garibaldi and his 'Redshirt' volunteers reunited Italy in a series of daring military campaigns. Garibaldi became hugely popular in Britain and received a hero's welcome when he visited London in 1864. Many were inspired by his political ideals.*

Jewels in the Crown

By 1869, ships could sail directly to Asia through the new Suez Canal. Passengers included troops and merchants, who were rapidly turning Asia's ancient empires into colonies from which they could reap rich rewards. Britain's Asian empire grew to take in the countries and ports now known as Aden, Pakistan, India, Bangladesh, Sri Lanka, Myanmar (Burma), Malaysia, Singapore, Brunei and Hong Kong.

← *Indian brokers examine bales of cotton in Bombay (Mumbai). British cotton mills obtained about 20 percent of their cotton from India. However this changed when the civil war in the United States (1861–65) interrupted supplies from America. The result was a boom in Indian cotton.*

BRITISH INDIA

British rule had a great influence on India, and India impressed the empire-builders in return. Generations of them came to know India's hot, dusty plains better than the distant islands of 'home'. They fought the Afghans along the Northwest Frontier, built railways, planted tea or played polo. Many of them were racists, who believed themselves to be superior to the Indians. Others worked hard for the country and its people, but British rule did not bring an end to poverty or starvation.

THE CHINA TRADE

One crop grown in India was the opium poppy. It was made into a very addictive drug. Britain exported Indian opium to China. When the Chinese government tried to ban this deadly trade in 1839, Britain declared war. Britain won this shameful conflict and as a result gained the Chinese port of Hong Kong as a colony. The rest of China remained an independent empire, but was forced to grant more and more trading rights to Western nations. British and French troops sacked Beijing, the Chinese capital, in 1860.

➡ One of China's chief exports was tea. Fast merchant ships called clippers raced back to Britain with their cargo. Clippers were the finest sailing vessels ever built. One of them, the Cutty Sark, can still be seen beside the River Thames at Greenwich, London.

1841
James Brooke becomes Rajah of Sarawak.

1842
Britain gains South China port of Hong Kong
as colony.

↓ *British government rule in India
(the 'Raj') lasted from 1858 to 1948.*

IN SOUTHEAST ASIA

The British, French and Dutch all
sought to control the rich Southeast
Asian trade in spices, rubber, timber
and minerals. An Englishman called
Stamford Raffles founded Singapore in
1819, and in 1826 it joined Penang
and Malacca as the Straits Settlements.
In 1841 another Englishman, James
Brooke, helped to defeat a rebellion
against the Sultan of Brunei, on the
island of Borneo. As a reward he was
made the ruler, or Rajah, of Sarawak.

WORDS FROM THE EMPIRE

As the British empire spread, the English
language reached new areas of the
world. It is still widely spoken today in
many parts of Asia and Africa.
Sometimes English became mixed up
with local languages and formed new
dialects or simplified forms to create
'creole' or 'pidgin' speech. At the same
time, English picked up many foreign
words in return. From India alone came
the words 'pyjamas', 'bungalow', 'curry',
'shampoo', 'bangle', 'cot', 'punch' (the
drink), 'thug', 'chintz', 'loot' and 'jungle'.

THE JUNGLE BOOKS

Rudyard Kipling was an English writer born at Bombay, India in 1865. He was fascinated by India and wrote short stories and poems about common soldiers, officers and Indian life. For children he wrote the two classic *Jungle Books*. Although Kipling was inspired by the empire, he often criticized imperialism and realised that it must pass.

REBELLION IN INDIA

In 1857 Indian soldiers (or 'sepoys') serving Britain's East India Company rose up against their commanders in northern India. In some regions this mutiny turned into a general uprising. The rebels captured Delhi and laid siege to Kanpur and Lucknow. They were defeated in 1858. From now on, however, India would be ruled not by the Company but by the British government itself. In 1877 Queen Victoria was declared Empress of India.

⬇ *During the Indian Rebellion, the city of Delhi was held by the rebels for three months. British troops under the command of Sir Colin Campbell stormed its defences in September 1857.*

To the Ends of the Earth

Britain's empire grew to take in the vast, unknown land of Australia, as well as New Zealand and many South Pacific islands. At first, the British only used Australia as a place to send prisoners. Many convicts died on the outward voyage and life in the prison colonies was harsh. Some escaped and sailed to New Zealand.

Aborigines were masters of survival in a harsh environment. They had lived in Australia for over 50,000 years, but the settlers claimed that they had no right to their own land.

BRITAIN'S AUSTRALIAN COLONIES

By 1793 the first free settlers had arrived in New South Wales, but it was 1868 before all transportation of convicts to Australia came to an end. Settlers gradually opened up the dry lands of the interior. New or breakaway colonies were founded – Van Diemen's Land (Tasmania) in 1804, Western Australia in 1829, South Australia in 1836, Victoria in 1851, Queensland in 1859. While farmers and itinerant workers struggled to tame the dry and dusty lands of the 'outback', new cities sprang up around the coast. Railways and roads and seaports were built, and more and more colonists arrived to seek a new life 'down under'. The Aborigines, the first Australians, suffered greatly. Some were employed as police scouts or as hands on the farms, but many were chased off their own land, moved to reserves or murdered.

1845
Start of First Maori War, New Zealand
(Second War 1860).

1851
Start of the gold rush in Australia.

GOLD NUGGETS, WOOLLY SHEEP

In 1851 gold was discovered in New South Wales.
Settlers poured into Australia in search of a fortune.
The miners had few legal rights and a major
revolt took place at Eureka, near Ballarat
in Victoria, in 1854. Thirty miners were
killed by mounted police. Another great
source of wealth was sheep farming. By
1890 there were 100 million
sheep in Australia.

⬇ *In 1860, Robert O'Hara Burke and
William John Wills set out on an
expedition across the unknown interior of
Australia. The explorers travelled with
camels, horses and wagons. However
seven of the explorers died, including the
two leaders, on the return journey in 1861.*

NED KELLY THE OUTLAW

Ned Kelly, the son of an Irish convict, was born in Victoria in 1855. He became an outlaw, or 'bushranger', whose gang robbed banks and stole cattle. After a train was held up at Glenrowan, three of the gang were killed. Ned Kelly was captured and hanged in 1880.

▶ *When Ned Kelly was finally captured he was dressed in home-made armour.*

NEW ZEALAND AND THE MAORIS

New Zealand was inhabited by the Maoris, a Polynesian people, and by a small number of mostly British settlers. In 1840 the British signed a treaty with Maori chiefs at Waitangi and New Zealand became a British colony. The settlers failed to honour the treaty and Maoris fought them from 1845 to 1847 and again from 1860 to 1872. From 1856, the settlers had their own Parliament. Many gold miners and farmers now arrived in New Zealand. From the 1880s, advances in refrigeration meant that lamb could be shipped back to Britain.

WHOSE AUSTRALIA?

Between 1823 and 1855, the Australian colonists gained increasing rights to govern their own affairs, and by 1901 the various colonies had come together to form a federation, the Commonwealth of Australia. There was a new Parliament – but the true Australians, the Aborigines, were denied the vote until 1967.

⬇ *This war canoe was made by Solomon Islanders. Britain gained control of these Pacific islands between 1893 and 1900.*

1901
Australian colonies unite as a federal Commonwealth.

1907
New Zealand becomes a Dominion of the British empire.

ACROSS THE PACIFIC

European seafarers, planters and Christian missionaries were now spreading out through the islands of the South Pacific. Many islanders fell victim to kidnappers called 'blackbirders', and were shipped off illegally to forced labour in Australia. Fiji became British in 1874 and Britain claimed southeastern New Guinea (Papua) in 1884. By the end of the century, most Pacific islands were under foreign rule.

HMS CHALLENGER

In 1872, a ship set out to explore a new world – the bottom of the sea. But the *HMS Challenger* wasn't a submarine. It measured the seabed, using ropes to find out the depth of the ocean. On its round-the-world voyage, *Challenger*'s crew also found many new species of sea creatures.

▼ *HMS Challenger*

Into Africa

The British may have ended their part in the slave trade, but it remained a curse in many parts of Africa. European explorers and Christian missionaries were now braving lions, spears and tropical fevers as they led expeditions into Africa. They were followed by traders, prospectors, colonists, hunters – and soldiers. By the end of Victoria's reign, most of Africa was under European rule.

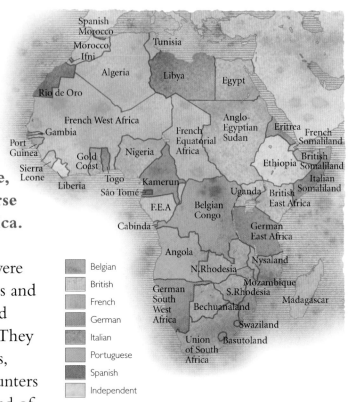

Key:
- Belgian
- British
- French
- German
- Italian
- Portuguese
- Spanish
- Independent

⬆ European powers competed with each other to control Africa. There were wars of resistance all over Africa, but people were helpless against troops armed with modern firearms. This map shows who ruled Africa in 1890.

SHARING THE SPOILS

Africans were used as a labour force, but were little better off than slaves. Their job was to extract the riches of the continent for colonial rulers. In southern and eastern Africa the best farmland was seized by white settlers.

At the Conference of Berlin in 1884–85, regions of Africa were shared between European powers. They knew little about the peoples living there and did not care about their needs.

STANLEY AND LIVINGSTONE

In 1869, Livingstone went missing. He had gone exploring in East Africa and no one had heard from him. Everone thought he had died. A Welsh-born American journalist, HM Stanley, turned explorer and went to look for Livingstone. He found him in the town of Ujiji, in Tanzania. He greeted him with the words: "Dr Livingstone, I presume?"

 ▶ It took Stanley eight months to find Dr Livingstone in Africa.

SCOTTISH EXPLORER

Dr David Livingstone was one of the most famous explorers of Africa. He went there in 1840 as a missionary, to try to teach African people to be Christians. He trekked right across the dusty Kalahari Desert with his wife and young children and discovered Lake Ngami. Livingstone became the first European to travel all the way across Africa. On the way, he discovered a huge, beautiful waterfall on the Zambezi River. The locals called it *Mosi Oa Tunya*, meaning 'the smoke that thunders'. Livingstone renamed it Victoria Falls, after Britain's Queen Victoria.

EAST AFRICAN LANDS

In 1887 the British East African Company leased the Kenya coast from its ruler, the Sultan of Zanzibar. Eight years later, Britain claimed the interior, eventually creating a colony called Kenya. British rule extended into neighbouring Uganda and (after 1918) into Tanganyika (now the mainland of Tanzania). Railways were built by labourers brought in from India, while farmers seized the highlands and planted coffee.

INTO AFRICA 311

SUEZ TO SUDAN

In 1875 Britain became chief shareholder in the new, French-built Suez Canal, which cut through Egypt. Britain soon became more powerful in Egypt than the government itself. It also took control of Sudan, to the south. In 1877 British General Charles Gordon became governor of Sudan. He was killed at Khartoum in 1885, after an uprising led by the fiery religious leader Muhammad Ahmed, known as the *Mahdi* ('saviour'). In 1898 the British avenged Gordon's death at Omdurman, killing 11,000 Sudanese warriors.

→ *A Zulu impi (armed unit). In South Africa, the British clashed with the highly disciplined armies of the Zulu nation. These inflicted a crushing defeat on British troops at Isandlhwana in 1879. Away from the battlefield, a British force at Rorke's Drift fought off Zulu attacks. The Zulu warriors fought with stabbing spears, clubs called knobkerries, and long shields.*

Ostrich plumes

Headband of fur

Fringes made from cows' tails

Spear

SOUTHERN AFRICA

In 1806 the British gained control of Cape Colony, South Africa. The Dutch had settled the area since the 1650s and resented British rule.

In 1837 these 'Afrikaners' or 'Boers' ('farmers') left the Cape. They headed for the interior, where they founded independent republics. When reserves of diamonds and gold were found there, British businessman Cecil Rhodes saw this as an opportunity. His miners poured into the area, but Afrikaner president, Paul Kruger would not give them rights. In 1899 a war broke out between the British and the Boers. Peace was made in 1902 and the Union of South Africa was formed in 1910. British rule spread from South Africa into the countries we now call Lesotho, Botswana, Eswatini (Swaziland), Malawi, Zambia and Zimbabwe.

Knobkerrie

Shield made from cow hide

North and South Atlantic

Queen Victoria's empire took in remote Atlantic outposts such as St Helena, Tristan da Cunha and the Falkland Islands. It governed Bermuda and many Caribbean islands. On the American mainland, the lands now known as Guyana and Belize were all part of her empire, as well as Canada's vast forests and prairies.

↑ *The Inuit or Eskimo people lived in scattered settlements in the Canadian Arctic.*

CANADA BECOMES A DOMINION

In 1791 Canada had been divided along the Ottawa River. Lower Canada was the French-speaking area, while Upper Canada was English-speaking. These two were united in 1840, taking in the provinces of Ontario, Quebec, Nova Scotia and New Brunswick. A parliament was set up in 1849 and in 1858 Ottawa became the Canadian capital, the personal choice of Queen Victoria. In 1867 Canada was made a self-governing Dominion of the British empire. This was set up along federal lines, with each province keeping its own elected assembly.

PRAIRIES AND FORESTS

Canada continued to expand into lands occupied by its First Peoples and by the Métis (people of mixed French–Indigenous descent). They rose up in rebellion in 1867, under the leadership of Louis Riel, but were defeated. Manitoba joined Canada (1870), British Columbia (1871), Prince Edward Island (1873), Alberta and Saskatchewan (1905). Poor farmers from all over Europe arrived to settle the Canadian prairies, and prospectors searching for gold arrived in the remote Northwest in 1896. Canada prospered from its timber, oil, mineral wealth and fisheries. The last province to join the Canadian federation was Newfoundland, in 1949.

⬇ *The building of railways encouraged settlement of Canada's prairie provinces and the far west. The Canadian Pacific Railway spanned the country coast-to-coast by 1885.*

⬇ *Prospectors pose at a goldmine in British Columbia in about 1868.*

1831
British Guiana (Guyana) becomes a colony.

1834
Slavery ends in Britain's Caribbean islands (to 1838).

THE CARIBBEAN ISLANDS

In the 1830s, slavery was ended in Britain's Caribbean colonies, which were known as the 'West Indies'. Many freed slaves moved off the plantations and lived by farming small plots of land, or fishing. They remained desperately poor and there was an uprising against the British governor on Jamaica in 1865, led by George William Gordon and Paul Bogle. On Trinidad, contracted labourers were brought in from Asia to work on the sugar plantations, but the majority population throughout the Caribbean region was now of African descent.

IN CENTRAL AND SOUTH AMERICA

In 1862 a small region of the Central American coast, occupied by British loggers, was made into a colony called British Honduras (modern Belize). In South America, sugar-producing British Guiana (modern Guyana) had become a colony in 1834. British people played an important part in the development of other South American lands, too, building railways high into the Andes mountains.

CARIBBEAN CARNIVAL

Trinidad and some other Caribbean islands began to celebrate Carnival in the 1800s. This festival had been brought to the region from Catholic Europe. At first, slaves were not allowed to take part, but after they were freed they made it their own, with dancing, singing and drumming to African rhythms. From the Asian community came spectacular costumes and masks.

▶ Carnival originally marked the beginning of Lent, the Christian period of fasting. It is still celebrated in the Caribbean today.

BANANAS AND LOGWOOD

Slavery was over, but the people of the Caribbean or 'West Indies' were still poor and working for colonial masters. Sugar, molasses and rum were mainstays of the economy, although internationally sugar was now being made from beet as well as from cane. By the end of the 19th century, other exports were becoming more important, such as bananas, coffee and logwood – a timber used in making dyes.

▶ Bananas have been grown on the Caribbean islands since the beginning of the 16th century.

⬇ Slavery had dominated the culture and economy of the Caribbean for 300 years, when it was finally phased out in the 1830s.

The Modern Age

1901–

ELSEWHERE IN EUROPE	ASIA	AFRICA
1914 The First World War, fighting across Europe (until 1918).	**1912** The last Chinese emperor, a young boy, is forced to give up the throne.	**1914** First World War: colonial powers fight in Africa, Germany loses empire (1918).
1917 Revolutions in Russia, Bolsheviks (Communists) seize power.	**1940** Japan starts invasion of Southeast Asia in Second World War.	**1953** Egypt becomes a republic (nationalises Suez Canal 1956).
1933 The National Socialist (Nazi) party comes to power in Germany.	**1945** United States drops atomic bombs on Hiroshima and Nagasaki in Japan.	**1957** The Gold Coast becomes the independent nation of Ghana.
1939 Second World War, Germany overruns Europe (defeated 1945).	**1947** British India divided into two independent states, India and Pakistan.	**1960** Nigeria gains independence from Britain.
1948 Start of 'Cold War'. Europe divided into Communist East and Capitalist West.	**1948** Israel declares an independent state in Palestine, southwest Asia.	**1960** Belgian Congo becomes independent, start of long civil war.
1957 Treaty of Rome: the European Economic Community (later European Union).	**1949** Communists defeat Nationalists in China, found a People's Republic.	**1961** Tanganyika becomes independent (Uganda 1962, Kenya 1963).
1990 Communist governments fall in Eastern Europe, end of the Cold War.	**1979** An Islamist revolution in Iran, the Shah (emperor) is overthrown.	**1994** Democracy introduced in South Africa: Nelson Mandela first black president.
2002 Introduction of the Euro currency.	**2003** The United and States and its allies invade Iraq.	**2011** The 'Arab Spring': Governments overthrown in Tunisia, Egypt and Libya.

> *"World science, world wars and the search for world peace…"*

NORTH AMERICA

1914
Canada enters the First World War
(United States, 1917).

1929
Wall Street 'crash' – US economic problems
lead to Great Depression.

1939
Canada enters the Second World War
(United States, 1941). War ends 1945.

1959
Revolution in Cuba, Fidel Castro
seizes power.

1961
USA becomes involved in Vietnam War,
in Southeast Asia (until 1973).

1962
Jamaica and Trinidad gain independence
from Britain.

1963
US President John F Kennedy is assassinated
in Dallas, Texas.

2009
Barack Obama is the first African American
to become US President.

SOUTH AMERICA

1910
Massive oil reserves discovered in Venezuela.

1946
Juan Perón wins general election
in Argentina.

1949
Bitter civil war in Colombia, La Violencia.

1960
Brasília replaces Rio de Janeiro as the capital
of Brazil.

1966
Guyana gains independence from Britain.

1973
Chile's elected government is overthrown,
Pinochet dictatorship.

1975
Independence for Suriname, mass emigration
to Netherlands.

1982
Falklands War between Britain and Argentina
in South Atlantic.

2010
Rapid growth of Brazilian economy.

OCEANIA

1907
New Zealand becomes a Dominion within
the British Empire.

1914
Australia and New Zealand enter First
World War (until 1918).

1931
Statute of Westminster confirms Australian
independence.

1939
Australia and New Zealand enter the
Second World War (until 1945).

1941
Japan bombs Pearl Harbor (Hawaii), invades
Pacific islands (until 1945).

1967
Aborigines granted citizenship rights
in Australia.

1968
Independence for Nauru (Fiji and Tonga
1970, Vanuatu 1980).

2011
Earthquake in Christchurch, New Zealand.

The Edwardian Age

Queen Victoria's funeral was held on 2 February 1901. It was attended by rulers from all over Europe, many of them her relatives. The new king was Edward VII. During his 60 years as Prince of Wales, he had led a roguish life of pleasure. How would he fare as a ruler?

Queen Victoria's funeral cortege passes through the High Street, Windsor, on 2 February 1901. After lying in state, the queen was laid to rest at Frogmore Mausoleum on 4 February 1901.

1904
The *Entente* ('Agreement') is signed between France and Britain.

1906
Germans and British compete in building of battleships.

UPSTAIRS, DOWNSTAIRS

The reign of Edward VII is often remembered as a golden age, a brief period of peace before the tide of war broke over Europe. For the aristocracy, it was a time of lavish weekend house parties, of balls, regattas and visits to the theatre. The middle classes in the growing suburbs worked in banks or businesses, played tennis and sang songs around the piano. Even middle class homes could afford servants and cooks. These worked 'below stairs', polishing boots or cleaning the silver. Upstairs were the halls, landings and family rooms, often furnished with umbrella stands, drapes and dark wooden furniture.

> **RULERS OF THE UNITED KINGDOM**
> **House of Saxe–Coburg and Gotha**
> ✤ Edward VII   1901–1910
> **House of Windsor**
> (new name as from 1917)
> ✤ George V   1910–1936
> ✤ Edward VIII (abdicated)   1936
> ✤ George VI   1936–1952
> ✤ Elizabeth II   1952

→ *Edward VII's reign would only last nine years, but he was an active and effective ruler. His visit to Paris in 1903 helped to prepare the ground for close ties between Britain and France.*

↓ *Edwardian ladies and gentlemen enjoying the Henley Regatta.*

THE EDWARDIAN AGE

POVERTY AND UNEMPLOYMENT

For the working class, this age was far from golden. By 1904 there were 800,000 people in England and Wales registered for poor relief. In 1913, half a million school children were reported suffering from disease or a poor diet. There were many tragic mining accidents and industrial disasters – and an ever-growing number of strikes, as trade unions campaigned for fairer and safer working conditions. In 1909 the Liberal government brought in the first old age pensions.

⬆ *Many working class women were employed in 'service', as maids in private homes.*

1912
Robert Falcon Scott and his team die on
South Pole expedition.

1914
Two million British workers are on strike.

THE GROWING CRISIS

Europe was arming for war. The
German *Kaiser* was building up a naval
fleet to challenge British rule of the
seas. Britain made alliances with France
in 1904 and with Russia in 1907. In
1914, these treaties were put to the test.
The heir to the Austrian throne,
Archduke Franz Josef, was assassinated
in Bosnia by a young Serbian
nationalist. Austria, encouraged by
Germany, went to war with Serbia.
Serbia was in turn supported by Russia.
Within just a few weeks, almost the
whole of Europe was on the brink of
war – including the United Kingdom.

↑ *The German emperor or Kaiser, Wilhelm II, a
grandson of Queen Victoria, came to the throne in
1888. He was disabled, a fact that he tried to
conceal, and was conservative, rash, militaristic and
jealous of British power.*

GOING SHOPPING

In Edwardian shop windows there were
elaborate displays of goods or produce,
and well-known advertisements for tea
or soap. Shop assistants were formally
dressed, with starched white aprons and
cuffs. Goods could be delivered to the
home by bicycle. Department stores,
which had first arrived in Britain in the
Victorian period, were now popular in
cities. Here, clothes and furnishings and
other assorted goods were all on sale
under the same roof.

The First World War

In August 1914 the United Kingdom
and Germany went to war. Most
people believed it would all be over by
Christmas, but this terrible conflict dragged
on for over four years. It was known as the
Great War. Today we call it the First World
War, for it was fought in many
different lands by
armies from
many nations.

THE ROAD TO WAR
The world order collapsed
like dominoes. Austria-
Hungary, backed by
Germany, threatened Serbia.
Russia, backed by France,
supported Serbia. Germany
attacked France via neutral
Belgium, which was backed
by Britain. The result? The
worst conflict the world had
ever known…

The assassination of the
Austrian heir, the Archduke
Franz Ferdinand, by a
Serbian nationalist triggered
the First World War.

Archduke Franz
Ferdinand, Sarajevo,
28 June 1914

1915
March: British fleet blockades German ports.

1915
April: Australians, New Zealanders and British land at Gallipoli, in Turkey.

THE WAR POETS

Before the First World War, poets used to celebrate victories and write of heroic deeds. Now many wrote of horror and anger at seeing so many young men being killed like cattle. Great poets who served as soldiers included Wilfred Owen (1893–1918) and Siegfried Sassoon (1886–1967).

NATIONS AT WAR

As well as British and Irish soldiers, empire troops included Indians, East Africans, South Africans, Canadians, Australians and New Zealanders. Their allies in the 'Entente' included France and its empire, Japan, Italy (from 1915), Russia (until 1918) and the United States (from 1917). Ranged against them were the 'Central Powers' – Germany, Austria–Hungary, Bulgaria and Turkey.

↑ Along the Western Front, the warring armies dug themselves into trenches defended by razor-sharp barbed wire.

THE PEOPLE'S WAR

In the 1800s, wars had been fought by professional soldiers, far from home. Now, warfare was coming home. Civilians found that they could be bombed in their houses by the new planes and airships, and that passenger liners as well as warships could be attacked by submarines. In 1916 the British government began to conscript members of the public, calling them up to serve in the armed forces.

▲ The Royal Flying Corps (forerunner of the Royal Air Force) was founded in 1912. During the war, its pilots could expect to live for just two weeks of combat. The most famous British fighter plane was the Sopwith Camel, in production from 1916.

◀ Ambulances carried wounded men from the front line. Severe wounds meant a return to 'Blighty' – the British Isles.

1916
May: Naval battle off Jutland.

1916
July–November: First Battle of the Somme,
1,043, 896 killed.

TRENCHES AND MUD

Fighting took place in the snowy forests of eastern
Europe, in Turkey and the deserts of Arabia, on the
plains of East Africa. There were great naval battles
and beneath the waves, submarines stalked Atlantic
shipping. The bloodiest fighting was on the Western
Front, a long line of defensive trenches that stretched
from Belgium, through France, down to the
Swiss border. Soldiers on both sides lived
and died in wretched conditions. Any
who fled were tried for desertion and
then shot.

*Troops are ordered 'over
the top', leaving their trenches
for a new assault. Thousands
of lives were often sacrificed to
gain just a few metres of land.
At the battle of
Passchendaele, fought in
Belgium in 1917, some
270,000 Germans died. Allied
losses, from British, Canadian,
South African, Australian and
New Zealand troops,
numbered about 300,000.*

ONE SILENT NIGHT

Along one sector of the Western front, on Christmas Eve 1914, the German troops raised Christmas trees from the mud of their trenches and lit candles. They began to sing German carols such as *Stille Nacht*. British troops recognised the tune as *Silent Night* and joined in. The guns fell silent. On Christmas morning troops from both sides left their positions and joined together in 'no-man's-land'. They exchanged rations and played a game of football. The troops were soon ordered back to their lines to resume the slaughter.

German infantryman 1915 nickname: 'Fritz'
The German soldier fought with a Mauser rifle. It was reliable but its magazine held only five bullets, so more time was spent reloading.

CHANGING ALLIANCES

There were changes in the alliances and armies during the course of the war. Italy joined the conflict in 1915, on the side of Britain and its allies. It suffered a dreadful defeat at Caporetto in 1917. The United States too entered the war in 1917, following a 1915 German submarine attack on the *Lusitania*, a liner carrying American passengers as well as munitions destined for Britain. By 1918 American troops (nicknamed 'doughboys') were pouring into Europe. However Russia, one of the original allies, collapsed in revolution during 1917, and many of its troops deserted from the Eastern Front. The new revolutionary government withdrew from the war.

British infantryman 1915 nickname: 'Tommy'
The British soldier fought with a Lee Enfield 0.303 rifle, which could be fitted with a bayonet. Its magazine held 10 bullets, and could be fired at the rate of about 12 shots a minute.

FIRST WORLD WAR 327

➡ HMS Dreadnought. By 1914 the most modern warships were encased in thick armour and carried large guns mounted in armoured turrets that could turn to face different directions.

◀ A British cavalryman and his horse charge forwards wearing anti-gas masks. The gas attack should have allowed the cavalry to break through the German lines and attack, but this failed to happen.

POISON WARFARE

Terrible new weapons were introduced by both sides during the First World War. The French used tear gas as early as 1914, but the following year the Germans used chlorine gas, a deadly choking poison, against French troops. The Allies soon also adopted gas warfare, and ever more deadly chemicals were developed, such as phosgene and mustard gas. Gas attacks were hard to control, as the chemicals drifted with the wind, and troops had to wear cumbersome gas masks over their faces. Those soldiers who survived gas attacks often suffered terribly from illnesses and mental problems for the rest of their lives.

➡ *Equipped with a small gun and carrying only three men this light tank could move quickly to attack enemy infantry, but was highly vulnerable to artillery fire.*

TANK ATTACK

The first tanks were known as 'land ships' and were developed by the British. They terrified the enemy, but they did not work very well and were often stuck in the mud. Conditions for the tank crews were appalling.

• The first use of British tanks was at Delville Wood in 1916. French tanks first appeared in the Aisne offensive of 1917.

• At the Battle of Cambrai in 1917, 474 British machines won the first major tank victory.

• German tanks attacked the British at Villers Bretonneux in 1918, the first battle in which tanks fought against tanks.

A LOST GENERATION

In 1914 the soldiers had marched off to war in a patriotic mood, singing the popular songs of the day. When the guns fell silent in 1918, some 10 million young men had been killed in all the armies. Countless more were left blinded, disabled, or in a state of severe stress called 'shell-shock'. The Allies had won the war, but at a terrible cost.

⬅ *A heavy howitzer with its barrel aimed to hurl shells at a high trajectory. Shells falling steeply onto enemy defences penetrated deep into the soil before exploding. This allowed them to burst under concrete defences and shatter them.*

1905
Sinn Féin founded, with aim of a united Irish republic.

1913
Ulster protestors threaten violence if Home Rule is passed.

Easter 1916

The question of Irish home rule had been a burning political issue for 100 years. In 1912 the proposal returned to Parliament in London. In Protestant Ulster, supporters of the union with Britain were prepared to use violence to oppose the bill. Their leader was lawyer Sir Edward Carson. Would Ireland be divided? Would there be civil war? The bill was passed in 1914 but immediately postponed. The First World War had broken out.

THE EASTER RISING

Many Irishmen were soon fighting in the war, but to others there was another priority – fighting against the Union. Sir Roger Casement, a well-known Irish diplomat, sought help from Germany for a rising – but was captured as he landed from a German submarine. It was Easter 1916 and an uprising was taking place in Dublin. The rebels seized the large General Post Office and their leader, Pádraig Pearse, proclaimed a republic. After five days they were shelled into surrender by the British army. At first they had little widespread support, but when 15 of them were executed by the British, Irish public opinion changed. At the general election of 1917, the republican party Sinn Féin ('Ourselves Alone') won an historic victory.

1914
Home Rule is passed, but postponed because of the war.

1916
The Easter Rising suppressed in Dublin. Fifteen executed.

↓ *Irish rebels defend ruined buildings in Dublin against British troops armed with machine guns.*

WRITERS AND DREAMERS

The new century was an inspiring time for Irish writers. George Bernard Shaw (1856–1950) was writing challenging essays and plays about great social issues. The playwright JM Synge (1871–1909) was director of Dublin's Abbey Theatre. The beautiful poems of WB Yeats (1865–1939) took Ireland as their theme and were inspired by the events of 1916. In 1914 James Joyce published *Dubliners*, short stories about life in the Irish capital. His later work, in the 1920s and 30s, shocked the world with a new kind of language that reflected humans' rambling thoughts, fears and dreams.

IRA AND THE 'BLACK AND TANS'

Sinn Féin, led by Éamon de Valera, did not take up its seats in Parliament. Instead, it set up its own Irish Assembly, or Dáil Éireann. In 1919 a ruthless guerrilla organisation, the Irish Republican Army (IRA), was set up to fight the British. It was countered by special military units sent in from England to help the police. Known from their uniform colours as the 'Black and Tans', their tactics were often brutal. In 1920 Ireland was split in two. In the north, six out of Ulster's nine counties were given their own parliament, while the rest of Ireland had theirs.

AN IRISH FREE STATE?

In 1921, Sinn Féin sent delegates to London, including Arthur Griffith and Michael Collins. They agreed to the partition of Ireland, with the south becoming a Free State, similar to a self-governing Dominion of the British empire. Back in Ireland their decision was rejected by de Valera, who wanted nothing short of an independent republic. A bitter war broke out within Sinn Féin. Collins was set to be head of the new Irish Free State government when he was murdered by the IRA.

⬇ *A pall of smoke hangs over central Dublin at Easter 1916. The rising by the Irish Volunteers and the Irish Citizen Army resulted in the death of 418 people.*

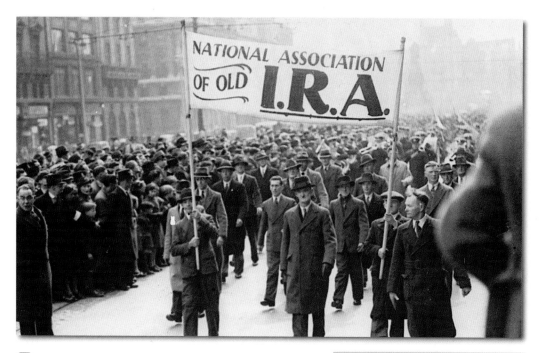

↑ *After 1919, the nationalist cause was fought by the IRA, which opposed the partition of Ireland. In 1969 a breakaway group was formed – the Provisional IRA.*

THE ROAD TO A REPUBLIC

Sinn Féin refused to recognise a Free State government, but in the end de Valera decided that it could be used as a step towards a full republic. In 1926 he founded a new political party, Fianna Fáil ('Soldiers of Destiny'), and in 1933 another party was founded, Fine Gael ('Tribes of the Gaels'). In 1938 the Irish Free State declared independence under the name of Éire. Éire remained neutral in the Second World War (1939–45) and in 1949 became the fully independent Republic of Ireland.

ARAN ISLANDERS

The Irish nationalists came from many different backgrounds, but they were inspired by the Gaelic culture, language and way of life. Nowhere had this survived in a more traditional form than amongst the fishermen and farmers of the Aran Islands, in Galway Bay. The islanders inspired the writer J M Synge and were the subject of a famous documentary film, *Man of Aran*, in 1934.

1889
A Women's Franchise League is founded by
Emmeline Pankhurst.

1893
New Zealand is first country in the world where
women can vote.

Votes for Women

In February 1913, the home of Chancellor David Lloyd
George was destroyed by a bomb. In May of that year, a
bomb was placed in St Paul's Cathedral, London. In June, during the
Derby event at the Epsom races, a woman called Emily Davison
dashed out and grasped the reins of a racehorse owned by the king.
She was trampled beneath the hooves and died the next day.

A STRUGGLE FOR EQUALITY

The 1913 protests were all by women
demanding suffrage – the right to vote.
Those calling for reform were called
suffragists, while more radical activists
were called suffragettes. Women had
never been allowed to take a democratic
part in choosing how the country was
governed. Most men were shocked by
the protests, for in those days women
were expected to obey their husbands
and raise children rather than take part in
political campaigns. In 1889 a campaigner
called Emmeline Pankhurst founded the
Women's Franchise League and in 1903
she and her daughter Christabel formed
the Women's Social and Political Union
(WSPU). The suffragettes met with
public ridicule and abuse, but they argued
their case loud and long.

← *Wearing sashes labelled 'votes for women', female
suffragists argue their case with labourers carrying out
road works.*

1903
A Women's Social and Political Union (WSPU) is founded.

1907
Women's Enfranchisement Bill is defeated in Parliament.

THE PANKHURSTS

Emmeline Pankhurst (1857–1928) campaigned for women's rights for 40 years. She and her eldest daughter Christabel were often imprisoned. They stopped campaigning when the First World War broke out in 1914. Emmeline later joined the Conservative Party. Emmeline's other two daughters were also suffragists. Sylvia and Adela (who moved to Australia) actively opposed the war and became socialists.

▼ *The Pankhursts all lived to see women gain equal voting rights with men.*

↑ *Suffragettes protested by breaking windows and chaining themselves to railings. Many were sent to prison.*

← *A woman bus conductor stands on the platform of a Number 19 double-decker bus. The 20th century saw a revolution in women's role in society.*

1912
Suffragettes smash shop windows and protest at the
House of Commons.

1913
WSPU member Emily Davison dies in Derby protest.

↓ The sight of women brandishing
placards and chaining themselves to
railings infuriated many men in the
Edwardian era.

PUBLIC PROTEST

The WSPU developed new
forms of protest in order
to gain publicity for their
cause. They committed
violent acts against property
like smashing shop windows.
When they raided the House
of Commons, it resulted in 96
arrests. When they were sent to
jail, they went on hunger strike,
refusing to eat. The prison officers
force-fed them through tubes. Under a
special law, the authorities could keep
releasing women hunger-strikers, only
to send them back to prison again
once they had recovered.

INTO THE WORKPLACE

During the First World War, men were
needed to fight in the armed services
and many were killed. Women took
over jobs once done by men. They
worked on the farms and in munitions
factories, making shells and weapons
for the front line. By the time the war
was over, women had become more
accepted as a part of the workforce.
Public opinion was changing.

1918
Votes granted to women over the age of 30.

1919
Nancy Astor is elected as Britain's first woman MP.

POLITICAL PROGRESS

In 1918, British women at last won
the right vote in general elections,
but only if they were aged over 30. It
was not until 1929 that the voting
age for men and women was
equalized, at 21. During the 1920s
more and more women found work
as office secretaries, typists or
telephone operators, but still received
lower wages than men.

➡ *In 1919 American-born
Nancy Astor became the first
woman to be elected as a
Member of Parliament,
winning Plymouth for the
Conservatives.*

⬆ *A suffragette prisoner on hunger strike,
being force-fed by prison authorities.*

1896
First cinema opens in United Kingdom.

1914
Charlie Chaplin goes to make films in Hollywood, USA.

Dance to the Music

People tried to forget the horrors of the First World War with dancing, popular songs and music, visits to the picture palace (cinema) or summer trips to the seaside. The stuffiness of the Edwardian era disappeared. Women wore shorter dresses. Their hair was now bobbed short, and was often curled into permanent waves ('perms'). They wore lipstick and face powder. They often smoked cigarettes – unaware of the risk to their health.

← *Film star 'Charlie' Chaplin (Sir Charles, 1889–1977) became one of the first human beings to be instantly recognisable around the world.*

GOING TO THE PICTURES

The first films were silent, in black and white. A pianist played music to fit in with the story. The best-known film star of all was Charlie Chaplin (1889–1977). During a childhood of poverty in south London, he performed on stage in the music halls. After 1914 he made comic films in Hollywood. In many of them he played a tramp. Chaplin hated social injustice and underlying the clowning there was often a serious message about the times he lived in.

← *Weekly visits to the cinema offered escape to the magical world of Hollywood stars.*

1919
First jazz record to be released in United Kingdom.

1922
Fashion for wide trousers, known as 'Oxford bags', for men.

JAZZ – AND JEEVES

The music of the new century was jazz, first played by African Americans in the USA. By 1919 this wild, free-flowing music was being heard in England. Wind-up record-players, or gramophones, now made it possible to play music and dance in the home. The good life of England in the 1920s and 30s was sent up by a witty writer called PG Wodehouse. His world was peopled by flappers, goofy young aristocrats and a butler named Jeeves – who was far wiser than his master.

↓ *Fashionable, flighty young women were known as flappers. They shocked their parents with 'unladylike' American dances such as the Charleston. They loved parties and driving motorcars. By the 1930s the age of fun was over as economic problems took hold, but after the flapper era, young women never looked back.*

↓ *One of the most famous jazz musicians was the American Louis Armstrong (1900–1971), a gifted trumpet player from New Orleans – the so-called 'birthplace of jazz'. He first visited England in 1932.*

TUNING IN

The 'wireless' was all the rage.
Schoolboys learned how to make very
basic radio receivers, called 'crystal sets'.
The British Broadcasting Company,
established in 1922, was made into a
Corporation (the BBC) in 1927. Soon
people were listening to plays,
music, sport, comedy shows and
news, all in their own living room.
King George V broadcast to the nation
on Empire Day, 23 April 1924.

↑ The radio soon became a part of everyday life.
News had once taken days to reach every corner of
the British Isles. Now it could be broadcast as it
happened.

← In 1932, George V became the first monarch to
make a Christmas broadcast to the nation.

1927
The first Ryder Cup golf match between Britain and the USA.

1935
First paperbacks published by Penguin Books.

A ROYAL CRISIS

In 1936 newspaper headlines reported a crisis in the royal family. George V had died and his eldest son Edward was due to follow him as king. However Edward intended to marry an American woman called Wallis Simpson, who was divorced. Divorce was considered to be scandalous in the 1930s. Public opinion forced Edward VIII to abdicate (resign) and his younger brother was crowned George VI in his place.

↑ *The Duke of York (second from right) became king as George VI. He was a shy man who became a popular ruler.*

⬇ *Edward VIII gave up the throne in order to marry Wallis Simpson (below). He became Duke of Windsor instead of king.*

The Hunger Years

T**he glitter of high society in the 1920s and 30s hid desperation and poverty.** After 1922, the British economy slowed down and countless men who had fought for their country now found themselves jobless, while their families went hungry. Germany too faced economic chaos after the First World War, made worse by the harsh terms of the 1919 Treaty of Versailles. This dragged down the economy of the rest of Europe.

Armoured cars take to London streets during the General Strike. The government feared a Communist revolution, as had happened in Russia in 1917.

THE JARROW MARCH

During the 1930s, 'hunger marches' were held as workers from Wales, Scotland and the north of England marched on London to protest against unemployment. In 1936, 200 men from Jarrow, on Tyneside, walked all the way to London on what they called a 'Crusade'. They were led by their Member of Parliament, Ellen Wilkinson, and were given food and sleeping places by supporters along the way.

▼ *The dignity and endurance of the Jarrow marchers impressed many people. It brought home to them the desperate poverty in Britain's industrial regions.*

THE GENERAL STRIKE

In 1926 a report on British coal mining called for wages to be lowered, yet the companies were demanding longer working hours. Miners went on strike and called on other workers to join them. Two million did and the country was paralysed. Middle-class volunteers tried to break the strike, driving buses and trains. The Trades Union Congress dropped their support within nine days, but it was another six months before the miners were defeated.

THE GREAT DEPRESSION

The United States now had the most powerful economy in the world. When it began to show signs of weakness in 1929, there was panic as people sold off their shares. The US economy crashed and European economies that depended on US credit came tumbling down too. Within a year, unemployment around the world had doubled. The crisis was so severe that British political parties joined together in a coalition government.

$100 WILL BUY THIS CAR MUST HAVE CASH LOST ALL ON THE STOCK MARKET

➡ The dire effects of the US stock market crash in 1929 (right) were soon felt on this side of the Atlantic.

JOINING THE FIGHT IN SPAIN

During the 1920s and 30s, capitalism seemed to be in a crisis, just as Karl Marx had predicted. Many young people in the British Isles looked to new political ideals such as socialism and communism. From 1936 many of them went as private volunteers to fight in Spain, where a bitter civil war had broken out. It was being fought between the elected Spanish government and their conservative and fascist opponents, led by General Franco. An 'International Brigade' was formed to help fight Franco, but the pro-government forces were defeated.

▼ The Spanish Civil War was bloody and chaotic. It was described by the British writer George Orwell (real name Eric Blair) in his book Homage to Catalonia (1938).

THE RISE OF FASCISM

A new political system took root amidst Europe's economic chaos. Fascism first developed in Italy in 1921. It aimed to replace 'weak' democracies with thuggery, dictatorship and extreme nationalism. Fascists went under various names. Racist 'National Socialists' (Nazis) seized power in Germany in 1934. In 1936 'Falangists' attacked the democratic government in Spain. Fascist groups were formed in England and Ireland too. London's East Enders came out to stop them marching through the streets.

→ The Nazi leader Adolf Hitler took power in Germany in 1933. He attacked Jewish citizens, built up the army and prepared for war. The storm clouds were building up yet again over Europe.

← Fascism had its sympathisers in Britain. Sir Oswald Mosley founded the British Union of Fascists in 1932. His black-shirted bullies fought with Communists and Jews on the streets of London.

The Second World War

The Nazi dictator of Germany, Adolf Hitler, was building up German military power. In 1938 British Prime Minister Neville Chamberlain made an agreement with Hitler at Munich, promising 'peace in our time'. It was soon broken. German tanks rolled into Czechoslovakia and Poland. By 1939, Britain and Germany were at war. The war spread around the globe like wildfire and claimed the lives of about 55 million troops and civilians, the bloodiest conflict in human history.

⬆ *The trench warfare of the First World War was a thing of the past. The Second World War was highly mobile. The Germans called it Blitzkrieg or 'lightning warfare'. Their rapid invasion of Europe was carried out by tanks, like this one, and by fighter aircraft. There were also huge tank battles in North Africa.*

DIVISION OF EUROPE

The map of Europe had been re-drawn by the Treaty of Versailles in 1919. The new borders did not survive for long. Germany annexed Austria, invaded Czechoslovakia, Poland and then France and much of continental Europe. It was 1941 before the Allies were joined by the Russians and the Americans. The Axis powers were joined by Japan in the same year.

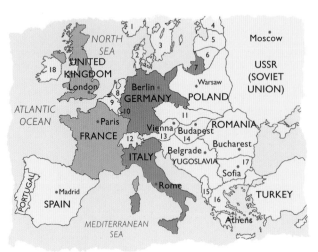

KEY

■ Allies	6 Lithuania	13 Austria
■ Axis powers	7 East Prussia	14 Hungary
1 Norway	8 Netherlands	15 Albania
2 Denmark	9 Belgium	16 Greece
3 Sweden	10 Luxembourg	17 Bulgaria
4 Estonia	11 Czechoslovakia	18 Republic
5 Latvia	12 Switzerland	of Ireland

1940
Rescue of British troops from Dunkirk. Italy joins
the war.

1940
Germans invade the Channel Islands. Battle of Britain
fought in the air.

➡ *Family air-raid shelters
were issued in Britain from
February 1939. Nearly
2.5 million shelters of this
type were erected in
gardens during the war. The
boy in the picture is trying
on a gas mask.*

Outside
view

Anderson
shelter

WAR BENEATH
THE WAVES

Submarines, called U-boats
by the Germans, played a major
part in the war around the
world. The submarines attacked
merchant ships, aircraft carriers
and warships with torpedoes.
The ships responded by
dropping underwater explosives,
called depth charges. Merchant
ships and troop transports
steaming between Britain and
the United States or the Soviet
Union were forced to travel in
convoys (large groups defended
by heavily armed naval vessels).
Submarines could be located
with a sound ranging
device called Sonar.

⬇ *The Messerschmitt Me-109 was a German
fighter plane, often used for 'reconnaissance' –
surveying enemy areas.*

⬇ *Submarines prowled the Atlantic Ocean in
search of their prey. Many sailors and submariners on
both sides were drowned during this deadly Battle of
the Atlantic.*

THE SECOND WORLD WAR 347

1941
Germany invades Soviet Union. Japan attacks USA
at Pearl Harbor.

1942
Japan captures Singapore, taking 70,000
Allied prisoners.

BRITAIN STANDS ALONE

In 1940, Germany rapidly invaded
Scandinavia, the Netherlands, Belgium and
France. Fascist Italy entered the war on
Germany's side, and the Balkans and Greece
were invaded. Britain was isolated in Europe.
In 1941 Germany attacked its former ally, the
Soviet Union (as Russia was then called), and
Japan declared war on Britain and the United
States. Japan had already invaded areas of
China and it now advanced through Southeast
Asia. Although Britain now had more
enemies, it had also gained powerful allies.

⬆ *St Paul's Cathedral rises above a
smouldering London. German night-time
bombing of Britain's major cities began on
7 September 1940. This 'Blitz' killed about
40,000 civilians and injured many more. Over
a million homes were pounded into rubble.*

V FOR VICTORY

In 1940 Winston Spencer Churchill (1874–1965) became
British Prime Minister. As a young soldier, he had fought
in Sudan and he later served both as a Conservative and
a Liberal MP. He was always a controversial politician,
but in wartime he inspired people with his gritty
personality, his brilliant speeches – delivered in a
growling voice – and his shrewd judgement.

▶ *Winston Churchill
gestures V – for
'Victory'.*

1942
Allied victory at El-Alamein, in the North
African desert.

1944
D-Day: Allies land on beaches of Normandy.

↑ In the late summer of 1940,
the skies of Britain were filled
with vapour trails and the sound
of fighter aircraft from the Royal
Air Force battling in 'dogfights'
with the German Luftwaffe. By
the end of October, the Germans
had lost 1733 planes, and the
Allies 915. The 'Battle of Britain'
had been won.

← RAF fighter pilots relax next
to their Spitfires while waiting for
the signal to 'scramble' (take off)
and battle with the enemy.

THE SECOND WORLD WAR   **349**

In 1944, British troops were combing the jungles of Burma (Myanmar) in a desperate conflict with Japanese invaders.

A COMMANDO RAID

From 1940 the British formed small military or naval units known as commandos, which specialised in night-time raids or reconnaissance behind enemy lines. Hitler commanded that all commando prisoners be shot, but most German officers ignored this order.

Helmet
A camouflaged helmet was generally used in action, but commandos also wore dark woollen caps.

Backpacks
Equipment might include explosives, ropes and rations.

Weapon
Commando units might carry sub-machine guns, daggers, sniper rifles and pistols.

WAR IN THE PACIFIC

The Second World War really was a global conflict. Much of the fighting took place in Asia and the Pacific, where the militaristic empire of Japan overran British and Dutch colonies in a bid to control the entire region. Even before the Second World War had begun, Japan had invaded China. Many of the captured troops and civilians now suffered greatly in Japanese prisoner-of-war camps. British troops fought alongside Australian, New Zealand and large numbers of US troops to liberate the region.

British commando units carried out daring raids in German-occupied Norway and France, in the Middle East and Burma.

1945
14 August VJ Day (Japanese surrender): End of
the war.

1945
November: leading Nazis put on trial in
Nuremberg, Germany.

THE TIDE TURNS

By 1943 the tide of the war was
turning. The Soviet Red Army was
pushing back the Germans in eastern
Europe. The Allies had defeated them in
North Africa and were advancing through
Italy. On 6 June 1944, ('D-Day'), Allied
troops landed in occupied France and began
to battle their way eastwards. Germany was
devastated by Allied bombing raids and surrendered
in 1945. After long and bitter fighting in the
Pacific, the United States dropped two terrifying
weapons of mass destruction on Japan – atomic
bombs. Surrender was immediate.

*The atomic bombs that were dropped on the Japanese cities
of Hiroshima and Nagasaki by the United States in August 1945
brought the Second World War to a terrible end. Tens of
thousands of Japanese civilians were killed instantly, while others,
sick with radiation, died lingering deaths over many years.*

▼ *Slave labourers in Buchenwald camp, April
1945. Cameramen entering the death camps with
Allied troops took the first pictures to reveal the full
extent of Nazi cruelty.*

HORROR OF THE CAMPS

The Nazis were racists. They blamed all
the troubles of Europe on Jews, Slavs and
Roma (Gypsies). They built secret
'concentration camps' where these peoples
– alongside political opponents, disabled
people and homosexuals – were forced
into labour, shot, hanged or gassed to
death. No fewer than six million
Jews were murdered in this
'Holocaust'. As Allied troops invaded
Germany and the lands that had been
occupied, they were sickened to find
starving prisoners and piles of corpses.

1946
Nationalisation of Bank of England, coal mines and railways.

1948
The National Health Service is founded in Britain.

Post-war Britain

Soldiers returned to a Britain that was victorious but **battered.** In the cities there were bomb sites to be cleared. Barbed wire, concrete and mines had to be removed from British coasts. Shortages of food and other goods meant that these had to be strictly rationed – and the birth rate was suddenly rising as families looked forward to a safer, more peaceful world.

GAMES AND FESTIVALS

Post-war life was far from easy, but the British people still had time for celebrations. London staged the first post-war Olympic Games in 1948, and in 1951 a Festival of Britain was held. It looked to the future and was marked by the construction of many very modern-looking public buildings.

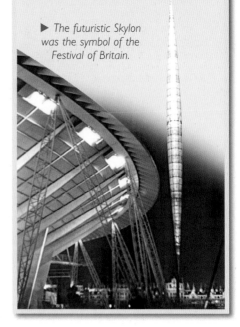

▶ *The futuristic Skylon was the symbol of the Festival of Britain.*

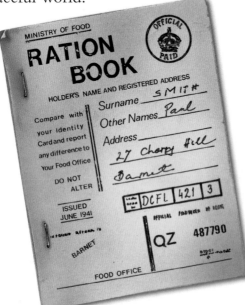

⬆ *Ration books, brought in during the shortages of the Second World War, were still necessary in the post-war years. Certain goods could only be purchased with government-issued coupons.*

1952
King George VI dies of cancer. Elizabeth II
succeeds him.

1954
Food rationing ends in Britain.

THE WELFARE STATE

The Second World War had convinced
many British people of the need for
social change. In 1945 the wartime
leader Sir Winston Churchill lost the
election to the Labour Party under
Clement Attlee. By 1950, 650,000 new
publicly owned, low-rent 'council
houses' had been built across the
country. A National Health Service was
founded in 1948, with free medicine
for all. This 'welfare state', which aimed
to provide care for all its citizens, was
also supported by Conservative
governments, from their re-election in
1951 until 1979.

⬇ The radical Welsh Labour politician Aneurin
('Nye') Bevan founded the National Health Service.
Here, he is at a London health centre site in 1949.

⬇ A council estate in Glasgow in 1950. The housing
on offer was not always beautiful, but it was cheap to
build, affordable to rent, and generally better equipped
and healthier than the old slums and tenements.

Winds of Change

SUN SETS ON THE BRITISH RAJ

The campaign for Indian freedom had begun as early as 1885, with the founding of the Indian National Congress. From the 1920s this movement was led by a former lawyer called Mohandas K Gandhi. He used non-violent methods to oppose the British, organising marches and fasts. He was often imprisoned. Amidst bloody riots in 1947, Britain partitioned India into a mainly Hindu India and a mainly Muslim Pakistan. These two nations achieved independence, making the nationalists' dream come true. However Gandhi was dismayed by the religious hatred. He was assassinated by a Hindu fanatic in 1948.

◀ *Gandhi championed the poor and he himself led a very simple lifestyle. He became known as the Mahatma ('great soul').*

In 1960 the Conservative Prime Minister Harold Macmillan spoke in South Africa of a 'wind of change' blowing through the African continent. In reality this wind had been blowing throughout the world for some years. With the Second World War, the age of colonial empires had come to an end. In Africa, Asia and the Caribbean, people were demanding independence from Britain. At the same time, self-governing nations such as Canada, Australia and New Zealand were increasingly breaking ties with 'the mother country' and going their own way.

1949
The modern form of the Commonwealth replaces the old empire.

1957
Independence for Gold Coast (Ghana) and Malaya.

INDEPENDENCE STRUGGLES

Nationalist movements were founded in many parts of the British empire from the 1920s to the 1950s. Their leaders were often jailed and in some lands the independence campaigns turned violent. In Kenya, there was a bitter uprising from 1952, the Mau-Mau Rebellion. By the end of the 1950s, Britain was forced to realise that it no longer had the power to rule the world. Local political leaders were released from jail and became the leaders of independent nations.

⬇ *During Kenya's Mau-Mau Rebellion, about 100 white settlers were killed. Many African Kenyans, mostly Kikuyu people, were also killed and tens of thousands were imprisoned in camps.*

⬇ *Britain's Princess Margaret reads an address in the name of her sister, Queen Elizabeth, as she open the first meeting of the Jamaican parliament in 1962. Her husband the Earl of Snowdon stands on her left.*

A COMMONWEALTH OF NATIONS

In 1931 the lands of the British empire had been formally joined together within a 'British Commonwealth'. After 1947 this became a union of independent nations, most of which had formerly had links with Britain. 'British' was dropped from the title. While some newly independent nations kept the British monarch as their head of state, others became republics. The Commonwealth fostered economic and cultural links between its members.

1960
Nigeria independent.

1961
South Africa leaves the Commonwealth; Tanganyika
becomes independent (Tanzania 1964).

WHITE MINORITIES

In some parts of the former empire, the
ruling Whites were not prepared to allow
democracy or independence. In South Africa,
governments refused to give the vote to
people of African or Asian descent. South
African society was cruelly segregated along
racial lines until democratic government was
introduced in 1994. In 1965 the White
minority government in Rhodesia broke
away from British rule, preventing
independence (as Zimbabwe) until 1980.
Years of bush warfare followed. Black
majority rule also failed to deliver
democracy, with elected president Robert
Mugabe suppressing free opposition.

⬆ The apartheid system of racial
segregation was introduced in South Africa in
1948. As a result, South Africa was expelled
from the Commonwealth in 1961 and not
readmitted until 1994, when all South
Africans won the vote. In Britain, supporters
and opponents of apartheid clashed
throughout that period.

⬅ Nelson Mandela, born in 1918, was a tireless
campaigner against the system of apartheid in South Africa.
He was a leader of the African National Congress (ANC)
and demanded votes for all South Africans, regardless of
colour. He was imprisoned for 27 years and finally released
in 1990, after a long international campaign for his
freedom. From 1994 to 1999 he served as the first
president to be elected by all the people of South Africa. On
5th December 2013, after a prolonged respiratory infection,
Mandela died, aged 95, at his home in Johannesburg.

AFTER THE EMPIRE

After independence, some former colonies became republics, but others remained monarchies, still recognising Queen Elizabeth II as head of state. Today the British monarch still reigns in 16 'Commonwealth Realms'. These are Antigua and Barbuda, Australia, the Bahamas, Barbados, Belize, Canada, Granada, Jamaica, New Zealand, Papua New Guinea, St Kitts and Nevis, St Lucia, St Vincent and the Grenadines, Solomon Islands, Tuvalu and the United Kingdom. Australia has so far voted to remain a monarchy, but has a strong republican movement.

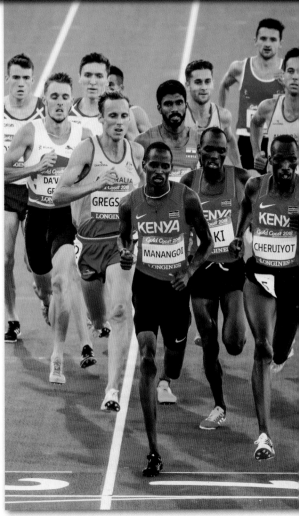

↑ The Commonwealth has encouraged sporting and cultural links among its members. This Commonwealth Games was held on the Gold Coast, Queensland, Australia, in 2018. Winner of the men's 1500 metres was Elijah Manangoi of Kenya.

← Elizabeth II is also Queen of Canada. Here she meets well-wishers while on a walkabout during her visit to the country in 2010.

1958
White youths attack Black immigrants in
Notting Hill, London.

1965
Race Relations Act makes discrimination illegal
(also in 1968).

New Britons

The British Isles have been settled by many different groups of people throughout their history. Black people were in Britain as early as Roman times. In the 1950s a new wave of immigration began from the lands of the former British empire. Like others before them, these immigrants came either to find work or to escape persecution in their homelands.

⬆ *The golden dome of a mosque rises above Regent's Park, London. Islam, Sikhism and Hinduism now play an important part in modern British life, alongside Judaism and Christianity.*

ARRIVING IN HOPE

The first Caribbean immigrants to arrive in Britain came on board the *Empire Windrush*, a ship that docked at Tilbury in June 1948. Many were ex-servicemen hoping to make use of skills they had learned while fighting for Britain in the war. This 'Windrush generation' and their children were soon a valuable part of British society, but often faced racial prejudice. In 2018 there was a scandal when some of them wrongfully recieved official notices that they had to return to the Caribbean.

◀ *Young Caribbeans came to England in search of a decent wage, but found that there was little money left to save or send home.*

THE NEWCOMERS

In the 1950s, British governments recruited many workers from the Caribbean region – where there was widespread unemployment – to staff National Health Service hospitals or to work in public transport. Others came in search of jobs and were joined by their families. Indians and Pakistanis arrived too during the 1960s. In 1972 Asians, including many who held British passports, were expelled from their homes in Uganda. Most of the new arrivals settled in large industrial cities such as London or Birmingham.

➡ *A Caribbean carnival, first held in London's Notting Hill district in 1965, soon developed into one of Europe's most popular street festivals. A love of Caribbean music and dance styles have forged links between young people for over 50 years.*

A MIXED WELCOME

It was the ancestors of the 1950s and 60s immigrants who had created the wealth of the British empire. The new arrivals were often hard-working and enterprising, Some were trained as doctors, nurses and teachers. However they were often met with a lack of understanding and racial prejudice. Some politicans stirred up trouble, but new racist political parties remained very small. Laws were passed against discrimination. Britain began to absorb new cultures, as it had throughout its history.

1946
Churchill warns of an 'Iron Curtain' dividing Europe.

1948
West Berlin is blockaded by Communists. Allies fly in vital supplies.

The Cold War

The period from 1945 to 1990 is often called the Cold War. This refers to the tension between Russia (the 'Soviet Union') and the countries of the West, led by the United States. The Soviet Union was still ruled by the Communist Party, although supporters of its ruthless leader Joseph Stalin (who died in 1953) had by now killed most of the idealists who had taken part in the revolution. The West remained capitalist. In the United States anti-Communist feelings reached fever pitch in the 1950s. The world teetered on the brink of war.

↑ In 1948 the Allies airlifted supplies into Berlin's Tempelhof airport to beat a Russian blockade.

→ Just before the end of the Second World War, in February 1945, the Allied leaders Winston Churchill of Britain, Franklin D Roosevelt of the USA and Joseph Stalin of the Soviet Union, met at Yalta, in the Crimea. They discussed the post-war settlement and how Europe would be divided between the great powers.

1949
China becomes a Communist republic under
Mao Zedong.

1949
British troops fight Communist rebels in
Malayan jungle.

NATIONAL SERVICE

During the Second World War, young men had been
called up into the armed services. Conscription
continued until 1962, even though the United
Kingdom was no longer at war. Some said that this
National Service was good for young people,
teaching them discipline and a trade.

▶ *Many recruits felt that weapons drill and army
routine served little use in peacetime.*

THE IRON CURTAIN

After the Second World War, Europe
was divided into two power blocs.
Winston Churchill said it was as if an
'iron curtain' had fallen across the
continent. In 1949 Western Europe and
North America joined in a military
alliance, the North Atlantic Treaty
Organization (NATO). Eastern and
Central Europe were now in
the hands of Communist governments
and in 1955 they united within the
Warsaw Pact. The rival blocs faced each
other in Germany, which was divided
in two. The former capital, Berlin, was
itself divided and surrounded by
Communist territory. British troops
were stationed in the west.

⬇ *Polaris was the first missile system
developed in the United States in the
1950s and came into service in
1960. By 1968 it was being used
by Britain's Royal Navy. It was
the first missile to be fired
from submarines.*

Polaris missile
Each missile was 9.4 metres long and
1.4 metres thick. It carried a nuclear
warhead. The first Polaris missile had a
range of 2200 kilometres. The final model,
adopted by the United Kingdom in 1969,
had a range of 4800 kilometres.

1950
Korean War (to 1953). Multi-national force fights
Communists.

1952
Britain's first atomic bomb is tested in Monte Bello
islands, Australia.

WHEN THE WAR TURNED HOT

In Asia the Cold War turned hot,
especially after China too became
ruled by Communists in 1949. The
newly formed United Nations
Organization sent a multi-national
force, including many British troops,
to fight a Communist invasion of
Korea. This war lasted from 1950 to
1953. From 1965 the United States
also fought a bitter war against
Communists in Vietnam, but was
defeated in 1973. Cold War tensions
spread around the world, preventing
peaceful development in Africa, Asia,
Central and South America.

⬇ *Many British people thought that the Vietnam
War was unjust and protested against it on the
streets. British governments supported the United
States' policy, but – unlike Australia – sent no troops.*

⬇ *British Troops arriving in Korea in September 1950.
They are seen marching from the quay after landing at
the southern port of Pusan (now Busan).*

1958
Campaign for Nuclear Disarmament (CND) founded in London.

1961
East Germans divide Berlin with fortified wall (until 1989).

BOMBS AND PROTESTS

The chief danger of the Cold War was the rapid increase in the number of nuclear bombs and missiles, just a few of which could destroy the world. Britain held nuclear weapons as a 'deterrent', so that no other country would risk an attack. The United States set up large air and naval bases in the United Kingdom. Many British people protested against nuclear weapons and a Campaign for Nuclear Disarmament (CND) was founded in 1958.

END OF THE COLD WAR

Many Western leaders believed that once one nation had turned Communist, its neighbour would soon follow, one falling after the other like so many dominoes. This did not happen, for the Communist nations were divided amongst themselves. The Soviet Union tried to bring in political reforms in the 1980s, but its economy finally collapsed. By 1991 the old Soviet Union was finished and the Cold War was over.

SPIES WHO CAME IN FROM THE COLD

Much of the conflict between the Cold War powers was secret, carried out by spies and undercover agents. Some Russian and Central European spies were secretly working for the west, while some members of the British secret service gave away secrets to the Soviet Union. These included Guy Burgess, Donald Maclean, Kim Philby and Anthony Blunt. British writers loved to create Cold War thrillers with spies as heroes, such as Ian Fleming's James Bond or Len Deighton's Harry Palmer.

▼ Spy Harry Palmer (played by Michael Caine) slips through Checkpoint Charlie in the Berlin Wall, in a scene from the thriller Funeral In Berlin, 1966.

1952
The first Top Ten pop music chart is published in Britain.

1955
Britain's first television commercial.

Rocking and Rolling

In the second half of the 1950s, the European economy began to recover from the war years. More and more families watched television. Glossy magazine advertisements offered dreams of foreign travel or the ideal home. British car designer Alec Issigonis produced the classic Morris Minor in 1948 and the world famous Mini in 1959, the year in which England's M1 motorway opened. High-rise flats began to tower above Britain's cities in the 1960s.

⬇ *Four young lads from Liverpool formed a pop group in 1960. Paul McCartney, Ringo Starr, George Harrison and John Lennon made up The Beatles. During the 1960s they became the most successful band the world has ever known.*

Ringo Starr (b.1940)

George Harrison (1943–2001)

John Lennon (1940–80)

Paul McCartney (b.1942)

1958
First section of motorway opens in England, M6.

1961
The first contraceptive pills go on sale in Britain.

← *Putting on the style… rock 'n' roll music took over dance halls in the years 1957–59.*

TEENAGE REBELS

It was in the post-war years that teenagers began to be seen as a separate social group. For the first time they had money and leisure, which they devoted to pop music and outrageous fashion. In the 1950s came American rock 'n' roll music, skiffle and modern jazz. Rebels were known as 'teddy boys', 'teddy girls' and 'beatniks'. They were followed in the 1960s and 1970s by gangs of 'mods' and 'rockers', mini-skirted girls, long-haired 'hippies', and shaven-headed 'skinheads'. British popular music became famous all over the world.

→ *The 'punks' of the late 1970s despised the hippies for going soft. Punks listened to loud, discordant music. They pierced their bodies, dyed their hair in bright colours and wore torn clothes and metal chains.*

ROCKING AND ROLLING 365

1945
The founding of the United Nations (UN) Organization.

1959
UK is a founder member of the European Free Trade Association (EFTA).

Conflict, peace and Trade

↑ *A British teacher working for Voluntary Service Overseas (VSO) talks with pupils in Thailand.*

I n 1919 an international body called the League of Nations was founded, in order to prevent the outbreak of another world war. It failed completely, so in 1945 a new organisation was set up, the United Nations (UN). Its aim was to promote peace, health, human rights, economic and cultural co-operation.

WORKING FOR WORLD PEACE

The United Kingdom (from 1945) and the Republic of Ireland (from 1955) played an important part in the United Nations. Both committed troops to international peacekeeping operations and to military task forces. The blue berets of UN soldiers became a familiar sight in trouble spots around the world. Individual citizens also began to get involved in tackling the world's problems. Volunteers from Britain and Ireland went to some of the world's poorest countries, teaching, building and distributing food.

1973
UK, Ireland join EEC – known as European Union (EU) from 1993.

2003
Britain joins the US-led invasion of Iraq.

No end to the fighting

British troops served in many smaller conflicts after the Second World War. They were in Palestine before the creation of the Israeli state in 1948. In 1956 Britain and France launched a bid to prevent Egypt from nationalising the Suez Canal. Britain fought a war with Argentina over the Falkland, or Malvinas, Islands in 1982 and in the 1990s Britain sent troops to the Balkans and the Gulf. In 2003 Britain joined the United States in invading Iraq, a costly and prolonged conflict, during which Iraq plunged into chaos. In 2001 British troops were deployed to Afghanistan, as part of a multi-

Arrest of Iraqi militiamen by British soldiers on the road to Basra in 2003.

national action that toppled the Taliban – an Islamist political movement that had governed the country from 1996. By 2004, Taliban forces had regrouped and a guerrilla-style war commenced, with British troops seeing ten years of action in the southern province of Helmand.

The new Europe

After the Second World War, people wanted to safeguard the future peace of Europe. As early as 1946, Sir Winston Churchill was calling for a United States of Europe. In 1949 Britain and Ireland joined the new Council of Europe, and in 1973 they finally joined the European Economic Community (EEC) – an economic and political alliance known since 1993 as the European Union (EU). Many enjoyed the economic benefits of EU membership and the Irish economy was transformed. Critics of Britain and Ireland's EU membership complained of bureaucracy and loss of national sovereignty, and of economic problems with the Euro. Supporters believed that membership offered economic benefits and more peaceful international relations.

Ireland North and South

By 1949 most of Ireland was a republic, fully independent from the United Kingdom. However six counties of the northern province of Ulster remained part of the UK. The Irish Republic still claimed those counties, and the Irish Republican Army (IRA) continued its campaign of violence against Britain during the 1950s and 60s.

⬆ *Michael D Higgins has been a politician, writer and broadcaster. He was elected President in 2011, and in 2014 became the first President of the Republic of Ireland to make a state visit to the UK. He was re-elected for a second term in 2018.*

IN THE REPUBLIC

In the 1950s, Ireland remained a conservative, largely agricultural society. The Roman Catholic Church dominated public and political life. The Irish language, although taught in schools, was no longer widely spoken. The pockets where it survived were called *Gaeltachtaí*. After the 1960s, the power of the Church began to lessen. Ireland opened up more to the world and tourists poured into the west. After Ireland joined the European Economic Community (EEC) in 1973 its economy grew rapidly, developing new industries. However after 2008 the Irish economy suffered during a global financial crisis.

PRESIDENTS OF IRELAND

✤ Douglas Hyde	1938–1945
✤ Séan O'Ceallaigh	1945–1959
✤ Éamon de Valera	1959–1973
✤ Erskine Childers	1973–1974
✤ Cearbhall ó Dálaigh	1974–1976
✤ Patrick Hillery	1976–1990
✤ Mary Robinson	1990–1997
✤ Mary McAleese	1997–2011
✤ Michael D Higgins	2011–

PRIME MINISTERS OF IRELAND

✤ Éamon de Valera (Fianna Fáil)	1932–1948
✤ John Costello (Fine Gael)	1948–1951
✤ Éamon de Valera (Fianna Fáil)	1951–1954
✤ John Costello (Fine Gael)	1954–1957
✤ Éamon de Valera (Fianna Fáil)	1957–1959
✤ Sean Lemass (Fianna Fáil)	1959–1966
✤ Jack Lynch (Fianna Fáil)	1966–1973
✤ Liam Cosgrave (Fine Gael)	1973–1977
✤ Jack Lynch (Fianna Fáil)	1977–1979
✤ Charles Haughey (Fianna Fáil)	1979–1981
✤ Garret FitzGerald (Fine Gael)	1981–1982
✤ Charles Haughey (Fianna Fáil)	1982
✤ Garret FitzGerald (Fine Gael)	1982–1987
✤ Albert Reynolds (Fianna Fáil)	1987–1994
✤ John Bruton (Fine Gael)	1994–1997
✤ Bertie Ahern (Fianna Fáil)	1997–2008
✤ Brian Cowen (Fianna Fáil)	2008–2011
✤ Enda Kenny (Fine Gael)	2011–2017
✤ Leo Varadkar (Fine Gael)	2017–

MORE TROUBLES

A new round of 'troubles' broke out in Northern Ireland in 1969, as the minority supporting the Republic, mostly Catholics, clashed with the Protestant majority who supported the union with Britain. British troops were drafted in and the situation became worse after 'Bloody Sunday' in 1972, when 13 civil rights protestors were shot dead by British troops in Derry. New paramilitary groups were formed on both sides, engaging in murder and terrorist bombing, often in English cities.

THE ROAD TO PEACE

In 1998 a peace accord known as the Good Friday Agreement was approved by all sides in Britain, Northern Ireland and the Irish Republic. The Irish Republic dropped its claim to the six counties of the north. Prisoners were to be released, weapons handed in, troops scaled down and the police force reformed and re-named. However the devolution of power faltered. A power-sharing agreement between the Democratic Unionist Party and Sinn Féin functioned from 2007, but collapsed once again in 2017.

⬆ *Since 2017 the devolved Northern Ireland administration has been in suspension due to a deadlock between Sinn Féin, represented here by vice president Michelle O'Neill (left) and the DUP, led by Arlene Foster (right).*

1964
Harold Wilson ends 13 years of
Conservative government.

1979
Margaret Thatcher becomes first woman Prime
Minister of UK.

Left, Right or Centre?

➡ *Harold Wilson, MP for Huyton, won three elections for Labour – in 1964, 1966 and 1974.*

After the Second World War, the three chief political parties within the United Kingdom were the Conservative, Labour and Liberal Parties. The Liberals never achieved government during this period. It is common to talk about parties as 'right-wing' (following conservative policies) or 'left-wing' (inclined to more liberal or socialist policies). Which course would British politics follow, left or right?

'YOU'VE NEVER HAD IT SO GOOD'

In 1951 Sir Winston Churchill regained power for the Conservative Party. They kept it for 13 years. Sir Anthony Eden lost votes over the Suez Crisis. Harold Macmillan was nicknamed 'Supermac' by the press. His slogan was 'You've Never Had It So Good' – which in economic terms was probably true. Sir Alec Douglas Home, like his predecessors, came from the upper classes and lacked the common touch. By contrast Harold Wilson, who brought Labour back to power in 1964, prided himself on being a man of the people. Between 1951 and 1979 both Labour and Conservative parties moved towards the centre ground. Edward Heath, the Conservative who took Britain into Europe in 1973, was a centrist, as was Labour leader James Callaghan.

1984
Coal miners strike against pit closures, led by
Arthur Scargill.

1997
Victory for 'New' Labour under Tony Blair.

THE THATCHER YEARS

During the 1970s,
unemployment rose. Both
Heath and Callaghan came
under pressure from striking
trade unionists. Conservative
Margaret Thatcher who came
to power in 1979, was
Britain's first woman Prime
Minister. She moved her party
to the right, attacking trade
union rights and defeating a
national miners' strike in
1984. Nationalised industries
were now privatised.

PRIME MINISTERS OF THE UNITED KINGDOM

✤ Clement Attlee (Labour)	1945–1951
✤ Sir Winston Churchill (Conservative)	1951–1955
✤ Sir Anthony Eden (Conservative)	1955–1957
✤ Harold Macmillan (Conservative)	1957–1963
✤ Sir Alec Douglas Home (Conservative)	1963–1964
✤ Harold Wilson (Labour)	1964–1970
✤ Edward Heath (Conservative)	1970–1974
✤ Harold Wilson (Labour)	1974–1976
✤ James Callaghan (Labour)	1976–1979
✤ Margaret Thatcher (Conservative)	1979–1990
✤ John Major (Conservative)	1990–1997
✤ Tony Blair (Labour)	1997–2007
✤ Gordon Brown (Labour)	2007–2010
✤ David Cameron (Cons./Lib. Dem. Coalition)	2010-2016
✤ Theresa May (Conservative)	2016-

MAJOR, BLAIR AND BROWN

Thatcher was relected, but introduced some unpopular
policies, and was ousted in 1990. Her successor, John
Major, led a divided party. Labour too had seen years
of division, with a Social Democratic Party breaking
away in 1981. This merged with the Liberals in 1988,
forming the Liberal Democrats. Labour rebranded
itself as 'New' Labour, winning 13 years of power with
Tony Blair and Gordon Brown. They were replaced by
a coalition of Conservatives and Liberal Democrats in
2010. The main parties were competing for much the
the same ground, and voters became disillusioned or
turned to smaller parties. The
Green Party won their first
Westminster seat in 2010.

⬇ Parliament is still
organised into two
Houses. Arguments
about reforming the
House of Lords have
continued for over
a century.

Wales, Scotland, England

In the 1920s and 30s more and more people in Scotland and Wales were looking at ways of reforming or abolishing the union of nations within the United Kingdom. By the 1960s they were beginning to make their mark at general elections. Devolution of power from the parliament at Westminster became an important issue. Across Europe, regional cultures were gaining more political recognition.

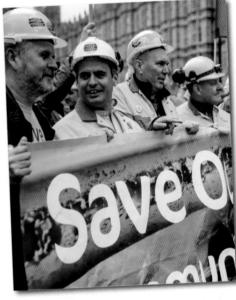

⬆ *Welsh steel workers from Port Talbot call on the UK government and Tata Steel to protect their jobs, in 2017.*

A WELSH ASSEMBLY

Wales went through great social changes in the 20th century. The upheaval of the world wars disrupted towns and rural communities. The coalmining industry of the south and northeast was closed down after 1984. The Welsh Nationalist Party (later, Plaid Cymru) was founded in 1925, and after the 1960s moved leftwards in its politics. The flooding of the Tryweryn valley to make a reservoir, pushed through the Westminster Parliament against the wishes of Welsh MPs, increased support for nationalists. The unionist policies of the Conservative governments in the 1980s and 90s were also opposed by Liberals and many Labour supporters. A Welsh Assembly, based in Cardiff, was voted into existence in 1997.

A SCOTTISH PARLIAMENT

In Scotland as in Wales there was wide-scale emigration, a decline in heavy industry and a rural population that struggled to make a living. The 1990s saw extensive clearance of poor housing from cities such as Glasgow. Scotland too was a Labour party stronghold. It was not until the 1960s that the Scottish Nationalist Party (SNP, founded in 1928) began to make inroads. When oil was discovered in the North Sea in 1975, many Scots wanted to control this resource for themselves. Scotland already had its own legal and education system. In 1997 it voted in its own Parliament too. However in a 2014 referendum on full Scottish independence, 55.3 percent voted No, with 44.7 percent voting Yes.

➡ *The Scottish National Party (SNP) lost the 2014 referendum for independence, but tensions over leaving the European Union have kept Scottish independence on the agenda.*

ENGLISH REGIONS AND CITIES

Where did the devolution of power to Wales and Scotland leave England? Some politicians proposed regional assemblies for England. Regions such as the Northeast or Cornwall certainly saw themselves as culturally different from the Southeast. Some people believed that the real problem was economic, a North-South divide based on prosperity. Some wanted to bring life back to local government. Major change was introduced in London, which gained its own Assembly. London's first elected mayor, in 2000, was a radical politician named Ken Livingstone.

Looking to the Future

↑ *The Shard soars above the dome of City Hall, home of the London Assembly.*

History helps us to learn from our past, so that we can face the challenges of a changing world, and plan for the future. There are periods of the world's history when huge changes happen very quickly. This happened during the Industrial Revolution of the 1800s. Such times can be exciting, but also dangerous. Society has to change rapidly, and individuals may either suffer or benefit as a result. Today's revolution is an electronic one.

CONNECTED OR DISCONNECTED

In 1989 English computer scientist Tim Berners-Lee invented the World Wide Web. Today about 90 percent of the population are internet users, including 99 percent of adults under the age of 34. Electronic technology has transformed almost every aspect of our lives for the better, or worse, in just a few years – communications, education, leisure, business, crime, banking, warfare, politics, home appliances, and even personal friendships.

↓ *Learning new online skills – but is there too much screen time?*

GLOBAL MONEY

The economy is now global, not national. Products sold in Britain may be manufactured by workers in distant countries who are paid very low wages. Big companies can be more more powerful than national governments. How accountable are they? Do they pay their taxes as they should?

← *The City of London is a world centre of business and finance.*

RICH AND POOR

In 2007–2008 there was a worldwide banking crisis. The problems that caused it were never really dealt with. Could this happen again? In the UK the gap between the richest and poorest in society has become very wide. Homeless people sleep on the streets of our cities. Cuts in public spending ('austerity') have been severe for many years. Are they necessary? The welfare state created in 1945 has been cut back, leaving many people at risk.

→ *The gap between rich and poor in the UK has widened greatly in recent years. Many low earners rely on free food banks to feed the family.*

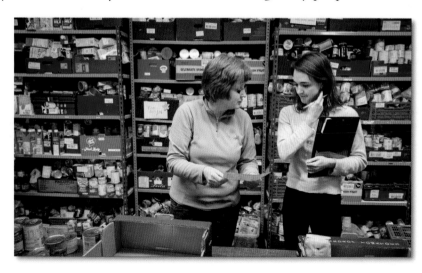

FACTS AND FIGURES
United Kingdom of Great Britain and Northern Ireland

Total area	243,610 sq km
Total population	65,105,250
England	55,268,100
Scotland	5,404,700
Wales	3,113,200
Northern Ireland	1,862,000
Average age	40.5 years
Life expectancy at birth	78.7 years (male)
	83.2 years (female)
Town and city dwellers	83.4 percent of total
Workforce:	
Agriculture	1.3 percent
Industry	15 percent,
Services	83.5 percent
Literacy (able to read and write)	99 percent

▲ Around 750,000 babies are born in the UK each year.

BREXIT BRITAIN?

In June 2016 Conservative Prime Minister David Cameron called a referendum on whether the UK should remain in the European Union or leave. In a surprise outcome, people voted to leave, by 17.4 million votes to 16.1 million. This Brexit ('British exit') result divided Labour as well as the Conservatives and raised more questions than answers. Scotland had voted Remain, so would it seek independence again? What would happen along Northern Ireland's border with the Republic? Did the economics make sense? At the start of 2019, opinons remained bitterly divided and the final terms of Brexit were still unclear.

TROUBLED TIMES

Endless wars, hunger and poverty have been driving families from their homes worldwide. Refugees go through great difficulties to reach anywhere that is peaceful and safe. Many kind people try to help migrants who reach Britain, but some prefer to blame these strangers for their own problems and worries. Racists whip up hatred on social media. They are listened to because many people themselves feel confused and insecure. Big shifts in economics and technology have left many workers in unrewarding or

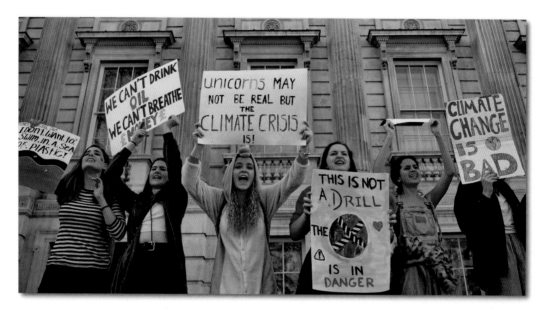

Young people gathered in London and cities across the country calling for urgent government action on climate change, February 2019. 'There is no planet B!'

poorly paid jobs. Around the world ordinary people have felt abandoned by millionaire politicians. Small parties with extreme policies have won popular support.

CHANGING CLIMATE

Scientists tell us that the world's climate is changing, and that the gases we pump into the air from factories, cars and airplanes are part of the problem. Britain will become warmer but stormier, with rising sea levels. Cleaning up our energy policies is essential. At the same time we humans are destroying the habitats that support our plants and wildlife, and choking our oceans with plastic.

MAKING A BETTER WORLD

If the problems of Britain and the wider world seem impossibly difficult at times, history tells us that humans can pull through when they work together. History can give us useful perspectives too. Even the Anglo-Saxons, ancestors of the English, originally arrived here as migrants. We cannot move forward without knowing where we came from. The other reason we must never despair is that across Britain and Ireland, and all over the world, there are young people full of good will and hope for the future.

Index

Entries in **bold** refer to main subject entries. Entries in *italics* refer to illustrations.

Acknowledgements

Front cover Airpowerart.co.uk

Alamy 55 Cary Clarke; 183 Michael D Griffin; 185 Painters; 242 & 269 The Picture Art Collection; 322 Interfoto; 372 Mark Kerrison; 375(b) Frank Schultze; 376–377 Steve Sparrow

Dover 323

Fotolia 19(tr) Richard Hannington; 62; 70 W. McKelvie 2005/Bill McKelvie; 101 davidmartyn; 103 Douglas Mcgilviray; 108 Jaspal Bahra; 145(b) Graham Lumsden; 145(tl) David Woods; 148–149 apeschi; 176 Richard Steinberg; 178 Johnny Lye; 216 Jean Philippe NAPPEY; 233 Pantera Rosa; 261 Artur Bogacki; 287(b) Tao Pang; 303 Eli Coory; 359 Jeff Gynane

Getty Images 11 Tony Howell/Photolibrary; 84 Ted Spiegel/Corbis Documentary; 173 Historical Picture Archive/Corbis Historical; 188 The Print Collector/Hulton Archive; 210 Kit Houghton/Corbis Documentary; 221 Historical Picture Archive/Corbis Historical; 262 Corbis Historical; 274(br), 274(t) 332, 333, 335(cr), 335(b), 337(b), 342, 353(t) & 353(b) Hulton Deutsch/Corbis Historical; 297 Corbis Historical; 338 & 341(b) Bettmann; 349 Hulton Archive/Fox Photos/Stringer; 355(t) & 355(b) Bettmann; 356(t) Bernard Bisson/Sygma; 357(b) Pool/Getty Images Entertainment; 362(b) Terry Disney/Stringer/ Hulton Archives; 365(t) Bettmann; 366–367 © Antoine Gyori/Corbis Historical; 368 Getty Images/News; 373 SOPA Images/LightRocket; 375(t) Daniel Sorabji/AFP; 377 Ben Stansall/AFP

iStock 60 pastie; 136 darrenturner; 147 ACMPhoto; 159 iwChameleon; 172 RMAX; 190 Rawpixel; 253 jorgeantonio; 358(t) tomwald

Mary Evans Picture Library 263 & 280

ShutterstockPremier 363 Paramount/Kobal/REX; 357(t) Mike Frey/BPI/REX; 149(t) walshphotos; 239 Nicku; 347 Nyvlt-art; 140 Andrew Roland; 369 James Gourley/REX; 374(t) Andrea Niotta; 374(b) Monkey Business Images

Topfoto 121 Topham Picturepoint; 281 Topfoto.co.uk; 292(br) 1999 Credit:Topham Picturepoint; 320 Topfoto.co.uk; 344(t) ©1999 Credit:Topham Picturepoint; 350 ©2004 Credit:Topfoto; 352 ©2000 Topham Picturepoint; 358(b) ©1999 Credit:Topham Picturepoint; 360(t) ©2000 Credit:Topham Picturepoint; 361 Credit:Topham Picturepoint ©1999; 362(t) ©2000 Credit:Topham/AP; 370 ©1999 Credit:Topham Picturepoint

Volunteer Service Overseas 366(t) Courtesy of Liba Taylor

All other photographs are from:
Corel, digitalSTOCK, digitalvision, John Foxx, PhotoAlto, PhotoDisc, PhotoEssentials, PhotoPro, Stockbyte
All artworks are from the Miles Kelly Artwork Bank

Every effort has been made to acknowledge the source and copyright holder of each picture.
Miles Kelly Publishing apologizes for any unintentional errors or omissions.